Chasing Demons

Reclaiming The Life They Stole

James Michael Williams

Staten House

CONTENTS

THE PRAYER OF THE PREPARED HEART

God,

Here I am. Standing at 3 AM about to take on demons I've been running from my entire life. The ones who've convinced me I'm not enough or too much or forever broken.

You see me in this moment when I feel most alone, most overwhelmed. I need You to remind me this isn't where my story ends.

I'm not asking You to make this easy. I'm asking You to make me ready.

Give me wisdom to see what I've been blind to. Strength to stand when everything in me wants to run. And grace to extend to myself as I do this hard work of reclaiming what's been stolen.

Where Your Spirit is, there is liberty. Let me chase that liberty with everything I have. Let me become the hunter instead of the prey.

Come what may, I will stand firm. Come what may, I belong to You.

This is my foundation. Now teach me how to build on it.

Amen.

AUTHOR'S NOTE

There's something I need you to know before you begin these pages.

I didn't write this book because I had it all figured out. I wrote it because I finally stopped pretending that I did.

The truth is, I've been working on these pages for years. Drafting. Deleting. Starting over. I had outlines that seemed perfect—until they weren't. I had chapters written that felt right—until I had to throw them out and start again. I thought I knew what needed to be written. I had a plan, a structure, a vision for what this book should be.

But what I wanted to write didn't align with what God wanted written.

And God, in His infinite wisdom, wouldn't let me finish. Not because the work wasn't good enough. But because I wasn't ready enough. Because I was trying to write the book I thought people needed instead of the book He called me to write. Because I was still trying to control the narrative instead of surrendering to the one He was shaping through my life.

So He made me walk it first.

He made me live the chapters before I could write them. He made me confront the demons I'd been naming from a distance. He made me break the chains I'd been theorizing about. He made me rewrite the narratives I'd been analyzing. He made me embrace the future I'd been too afraid to step into.

And more importantly, He woke me up. Eyes wide open. No more sleepwalking through my own life. No more performing versions of myself that felt safer than being real. No more running from the mantle my mother always knew God had placed on me.

My mother saw it before I did. She knew I was called to this —to education, to writing, to creating spaces for people to see themselves clearly and believe they can change. She knew I had something to say that needed to be said. Something to give that people needed.

But I ran from it. For more years than I can count, I ran from it. Because stepping into that calling meant being vulnerable in ways I wasn't ready for. It meant being open about things I'd spent a lifetime learning to hide. It meant admitting that I had demons of my own—not just theoretical ones I could write about from a safe distance, but real ones with real power over my life.

It meant being honest about who I was in spaces that didn't always feel safe. It meant being honest about grief that doesn't follow anyone's timeline. It meant being honest about trauma that doesn't have a tidy resolution. It meant being honest about the fact that I was still learning, still healing, still fighting, still becoming.

And I wasn't ready for that level of honesty. At least not yet.

So God waited. Not passively. Not patiently in the way we think of patience—as simply enduring the wait. But actively. Orchestrating. Positioning. Preparing me through tests I didn't want to take and lessons I didn't want to learn.

He let me survive COVID when I wasn't supposed to. He walked me through the loss of my mother when I didn't think I could. He showed me what favor looks like when circumstances are screaming otherwise. He taught me the difference between tracing and trusting. He revealed to me what liberty actually means when you've lived in captivity for so long you forgot what freedom felt like.

And slowly, painfully, beautifully, He made me ready.

Ready to stop running from the calling. Ready to embrace the mantle. Ready to write from the trenches instead of from the pedestal. Ready to be honest about my demons—not because I'd defeated them all, but because I'd finally stopped pretending they weren't there.

Ready to throw out the outline I'd been clinging to and write the book He wanted written instead of the one I thought I should write.

This book could not have been completed until I reached that place. Until I was willing to be seen. Until I was ready to tell the truth about the cost of freedom and the reality of the fight and the possibility of transformation—not as theory, but as lived experience.

So yes, I've been working on these pages for years. But the book you're holding? This version, these words, this honest testimony? This could only be written now. In this season. After these battles. On the other side of the tests that became testimonies.

God ordained the timing. Not to torture me with delay. But to prepare me for what this work would require. Because you can't give people what you don't have. You can't lead people to freedom you haven't experienced. You can't write about chasing demons if you're still letting them chase you.

I can't make the choice to confront your demons for you. But I can tell you what happened when I made it for myself.

I became free. Not perfectly. Not completely. Not in a way that means the struggle is over or the fear is gone or the tears have stopped.

But free enough to run. Free enough to write. Free enough to step into the calling I'd been running from. Free enough to be honest. Free enough to be myself.

Free enough to grieve the life I thought I wanted while chasing the life I was actually made for.

And that freedom? That's what made this book possible.

So as you turn these pages, know that what you're about to read isn't theory. It's not a workshop. It's witness work—testimony from the trenches. I'm not writing to you from a place of having arrived. I'm writing to you from the middle of the journey, honest about the demons I've named, the chains I've broken, and the future I'm still learning to chase.

You're about to embark on a journey that will require honesty you might not be ready for. You'll be asked to name demons you've been avoiding. You'll be challenged to break chains you've grown comfortable wearing. You'll be invited to chase a destiny you've been too afraid to claim.

It won't be easy. But it will be worth it.

Thank you for trusting me with your story as I share mine. Thank you for being brave enough to begin. Thank you for doing the work that most people spend their whole lives avoiding.

This book is my testimony. Now go write yours.

Come what may.

Dr. James Michael Williams

CHAPTER ONE
THE FOUNDATION

I didn't recognize the person staring back at me.

It was 3 AM, and I stood in my bathroom, hands gripping the edges of the sink, searching the eyes of a stranger who wore my face. My chest was tight. My breath was shallow. My heart was racing like it was trying to escape my ribcage. I didn't know it then, but I was having an anxiety attack.

One thing I can tell you is, the mirror doesn't lie. It reflects everything we try to hide from the world: the exhaustion we mask with smiles, the fear we cover with confidence, the battles we fight in silence while everyone else goes about their day. That night, although I didn't know it in the moment, I wasn't just looking at my reflection. I was facing my demon.

In my mind, I could see my future unfolding like a nightmare I couldn't wake from. Every scenario I imagined ended in failure. Every step forward I'd worked so hard to take was met with forces trying to knock me two, three steps back. The world felt increasingly hard, increasingly impossible. How on earth was I supposed to survive this? How was I supposed to keep going when every direction I turned seemed like a dead-end?

The panic was real and wrapped tightly around me like a Boa constrictor. The weight sat on my chest, chronicling every failure, every misstep, every moment I'd fallen short. I was drowning in questions that had no answers, suffocating under the weight of a future I couldn't control.

You know that demon, don't you? The one that whispers you're not enough when you're trying your hardest. The shadow that follows you through your brightest days, waiting for you to stumble so it can remind you of who you "really" are. That ever-present voice that wears your face, speaks in your tone, knows exactly which wounds to press and which dreams to poison.

The truth is, the most formidable opponent you'll ever face isn't out there in the world. It's right there in the mirror. And coupled with the inevitable trials and tribulations of life —the losses, the betrayals, the moments when everything you built crumbles—we gain a deep, often painful understanding of what it truly means to exist and navigate life's complexities.

But standing there at 3 AM, hands shaking, breath failing, I had forgotten something crucial.

I had forgotten that the same God who brought me to that moment was the same God who would carry me beyond it. I had forgotten that He would not suffer my foot to be moved. I had forgotten that He would not allow me to stumble.

The panic told me I was alone. The anxiety screamed that I couldn't make it. The demon in the mirror insisted that this was my final curtain call to this dark comedy I called life.

But they were all lying.

Here's what I eventually learned: that 3 AM moment in the mirror isn't the end of your story. It's the beginning of your breakthrough. Not because the fear disappears or the future suddenly becomes clear, but because in that moment of absolute panic, you have a choice. You can believe the demon. Or you can remember whose you are.

This book isn't about pretending your demons don't exist. It's about learning to chase them down, confront them, and reclaim the power they've stolen from you. Because the person staring back at you in that mirror? They're standing on a foundation that cannot be shaken, held by hands that will not let them fall.

They're stronger than they know. And it's time you both remembered that.

Come What May

My grandmother used to say it while making buttermilk biscuits, her hands working the dough in a wooden bowl that was older than I was, while humming some hymn I didn't recognize but somehow felt in my bones. I called her "Mama," because I had so many grandmothers alive at the same time that saying "grandma" would prompt them all to reply if they were in the same place at the same time. Mama was my grandmother on my father's side.

Both my grandmothers prepared me in their own ways. Mama taught me to stand firm when the punches come. Lil'Momma—my grandmother on my mother's side—would later show me grace that could withstand even the cruelest blows. Together, they uploaded into me everything I'd need for this tedious journey called life.

"Come what may, baby. Come what may."

I was nine the first time I really heard Mama say it—or at least, the first time I could remember. We were in her kitchen, and I'd just unloaded about some crisis that felt world-ending at nine years old. I was outside attempting to get a pomegranate off the tree, but instead of falling to the ground, it fell on the tin roof of the house. I couldn't get the buckles on the "My Buddy" doll loose. Oh, and don't get me started on the fact that I had a dream that a giant Sesame Street Big Bird was chasing me. I expected sympathy. I expected her to stop what she was doing and give me her full attention.

Instead, she kept mixing those biscuits by hand, flour dusting her dark hands white, her movements steady and sure.

"Come what may," she said, not even looking up from the bowl.

It seemed so random. So unprompted. Like she wasn't really responding to what I'd said at all, but to something she was hearing that I couldn't. These were her usual moments of wisdom—little uploads of truth she'd slip into my spirit right before turning on the TV to watch her soap operas. Or her "stories," as she called them.

At nine, I thought she was just talking to herself. At eighteen, I thought they were just old sayings that didn't mean much. At thirty, I thought I understood what she meant.

I was wrong. I didn't understand. Not really. Not until 2020.

2020 was the year the world broke. Or maybe it was the year the cracks that had always been there finally became visible. Either way, by October of that year, I had lost so many people, including my mother just months before, that I was numb. Completely numb. I stopped feeling the losses because if I started feeling them, I'd never stop. I moved through each day like I was underwater, everything muffled and distant and heavy.

That's when the call came. Mama had a heart attack.

And just like that, she was gone. No warning. No goodbye. No final words of wisdom uploaded into my spirit before she turned on her stories. She was making biscuits in her kitchen one moment, humming her hymns, and then she wasn't.

I remember just staring at my dad as he hung up the phone and feeling nothing. Just nothing. I'd felt so much loss already that year that my emotional circuit breaker had tripped. I was done. Empty. Shut down.

I retreated from the world, unable to attend another funeral. I spoke when spoken to. I refused to allow my last image of her to be of her in a casket, hands folded as if she was taking a nap after Guiding Light went off. Those same hands that had mixed biscuits in that wooden bowl, that had shaped dough and shaped me.

Everyone traveled to Georgia for the funeral, but I stayed behind. I was standing in my own kitchen, trying to make breakfast and failing because I couldn't remember what I was supposed to do next. Pancakes? Orange juice? Did I even eat breakfast? Nothing made sense. The numbness was cracking, and underneath it was something I wasn't ready to feel.

The clock on the wall ticked louder and louder, each second stretching into an eternity. Time was moving, but I was frozen. The sound filled the kitchen, filled my head, reminded me that the world was still turning even though mine had stopped.

That's when it hit me.

Like a ton of bricks, like a dam breaking, like the full weight of the sky falling on my shoulders all at once.

"Come what may."

Her voice in my head, clear as if she was standing next to me, mixing her biscuits and humming her hymns. Those three words I'd heard a hundred times, a thousand times, words I'd filed away as just another thing grandmothers say, suddenly detonated in my chest with the force of revelation.

Come what may.

Not "if things get hard." Not "when you're ready." Come. What. May.

She'd been preparing me. All those years. All those unprompted moments of wisdom slipped between biscuit-making and story-watching. She'd been uploading into me everything I would need for this journey called life. Everything I would need for 2020. Everything I would need for the moment when even she would be gone and I'd be standing in my kitchen, alone, trying to remember how to keep living.

"Come what may," she'd said. And now I understood.

It meant life was going to throw punches. It meant people I loved would die, dreams would crumble, plans would fail, and the world would break open in ways I couldn't predict or control. It meant I would stand at 3 AM facing demons in the mirror. It meant I would lose people I couldn't afford to lose. It meant 2020 would happen, and 2021 after it, and every hard year that would follow.

But it also meant something else.

It meant I would survive. Not because I was strong enough, but because I was standing on something that couldn't be moved. It meant that whatever came—and Lord, would things come—I had been given what I needed to stand firm. It meant her wisdom, uploaded into my spirit in fragments and moments I didn't even know I was collecting, would be there when I needed it.

Come what may. Not as a resignation to fate, but as a declaration of faith.

I stood in my kitchen and finally let myself cry. Not the numb, empty tears of someone who's lost too much to feel. Real tears. Grief tears. The kind that hurt because they mean you're feeling again.

And underneath the grief, I felt something else. Something solid. Something she'd been building in me all along with every unprompted word of wisdom, every hummed hymn, every batch of buttermilk biscuits made with hands that knew exactly what they were doing even when they didn't look up from the bowl.

She'd been teaching me how to stand firm.

Not by explaining it. Not by sitting me down and giving me a lecture on resilience. But by living it. By saying "come what may" while mixing biscuits, as if the truth was so woven into her being that it slipped out in the middle of ordinary moments. As if standing firm wasn't something you did in crisis, but something you practiced in kitchens, between flour and hymns and stories on TV.

The church elders in my granddaddy's congregation had a phrase they used for life. They called it a "tedious journey." I used to think that was such a depressing way to describe life. Why tedious? Why not beautiful, or precious, or meaningful?

But standing in my kitchen in October 2020, I finally got it.

They called it tedious because they were being honest. Life isn't one big dramatic battle you win once and then coast. It's the same struggles showing up over and over in different disguises. The same fears wearing new faces. The same doubts asking the same questions. It's *tedious* because you have to choose to stand firm not once, but every single day. Sometimes every single hour.

It's tedious because you don't get a break from being human.

But tedious doesn't mean meaningless. My grandmother made biscuits countless times. The same recipe, the same wooden bowl, the same movements of her hands. Tedious. But also sacred. Also necessary. Also the very thing that gave her the muscle memory to keep going when everything else fell apart.

"Come what may" is the anthem for the tedious journey. It's not the words you say once in a moment of crisis. It's the truth you upload into your spirit in ordinary moments—while making biscuits, while humming hymns, while watching stories on TV—so that when the crisis comes, you don't have to think about how to stand firm. You just do it.

Because it's already been uploaded. Because your grandmother's hands mixed it into you along with the flour and the butter and the love.

I think about her often now. I think about how she prepared me for loss by never pretending loss wouldn't come. How she taught me to stand firm not by shielding me from life's punches, but by showing me it was possible to take the hit and keep standing. Both my grandmothers did this.

Both of them had taken plenty of hits in life. They buried people they loved. Faced disappointments and betrayals and griefs I'll never fully know. Mama kept making biscuits. Kept humming hymns. Kept slipping wisdom into my spirit like she knew I'd need it someday. Lil'Momma showed me grace that would stand the test of time even when people spit in your face.

And when 2020 came, when the world broke and Mama left me, when I stood in my kitchen trying to remember how to keep living, her voice was there.

"Come what may, baby. Come what may."

Not because life would be easy. Not because I'd be strong enough on my own. But because both of them spent years uploading into me the truth that whatever came, I would stand firm. Because the same God who brought me to that moment would carry me beyond it. Because He would not suffer my foot to be moved.

Life will throw its punches. It's not a question of if, but when. And here's what I need you to understand: the punch isn't what defines you. Standing back up is. Or sometimes, just staying standing when everything in you wants to fall.

That's what "come what may" means.

It means you take the hit. You feel it. And then you stay standing.

Not because you're invincible, but because you've been prepared. Not because the pain doesn't hurt, but because underneath the pain is something solid. Something your grandmother mixed into you with flour and hymns.

Something God built in you before you even knew you'd need it.

Come what may, you will stand firm. Come what may, you will emerge victorious. Come what may, you are stronger than the storm.

Not because the punches won't come. But because when they do, you'll discover what was uploaded into your spirit all along: the truth that you're standing on something they can't touch.

My grandmothers knew that. And now, I'm uploading it into you.

Come what may.

Help My Unbelief

I've had many moments of doubt. Too many to count. Too many to confess comfortably in polite Christian company. But if I'm being honest, and this book demands honesty, the biggest moments of unbelief didn't come when life got hard. They came when life revealed that being good didn't matter.

Let me explain.

I watched people get promoted over me who didn't work half as hard. I watched colleagues cut corners, play politics, compromise their integrity, and climb ladders I couldn't even touch. Meanwhile, I showed up early. Stayed late. Did excellent work. Kept my word. Treated people with respect. And got passed over. Again. And again. And again.

The message was clear: integrity is a liability. Honesty is a handicap. If you want to get ahead, you have to be willing to cheat, steal, or lie. If you insist on being a person of character, you'll be left behind.

And I started asking dangerous questions.

Does God even care? Does He see this? Is He watching me work twice as hard for half the recognition while people with half the character and skill get everything I'm striving for? And if He's watching and doing nothing, what does that say about Him?

I cycled between two equally devastating possibilities: either God doesn't exist, or He does exist and we're nothing more than entertainment television for Him. Either way, the conclusion was the same—praying was pointless. Doing the right thing was naive. Striving to be a good person was just a human construct designed to keep us in line and under control.

The people who succeeded weren't the faithful ones. They were the ruthless ones.

So what was the point?

But here's the thing about unbelief: it doesn't usually announce itself with a dramatic renunciation of faith. It seeps in quietly, question by question, disappointment by disappointment, until one day you realize you've stopped believing that any of it matters.

That's where I was. Standing in the gap between what I'd been taught about God and what I was experiencing in the world. And the gap was getting wider.

But the workplace disappointments, as painful as they were, were just the surface wound. Underneath was something deeper. Something I hadn't talked about. Something I'd spent years suppressing, praying away, trying to reconcile with a faith that told me I was fundamentally wrong.

I grew up in a religious family. Church every Sunday. Bible studies. Youth group. Prayer before meals. I knew the scriptures. I knew the songs. I knew what was expected of me.

I also knew I was gay.

And according to everything I'd been taught, that made me an abomination.

Here's what made it even more confusing: the same people who called me an abomination for being gay would sit down to a seafood boil without a second thought. They'd wear polyester-cotton blend shirts to church on Sunday and think nothing of it. But Leviticus 11:10 says shellfish is an abomination. Leviticus 19:19 forbids wearing clothing made from two different fabrics. Yet somehow, my identity was singled out as the unforgivable deviation while their violations were conveniently overlooked.

I discovered something painful but clarifying: people will selectively use scripture to justify their beliefs, whether it's true or not. They'll weaponize certain verses while ignoring others that would indict their own lives. And in doing so, they reveal that their condemnation has less to do with God's Word and more to do with their own discomfort, their own biases, their own fear of what, or who, they don't understand.

So I did what so many others have done. I tried to pray away the gay. I begged God to change me, to fix me, to make me *normal*. I fasted. I wept. I memorized verses about transformation and new creation. I suppressed who I was because I believed it was out of the will of God.

But the prayers didn't work. I didn't change. The attraction didn't disappear. And every failed prayer became another brick in the wall of my unbelief.

Because here's the cruel logic that haunted me: if God is real, and if God is infallible, then He knew exactly what He was doing when He created me. He knew me before He formed the foundation of the world. He knit me together in my mother's womb with full knowledge of who I would be, who I would love, what I would struggle with.

And if that's true—if He made me this way—then either He's cruel, or the people calling me an abomination are wrong.

I couldn't reconcile it. How could a loving God create me as a contradiction to His own supposed will? How could He form me as something the church would reject, and then command me to live authentically? It didn't make sense.

So I cycled back to my earlier questions: Does God exist? And if He does, does He care?

The demon feeding my unbelief had a name: *Fear*.

But Fear itself was only a symptom. Behind it, orchestrating the whole performance, was a darker force— one of the ancient adversaries who specializes in creating doubt, sowing confusion, and building walls between who we are and who we're destined to be. The scriptures call this principality by many names, but its assignment is always the same: to separate us from truth by making us afraid of it.

This particular demon is skilled at twisting, at distorting what should be straight, at taking God's voice and garbling it until we can't distinguish His acceptance from their condemnation. It operates in the gap between what we know and what we fear, between who God says we are and who others tell us we must be. It feeds on silence, grows stronger in isolation, and builds its strongest fortresses in the minds of those who dare to ask honest questions.

I'll unmask this demon fully in a later chapter—its name, its tactics, its weaknesses, and how to chase it down when it comes for you. But for now, understand this: Fear is the weapon, but there's a calculating hand wielding it. And that hand knows exactly where to strike—at the intersection of identity and faith, at the place where your truth and God's truth are meant to unite.

Fear of rejection by the world. Fear of rejection by my friends. Fear of rejection by my family. Fear of losing everything I'd built if I admitted the truth. Fear that if I was honest about who I was, I'd confirm what I secretly believed —that I was too much, too wrong, too broken to be loved.

Fear built walls between where I was and where I was destined to be. It whispered that safety lay in hiding, in suppressing, in performing a version of myself that would be acceptable. It convinced me that my truth and God's truth were incompatible, and I had to choose.

But here's what I've learned about the difference between tracing God and trusting God.

Tracing God is what I was doing. Trying to follow the blueprint others had drawn for me. Trying to connect the dots between their interpretation of scripture and my lived experience. Trying to see God in the places they told me to look, using the language they told me to speak, becoming the person they told me I should be.

Tracing is exhausting because you're always following someone else's lines. You're never creating. You're never discovering. You're just trying to stay within the margins of what's been deemed acceptable.

Trusting God is different. Trusting God means believing that He knows what He's doing even when I can't see it. Trusting means accepting that His knowledge of me is deeper than any doctrine, any denomination, any human interpretation of who I should be.

We were not created to trace Him. We were created to trust Him.

And God has the ability to do and go beyond anything we can think or imagine. We do not have to see Him to know He works on our behalf.

The turning point for me didn't come with a thunderbolt or a burning bush. It came in the quiet. In the moments I thought were silence, God was orchestrating something I couldn't yet see.

He was changing hearts. He was shifting perspectives. He was moving in the lives of people close to me, preparing them to echo back to me the truth I'd been hearing in whispered prayers and midnight wrestling: I was who He made me to be.

My mother, who I thought would reject me, told me she loved me exactly as I was. My father, raised in the same religious tradition that taught me to be afraid, said he was proud of me. Friends I thought I'd lose became my fiercest advocates. One by one, the people I feared would abandon me began saying the same thing God had been whispering all along:

"You are who I made you to be. Before I formed the foundation of the world, I knew you."

And I realized: God wasn't silent. I just wasn't listening for His voice in the right places. I was listening for condemnation because that's what I expected. But He was speaking acceptance, orchestrating love, clearing a path for me to walk in truth.

The demon of Fear had convinced me that honesty meant rejection. But God was proving that honesty meant freedom.

Here's what I had to sit with, in the quiet of my own thoughts: Fear was creating a wall between where I was and where I was destined to be. And as long as I let Fear dictate my choices, I would never reach my purpose. I would never step into the fullness of who God created me to be. I would spend my entire life performing, suppressing, shrinking myself to fit into spaces that were never meant to contain me.

But then I understood something that changed everything:

I cannot worship God in spirit and in truth if I deny my own truth out of fear of rejection.

I want you to read that again and let it sink in.

You cannot worship God authentically while living inauthentically. You cannot approach Him in truth while hiding behind lies—even well-meaning lies, even self-protective lies, even lies you've been told are necessary for your salvation.

God doesn't want your performance. He wants you. The real you. The you that exists beneath the masks, beneath the fear, beneath the versions you've created to survive in spaces that don't know how to hold you.

When we engage in unbelief, it's because we are disconnected from the knowledge and understanding of God. We're listening to human interpretations instead of divine revelation. We're accepting someone else's limitations as if they were His.

But here's the truth scripture actually teaches:

"So faith comes from hearing the message. And the message that is heard is the message about Christ."

Romans 10:17 (NIrV)

Faith comes from hearing. But what are we hearing? Are we hearing the condemning voices of religion, or are we hearing the accepting voice of God? Are we hearing man's doctrine, or are we hearing divine truth?

I had to learn to distinguish between the two. And it wasn't easy. Because the condemning voices were loud and certain, backed by centuries of tradition and armed with proof texts. The accepting voice was quiet, almost imperceptible, requiring me to sit in silence and trust that what I heard in the stillness was more true than what I heard in the shouting.

My unbelief existed because I was governed by what I saw, what I thought, and what others told me to do. But belief—real belief—is rooted in what we hear from God Himself. And God was saying something different than the church was saying.

He was saying: You are mine. You are loved. You are exactly who I created you to be.

The problem wasn't me. The problem was that I'd been trying to fit into a version of faith that had no room for the fullness of who God made me. I'd been trying to trace someone else's blueprint instead of trusting God's design.

Let me tell you what happens when you finally stop tracing and start trusting.

Things don't immediately get easier. The workplace disappointment doesn't magically disappear. The people who judged you don't all suddenly change their minds. The systems that rewarded compromise over character don't reform overnight.

But something inside you shifts. The wall Fear built starts to crumble. The questions that once led to despair start leading to discovery. The silence you thought was abandonment reveals itself as God making space for you to hear His voice without the interference of everyone else's opinions.

You start to understand that His grace—not their approval—is what sustains you. That His favor—not their validation—is what positions you. That His knowledge of you before the foundation of the world is more authoritative than their interpretation of scripture written centuries after.

You realize that unbelief wasn't a sign of weakness. It was a sign that you were asking honest questions. And honest questions, when brought to God instead of buried in shame, lead to honest faith.

The kind of faith that doesn't require you to perform or suppress or shrink. The kind of faith that says: I don't understand everything, but I trust that You do. I can't trace the path You're leading me on, but I trust that You see where it goes.

I still have moments of doubt. I still wrestle with the gap between what I know about God and what I experience in the world. I still struggle with the reality that integrity doesn't always lead to promotion, that honesty doesn't always lead to reward, that being who God made me to be doesn't always lead to acceptance.

But now, when unbelief creeps in, I know what to do with it.

I don't suppress it. I don't shame myself for feeling it. I don't pretend I'm more certain than I am.

Instead, I bring it to God and say what the man in scripture said when Jesus asked if he believed:

"I do believe; help me overcome my unbelief!"

Mark 9:24, (NIrV)

I believe, and I struggle to believe. I trust, and I wrestle with trust. I know You're good, and I question what good means when the world feels cruel.

Help my unbelief.

And He does. Not by erasing my questions, but by meeting me in them. Not by making the world suddenly fair, but by reminding me that He is faithful even when the world is not. Not by changing who I am, but by confirming that He made me exactly as I was meant to be.

The demon of Fear wants you to believe that your questions disqualify you. That your doubts prove you're not faithful enough. That your struggle with belief means you're too far gone to be reached.

But here's the truth: God is not afraid of your unbelief. He's not surprised by your questions. He's not disappointed by your doubts.

He's present in them, waiting for you to stop tracing someone else's answers and start trusting His presence.

You were not created to trace Him. You were created to trust Him.

And trust doesn't mean having all the answers. Trust means believing that He has you, even when you can't see the path, even when the silence feels heavy, even when the world tells you you're wrong for being exactly who you are.

Stop trying to trace God through someone else's theology. Stop trying to perform your way into acceptance. Stop letting Fear build walls between who you are and who you're meant to be.

Start trusting that the God who knew you before the foundation of the world knew exactly what He was doing when He made you.

All of you. Including the parts you've been taught to hide.

I cannot worship God in spirit and in truth if I deny my own truth out of fear of rejection.

Neither can you.

So let's stop tracing. And start trusting.

Help our unbelief, Lord. And meet us right where we are.

Favor

There was no lightning bolt moment when I understood God's favor. No dramatic revelation on a mountaintop. No burning bush or angelic visitation.

It was quieter than that. More gradual. More like waking up slowly and realizing you've been held all night even though you don't remember falling asleep.

I started thinking about the absurdity of it all. The fact that even though we are unworthy of His love—even though we spit in His face with our choices, our doubts, our deliberate rebellion—He still loves us. Still gives us brand new mercies each day. Still shows up when we don't deserve it.

The Creator of everything. The One who spoke galaxies into existence. The One who holds atoms together with a word and knows the number of stars by name. The One who exists beyond what our finite minds can conceive, in dimensions we can't imagine, with power we can't comprehend.

That God favors us.

Not the impressive version of us we pretend to be. Not the cleaned-up, dressed-up, performance version we bring to church. Us. The messy, broken, questioning, struggling, sometimes-believing-sometimes-doubting us.

The depth of that favor should stop us in our tracks. But most of the time, we skim right past it because we've turned favor into a Christian buzzword instead of letting it wreck us with its implications.

I grew up hearing the phrase "Favor ain't fair." I can't recall exactly where I first heard it—probably in church when I was younger, thrown around like spiritual currency, used to explain why some people seemed to prosper while others struggled.

And for the longest time, I thought that's all it meant. A justification for inequality. A spiritual explanation for why some people get ahead and others get left behind. A way to make sense of the fact that life doesn't distribute success evenly, so we stamp "God's favor" on it and move on.

But I had to learn what this phrase actually means, because the true meaning is so much deeper, so much more profound, than I ever imagined.

"Favor ain't fair" doesn't mean God plays favorites. It doesn't mean some people deserve His attention more than others. It doesn't mean prosperity is proof of righteousness or struggle is proof of sin.

It means this: Even though we don't deserve it. Even though we could never measure up to His glory. Even though we fall short every single day in ways we're aware of and ways we're completely blind to. He still favors us.

Not in spite of who we are, but because of who He is.

That's what makes it unfair. Not that He gives it to some and withholds it from others, but that He gives it at all. That any of us receive it. That the Creator would look at His creation—broken, rebellious, constantly wandering—and choose love over judgment. Choose favor over what we actually deserve.

Let me tell you when I saw this unfair favor with my own eyes, even though I didn't recognize it at the time.

The year the world stopped. The year we all learned what the word "pandemic" actually meant. The year death tolls became daily news and hospital beds became scarce commodities and ventilators became the difference between life and whatever came after.

I got COVID. Not the mild version. Not the "I'll rest at home for two weeks" version. The version that put me in the hospital. The version that made breathing feel like drowning. The version that made the doctors start having quiet conversations about next steps.

The next step was a ventilator.

I remember hearing that and feeling nothing. I was too tired to be afraid. Too sick to process what it meant. But I remember the look on the doctor's face. The tone in her voice. The unspoken reality that once they put you on a ventilator, the odds shift dramatically.

I wasn't expected to survive.

But God had bigger plans for me.

I can't explain what happened medically. The doctors couldn't either. One day I was declining, spiraling toward that ventilator, toward becoming another statistic in a year full of devastating numbers. The next day, I turned a corner. Started showing signs of improvement. Started breathing a little easier. Started coming back from wherever I'd been slipping toward.

It didn't make sense to the doctors, but they were happy. Confused, but happy.

And I—lying in that hospital bed, weak and disoriented and grateful just to still be breathing—didn't fully understand what had happened. I didn't recognize it as favor. I didn't have the spiritual clarity to see God's hand in my survival. I was just relieved to be alive.

It took time for me to understand what 2020 really meant. What my survival actually signified.

So many people lost their lives during that time. More than I could count. More than I could bear to think about. Mothers and fathers. Grandparents who'd survived so much only to fall to an invisible enemy. Friends who were healthy one week and gone the next. Healthcare workers who gave everything and still couldn't save everyone.

The numbers were staggering. The losses were incomprehensible.

But somehow, God decided I would not be among those numbers.

He needed me in another number. The number of those who are testaments to being human and willing to show their struggles so that the works of God could be seen.

That's favor. Unmerited, inexplicable, unfair favor.

I didn't survive because I was more righteous than the people who died. I didn't make it because I prayed harder or believed stronger or lived better. I survived because God, in His sovereign wisdom, decided I had more work to do. More testimony to give. More story to tell.

That's what "favor ain't fair" actually means. It means the scales don't balance. It means you can't earn it, deserve it, or explain it. It means God's choice to love you, protect you, and position you has nothing to do with your merit and everything to do with His nature.

And here's the part that used to bother me: I struggled with this concept for a long time. Especially during the seasons when my faith was waning, when I was questioning whether God even cared, when I was wrestling with my identity and wondering if I wanted anything to do with a God who seemed so arbitrary in His affections.

I remember reading Psalm 23:6 (NIrV)—"*I am sure that goodness and love will follow me all the days of my life. And I will live in the house of the Lord forever*"—and thinking: Do I even want to dwell in that house?

If God blessed the wicked—if favor fell on people who lied and cheated and climbed over others—was that a God I wanted to belong to? If favor was as random as it seemed, what was the point of integrity? What was the point of trying to be good?

These questions haunted me because I was still thinking about favor through the lens of fairness. I was still trying to make it make sense according to human logic. I was still looking for the formula: if I do X, God does Y.

But favor doesn't work that way. It can't be systematized. It can't be earned. It can't be predicted or controlled or manipulated through the right prayers or the right behaviors.

Favor is simply this: God's love expressed toward you, not because of who you are, but because of who He is.

And once I started to understand that—once I stopped trying to trace the logic and started trusting the love—everything shifted.

I wouldn't say God's favor feels different now than it did before. I'd say I've grown spiritually enough to recognize it. To see it for what it is instead of what I thought it should be.

As I had to define who I was for myself—not by societal norms, not by religious expectations, not by fear of rejection—something started happening. With each step toward authenticity, I started feeling a newfound liberty. A lightness. A sense that I was finally breathing freely for the first time in my life.

Then someone said something to me. They probably didn't realize how profound it was. They probably thought it was just an encouraging word, a nice scripture to share. But their words landed like a key turning in a lock I didn't know was there.

"Where the Spirit of the Lord is, there is liberty!"

That was the moment I started to wake up on a deeper spiritual level.

If who you are feels like captivity, that's not God. If who you are feels like liberty, that's God.

Maybe you should read that again. Let it sink in.

For years, I'd been living in captivity—imprisoned by fear of rejection, shackled by religious expectations, trapped in a version of myself that wasn't real. And I'd been told that captivity was righteousness. That denying myself was holiness. That suppression was surrender to God's will.

But the Spirit of God doesn't produce captivity. The Spirit produces liberty.

And when I finally stepped into who God actually made me to be—when I stopped performing and started living authentically—I felt it. The liberation. The freedom. The sense that I was finally aligned with something true instead of fighting against it.

That's when I recognized favor for what it really is.

Not a reward for good behavior. Not a prize for spiritual performance. Not something I earned by praying hard enough or believing strongly enough or suppressing deeply enough.

Favor is God's love actively working on my behalf. Favor is the evidence that He sees me, knows me, and chooses me—not in spite of who I am, but exactly as I am. Favor is the unfair advantage of being loved by a God who doesn't operate by human standards of fairness.

Let me clarify something important: favor and blessing are related, but they're not the same thing.

Favor is God's love—the foundation, the source, the wellspring. Blessing is what flows from that favor. Blessing is the derivative, the result, the manifestation.

Because God loves us—because we are favored—we are able to overcome the world. His love is the favor. The blessing is the power to overcome any trials or tribulations we may face.

Think about it this way: I didn't survive COVID because I was blessed with good health or strong lungs or the right medical team (though I'm grateful for all of those). I survived because I was favored—held by a God who had plans for me that my circumstances couldn't cancel. The blessing was the recovery, the strength, the second chance. But the favor was the love that secured my survival before I even knew I needed it.

This distinction matters because we've gotten it backwards. We chase blessings—the tangible evidence, the material proof, the visible results—while taking favor for granted. We pray for blessings while questioning whether we're even favored.

But if you understand favor, blessings become almost secondary. Because if you know you're loved—if you know the Creator of the universe has chosen to set His affection on you, not because you deserve it but because that's who He is—then you can trust that whatever you need to fulfill your purpose will be provided.

You don't have to chase it. You don't have to perform for it. You don't have to prove you're worthy of it.

You're favored. And from that favor, blessings flow.

"I am sure that goodness and love will follow me all the days of my life."

I used to struggle with that verse. Now I cling to it. Because I've seen it proven true even when I questioned it. Even when I wondered if God blessed the wicked and ignored the righteous. Even when fairness seemed like a joke and favor seemed random.

Goodness and love—or as some translations say, goodness and mercy—follow me. Not because I'm good enough to deserve them. Not because I've earned the right to them. But because they are self-activating clauses in the contract Jesus secured when He rescued me from the curse of the law.

Goodness goes before grace because goodness is a trait of the assistance we receive from God, also called grace. Simply put, because He has such divine love for us, He gifts us grace.

Grace is undeserved favor.

And undeserved favor protects us from the destructive forces of doubt and unbelief. It shields us from the self-inflicted wounds of pessimism and self-destruction. This grace, this undeserved favor, is not something we earn but a gift freely given out of God's boundless love.

It's a beacon of hope in our moments of despair. A reminder that we are cherished and valued, even when we struggle to see it ourselves. Even when we're lying in a hospital bed wondering if we'll see tomorrow. Even when we're standing in the gap between who we were told to be and who we actually are.

If you remember nothing else from this, know that God's favor—His grace—is not a reward for good deeds but a reflection of His divine love for us. Our imperfections often lead to doubt and disbelief, but God's unmerited favor shields us from these self-destructive tendencies.

Favor serves as a beacon of hope in our darkest moments, a constant affirmation of our inherent worth. The "Favor of God" is a promise of His unyielding support, a gift of grace that transcends our comprehension.

Despite our flaws, His goodness and love persist, providing us the strength to resist any negativity that attempts to infiltrate our lives.

I survived 2020 not because I was special, but because I was favored. Not because I deserved it, but because He decided I had more work to do. More testimony to give. More truth to live.

And so do you.

Whatever you're facing—whatever odds are stacked against you, whatever voices are telling you you're not enough or you're too much or you're fundamentally wrong—remember this:

You are favored. Not because you've earned it. Not because you're perfect. Not because you've done everything right.

You're favored because the God who knew you before the foundation of the world chose to love you. And that love

—that unfair, unmerited, inexplicable favor—is stronger than any force working against you.

Where the Spirit of the Lord is, there is liberty.

If who you are feels like liberty, that's God. And if that's God, then you're exactly where you're supposed to be, exactly who you're supposed to be, covered by favor you could never earn and could never lose.

That's the unfair advantage of being loved by a God who doesn't play by our rules.

Favor ain't fair. Thank God it's not.

Because if it was fair, none of us would have it.

The Fight Isn't Physical

I can't pinpoint a specific moment when I realized the battles I was fighting weren't really against people or circumstances. It didn't come as a dramatic revelation or a supernatural encounter. It evolved. Slowly. The way most spiritual understanding does, not in lightning bolts, but in gradual dawning.

We all know the scripture. We've heard it quoted in sermons, seen it on social media graphics, recited it when things got hard:

> "*Our fight is not against human beings. It is against the rulers, the authorities and the powers of this dark world. It is against the spiritual forces of evil in the heavenly world.*"

> Ephesians 6:12 (NIrV)

We know the words. But knowing and understanding are two different things.

Understanding came for me as my spiritual awareness evolved. As I started to see patterns I'd missed before. As I began to recognize that people and circumstances, the things I'd been fighting against, the obstacles I thought were my enemies, were just vessels. Instruments. Tools being leveraged by something unseen to distract me from its true face.

What I had to realize is that the real enemy doesn't usually show up with horns and a pitchfork. It shows up wearing the face of a difficult colleague. It speaks through the voice of rejection. It operates through systems of injustice. It manifests in circumstances that seem designed to break you.

And if you're only fighting what you can see, you'll exhaust yourself battling symptoms while the disease remains untouched.

Spiritual warfare, I've learned, reveals itself as forces working against your peace, your prosperity, your good health, and your well-being. That's because the enemy doesn't like progress. Doesn't like momentum. Doesn't like when you start discovering who you really are and stepping into your purpose.

So it does what it does best: it creates resistance.

Remember when I said it felt like every step forward I took, there were two or three steps back? That's the essence of spiritual warfare. Not dramatic possession or Hollywood horror. Just strategic, calculated interference designed to distract you from your forward progress by forcing you to focus only on the failure or the setback.

And here's the trick: it only feels like a setback because we didn't get what we wanted or felt we deserved. The enemy doesn't have to stop you. It just has to slow you down. Discourage you. Make you question whether the effort is worth it. Make you think maybe integrity really is a liability and compromise really is the only way forward.

It makes you forget that the very fact you're facing resistance means you're moving in the right direction.

But here's what makes this fight so exhausting: it's not just external. The battlefield isn't just out there in the world. It's in here. Inside us.

I believe that's what the Apostle Paul meant when he said we must die daily. Not a morbid death wish, but a recognition that every single day is a tug-of-war between the light and dark that exists in us inherently because of the first sin.

It's a constant conversation with myself. Do I continue to act with integrity? Do I continue to sharpen my skills and knowledge? Do I maintain my standards even when no one's watching? Or do I cut corners? Do what others do to get ahead? Take the easier path that compromises who I am, but gets me closer to what I want?

Every. Single. Day.

The darkness whispers that integrity is overrated. That authenticity is too risky. That compromise is just being practical. And every single day, I have to choose the light again. Have to choose truth again. Have to choose to be who God made me to be even when being something else would be easier.

That's the fight. And it never stops. It just gets more sophisticated.

Let me give you an example of what spiritual warfare actually looks like when it manifests in the physical world.

I was a high school teacher. And one of my guiding principles, maybe the guiding principle, was to see each student as an individual and dedicate myself to teaching knowledge in a way that would bring out their deepest potential.

For me, "No Child Left Behind" wasn't a federal policy or a political slogan. It was a personal conviction. It meant that walking into my classroom every day and not performing at my best was not an option. It meant pushing students beyond what they thought they could do because I could see what they couldn't yet see in themselves.

It meant refusing to let potential go untapped just because a student was comfortable with mediocrity.

One year, I had a student who was coasting. Smart kid. Capable. But doing the bare minimum because the bare minimum had always been enough. I saw the potential. I saw what this student could become if they'd just push a little harder, dig a little deeper, stop settling for good enough when greatness was within reach.

So I pushed. I challenged. I raised the bar because I knew this student could reach it.

And a parent complained to the district.

Suddenly, I was under review. My gradebook was opened. My assignments were audited. My teaching philosophy and methodology were scrutinized. Everything I'd built, everything I'd poured into my students, everything I believed about education, all of it was on trial because one affluent family decided I was "too hard" on their child.

The investigation found nothing. No evidence of unfair targeting. No proof of bias or inappropriate conduct. In fact, the audit revealed the opposite: I was doing exactly what I said I was doing, holding all students to high standards because I believed in their potential.

I was cleared of any wrongdoing.

But it still felt like defeat.

It felt like punishment for caring. Like a penalty for refusing to bow to the will of an influential family who wanted their child's comfort prioritized over their child's growth. It felt like proof that the system rewards mediocrity and punishes excellence.

And for a moment, a long moment, I questioned whether it was worth it. Whether I should just lower my standards, stop pushing so hard, let students settle for less because fighting for more only brought me pain.

But then I recognized what was really happening.

This wasn't just about a parent complaint. This wasn't just about an administrative review. This wasn't just about a difficult circumstance I had to navigate.

This was spiritual warfare.

Though it manifested in the physical, through a parent, through a complaint, through a bureaucratic process, it was nothing more than the enemy trying to break my spirit. Trying to stop me from uplifting students. Trying to keep me from stirring up gifts that were lying dormant. Trying to convince me that settling for mediocrity was safer than fighting for greatness.

Because if the enemy could discourage me, it could silence me. And if it could silence me, it could keep those students from reaching their potential. And if it could keep them from their potential, it could rob them of their destiny.

That's how it works. It doesn't attack you directly. It attacks through the vessels available, people, circumstances, systems, and it aims for your spirit, hoping to break you before you break through.

I was reminded of 1 Peter 5:8 (NIrV):

"Be watchful and control yourselves. Your enemy the devil is like a roaring lion. He prowls around looking for someone to swallow up."

1 Peter 5:8 (NIrV)

The enemy is always seeking to devour us. Always prowling. Always looking for the opening, the weakness, the moment when our guard is down or our spirit is weary.

But through it all, here's what I learned: it's much harder to devour the pack than it is to devour someone tackling the world alone.

I've always sought to surround myself with people who will challenge me. People who aren't afraid to tell me when I'm wrong. People who will speak the truth even when it's uncomfortable. People who will stand with me in the fight, not as spectators but as fellow warriors.

Because if we cannot receive correction in love, then we need to re-evaluate our journey and where we are in that journey.

I want you to understand that there are times when you need to lean on the strength of others. Times when you need to call on the prayer warriors. Times when you just need someone to remind you why we must never give up the fight.

The enemy wants you isolated. Wants you thinking you're the only one struggling, the only one fighting, the only one who feels the weight of this battle. Because isolated prey is easy prey.

But when you're part of a community, when you have warriors who know your struggles and fight alongside you, the enemy has to work much harder. It can't pick you off as easily. It can't whisper lies as convincingly when you have voices speaking truth. It can't break your spirit as effectively when others are holding you up.

That's why community matters in spiritual warfare. Not as a nice addition to your spiritual life, but as a necessity. As armor. As a strength you draw from when your own runs dry.

I want to be clear about something: I believe that every battle we fight, even mental battles that require professional help, are rooted in spiritual warfare.

But that doesn't mean the solution is only spiritual.

Too often, we create a false dichotomy: either it's a mental health issue that needs professional help, or it's a spiritual battle that needs spiritual weapons. Either therapy or prayer. Either medication or faith.

But it's never either/or. It's always both/and.

Someone once said something to me that made everything click: God gave doctors and health professionals the knowledge to heal.

Think about that. If we believe God is the source of all wisdom, then the medical knowledge that helps treat depression is from God. The therapeutic techniques that help process trauma are gifts from God. The medications that balance brain chemistry are tools God provided through human discovery.

So the very notion that all we have to do is pray our way through circumstances is not just incomplete, it's dangerous. Because believing in something without doing the work associated with that belief is dead.

Simply put: faith absent of works is dead.

If you're struggling with depression, you pray and you see a therapist. If you're battling anxiety, you claim scripture and you take the medication your doctor prescribes. If you're processing trauma, you ask for spiritual covering, and you do the therapeutic work.

You use both the spiritual weapons and the practical tools. Because they're not in competition, they're in cooperation. They're both part of how God equips you to fight and win.

So when I talk about spiritual warfare, I'm not dismissing the reality of mental health. I'm saying that the enemy works through every available avenue, including mental health struggles, to steal our peace, kill our purpose, and destroy our destiny.

And we fight back with every available weapon, spiritual and practical, prayer and therapy, faith and action.

If a person ever thinks that spiritual warfare is outdated or dramatic, they need only understand this: there are powers and principalities within the air that try to take us away from the Fruits of the Spirit.

Love, joy, peace, patience, kindness, goodness, faithfulness, gentleness, and self-control, these aren't just nice virtues. They're evidence of God's presence in our lives. They're the very things that make us effective, whole, and aligned with our purpose.

And the enemy hates them. Hates when we walk in love instead of bitterness. Hates when we choose joy despite circumstances. Hates when we maintain peace in the middle of chaos.

So it attacks. It sends anxiety to steal peace. It sends offense to kill love. It sends chaos to destroy joy.

And if we don't recognize the spiritual dimension of these attacks, we'll spend all our time treating symptoms instead of addressing the source.

Jesus sacrificed His life for two main reasons that directly relate to this fight: so that we might have life and have it more abundantly, and to bring down the veil that separated God from humanity.

The abundant life He promised isn't just about heaven someday. It's about freedom now. Purpose now. Peace now. Wholeness now.

And the enemy's entire mission is to keep you from experiencing that abundant life. To keep you separated from the very thing Jesus died to give you access to.

That's the fight. That's why it matters. That's why we can't just ignore the spiritual dimension of our struggles.

When you realize that people and circumstances are only the instruments of the demonic powers and principalities that rule the air, everything changes.

You learn which tools you need to pick up at any given time to overcome the world.

You stop letting things bother you to the point that they detract from your journey to your place of destiny because you recognize exactly what they're trying to do: knock you off the path you were destined to walk.

You understand that you don't need to spend forty years in the wilderness to reach the promised land. The Israelites wandered for four decades not because the journey required it, but because they couldn't recognize the tactics being used against them. They kept fighting each other instead of fighting the real enemy. They kept blaming circumstances instead of recognizing the spiritual warfare.

But when you see clearly, when you understand that the difficult colleague is a vessel, the unjust system is a tool, the painful circumstance is a strategy, you stop wasting energy on the wrong battle.

You stop trying to change people who are just instruments. You stop fighting circumstances that are just symptoms. You stop exhausting yourself on surface battles while the real enemy operates unchallenged.

Instead, you address the source. You fight the actual fight. You use the spiritual weapons designed for spiritual enemies:

Prayer that isn't just religious routine but strategic warfare. Scripture that isn't just inspirational quotes but living truth that exposes lies. Community that isn't just social connection but spiritual reinforcement. Worship that isn't just emotional experience but declaration of whose you are. Truth that isn't just information but the light that exposes darkness.

And you pair those spiritual weapons with practical action, therapy when needed, medication when appropriate, boundaries when necessary, rest when required.

Because you're not fighting a phantom. You're fighting a real enemy with a real strategy aimed at a real target: your purpose, your peace, your progress, your destiny.

But here's the good news: the enemy wouldn't be fighting you this hard if you weren't a threat.

The resistance you're experiencing? It's confirmation that you're on the right path. The setbacks that feel like defeat? They're proof you're making progress. The spiritual warfare you're navigating? It's evidence that you matter in the kingdom, that your life has purpose, that the enemy sees what you can't always see—your potential to do damage to darkness.

So yes, the fight is real. Yes, it's exhausting. Yes, there are days when you wonder if you can keep going.

But the fight isn't physical. And once you understand that, once you see the real enemy and pick up the right weapons, you realize something powerful:

You're not fighting for victory. You're fighting from victory.

Because the battle was already won on a cross two thousand years ago. The enemy was already defeated. The veil was already torn. The separation was already ended.

You're not trying to win. You're enforcing what's already been won.

And that changes everything.

It means when the enemy sends resistance, you don't panic, you recognize the tactic. When circumstances try to discourage you, you don't give up, you adjust your strategy. When people become vessels for attack, you don't hate them, you see past them to the real enemy.

You keep moving forward. Keep standing firm. Keep choosing light over darkness, truth over lies, faith over fear.

Not because the fight is easy, but because you finally understand what you're fighting and why it matters.

The fight isn't physical. It's spiritual.

And you were built for this battle.

So pick up your weapons, all of them, spiritual and practical, and keep fighting.

Because the enemy prowls around looking for someone to devour.

But you're not someone. You're a warrior. Surrounded by warriors. Armed with truth. Standing on a firm foundation. Covered by favor you didn't earn.

And the pack is much harder to devour than the prey who stands alone.

Keep fighting. Keep standing. Keep moving forward.

The promised land is closer than you think.

CHAPTER TWO
THE TEST OF LIBERTY

Where The Spirit Of The Lord Is

I need to tell you something that might make you uncomfortable.

Not everything that calls itself freedom actually is.

We previously established something foundational: "*Where the Spirit of the Lord is, there is liberty*." That phrase became a turning point for me, a key that unlocked something I'd been missing. But here's what I had to learn the hard way: liberty isn't just about feeling free. It's about *being* free. And those two things aren't always the same.

You can feel liberated while still being in chains. You can mistake rebellion for freedom. You can confuse license with liberty. And if you're not careful, you can trade one form of captivity for another while calling it progress.

So we need a test. A way to distinguish God's voice from every other voice competing for our attention. A litmus test that helps us know whether we're moving toward authentic freedom or just a different prison with better marketing.

Let me take you deeper into 2 Corinthians 3:17.

"Now the Lord is the Spirit. And where the Spirit of the Lord is, people are free."

2 Corinthians 3:17 (NIrV)

Paul wrote these words in the context of talking about the old covenant versus the new covenant. He was explaining how the law, which was supposed to bring life, had become a veil that obscured people's understanding. The letter kills, but the Spirit gives life.

But here's what I want you to catch: Paul isn't saying the Spirit gives you permission to do whatever you want. He's saying the Spirit produces a specific result—liberty. Not chaos. Not self-indulgence. Not the absence of boundaries or discipline or commitment.

Liberty.

And liberty, real liberty, looks a specific way. It feels a specific way. It produces specific fruit in your life.

That's the test.

The Liberty Litmus Test

To understand if something is from God ask yourself: Does it produce liberty in your spirit, or does it produce captivity?

Not comfort. Not convenience. Not what feels good in the moment or what other people approve of or what seems most spiritual on the surface.

I am talking about true liberty.

When I started applying this test to my life, everything changed. Suddenly I had a way to evaluate the voices in my head, the expectations placed on me, the religious obligations I'd been carrying, the relationships I'd been maintaining, the career decisions I was making, the version of myself I was performing.

I started asking: Does this produce liberty, or does it produce captivity?

And let me tell you, the answers were not what I expected.

Some things I thought were freedom turned out to be chains. Some things I thought were captivity turned out to be the path to liberation. Some voices I thought were God's turned out to be demons in disguise. And some truths I'd been afraid to face turned out to be the very things that would set me free.

The test sounds simple. But applying it requires honesty, and honesty requires courage.

Let me give you some markers to help you distinguish liberty from captivity.

The Markers Of Liberty

Liberty produces peace, not just excitement.

There's a difference between the adrenaline rush of rebellion and the settled peace of alignment. When you're living in true liberty, there's a deep sense of rightness, even when the path is difficult. You're not constantly second-guessing yourself. You're not performing for an audience. You're not white-knuckling your way through each day.

You're at peace.

Not because everything is easy. Not because everyone approves. Not because you've arrived at some perfect destination. But because you're finally aligned with who you were created to be.

Liberty produces growth, not stagnation.

When you're living in God's liberty, you grow. You stretch. You become more, not less. You discover capacities you didn't know you had. You develop character you didn't think you could possess.

Captivity keeps you small. It keeps you safe, sure, but it also keeps you stuck. It tells you this is as good as it gets, this is all you're capable of, this is who you'll always be.

Liberty says: you're not done yet. There's more in you. Let's see what you can become.

Liberty produces authenticity, not performance.

This one was huge for me. For years, I was performing. Playing a role. Presenting a version of myself that I thought people needed to see, that I thought God wanted to see, that I thought would keep me safe and accepted and loved.

And I was exhausted.

True liberty let me stop performing. It gave me permission to be exactly who I am—flaws and all, questions and all, struggles and all—without fear that God would reject me or that His favor would evaporate.

When you're free, you don't have to pretend anymore. You can show up as yourself and trust that's enough.

Liberty produces love, not fear.

This is the big one. The ultimate test.

"There is no fear in love. Perfect love drives fear away."

1 John 4:18 (NIrV)

If what you're experiencing produces fear, it's not from God. If your identity feels like something you have to defend constantly, if your faith feels like something you have to prove repeatedly, if your worth feels like something you have to earn continually—that's captivity, not liberty.

God's Spirit produces love. And love casts out fear.

So if you're afraid—afraid of rejection, afraid of punishment, afraid of not measuring up, afraid of being too much or not enough—that fear is not coming from God. It's coming from somewhere else.

And we need to identify where.

What Captivity Feels Like

Because here's the thing: captivity doesn't always announce itself. It doesn't show up wearing a sign that says

"I'm here to trap you." It's often subtle. Insidious. It masquerades as righteousness, as wisdom, as protection.

So let me tell you what captivity actually feels like, so you can recognize it when it shows up.

Captivity feels like constant striving with no arrival.

You're always working, always trying, always pushing, but you never feel like you've done enough. There's no rest. No satisfaction. No moment where you can exhale and say, "It is well."

You're on a treadmill that speeds up every time you think you're catching your stride.

That's not God. God's yoke is easy, His burden is light. If what you're carrying feels crushing, if the expectations feel impossible, if you're exhausted from trying to be good enough—that's captivity.

Captivity feels like shrinking, not expanding.

When you're in captivity, you get smaller. Quieter. Less. You start editing yourself, censoring your thoughts, hiding your questions, suppressing your gifts.

You learn to make yourself palatable. Acceptable. Safe for public consumption.

And in the process, you lose yourself.

Captivity feels like performance, not presence.

You're so busy managing how people perceive you that you're never actually present. Not with yourself. Not with God. Not with the people you love.

You're always calculating. Always monitoring. Always adjusting your mask to fit the room you're in.

And it's exhausting.

Captivity feels like fear disguised as faithfulness.

This one is tricky because it looks so much like obedience. It sounds so much like righteousness.

But underneath the religious language and the spiritual performance, there's fear. Fear of rejection. Fear of punishment. Fear of losing approval. Fear of discovering that who you really are isn't acceptable.

So you stay in line. Not because you want to, but because you're afraid not to.

And you call it faithfulness. But it's actually bondage.

Captivity Vs. Freedom

Let me tell you about a conversation I had with someone who was convinced they were walking in freedom.

They'd left the church. Left the faith tradition they grew up in. Left the expectations, the rules, the constraints that had been suffocating them for years. And they felt free. Lighter. Like they could finally breathe.

"I'm finally living authentically," they told me. "No more pretending. No more performing. No more trying to be someone I'm not."

And I understood that. I really did. Because I've felt that same relief, that same sense of breaking free from something that was crushing me.

But then I asked them a question: "Are you at peace?"

They paused. And in that pause, I saw something flicker across their face. Not peace. Not the settled assurance of someone who's finally found their way home.

Defiance.

"I'm free," they said again. But this time it sounded less like a declaration and more like a defense.

Here's what I've learned: freedom and liberation are not the same thing as rebellion and license. And sometimes, in our rush to escape captivity, we run straight into a different kind of bondage without realizing it.

The Difference Between Liberation and Rebellion

Liberation moves you toward something. Rebellion moves you away from something.

Liberation is about discovering who you were created to be. Rebellion is about rejecting who others told you to be.

Liberation produces peace. Rebellion produces defiance.

And here's the tricky part: they can look identical from the outside. They can even feel similar on the inside, especially in the beginning. Because both involve breaking free from constraints. Both involve saying no to expectations. Both involve stepping away from what's familiar.

But the fruit is different.

Rebellion says, "I don't need anyone telling me what to do." Liberation says, "I'm finally free to become who I was created to be."

Rebellion is reactive. Liberation is proactive.

Rebellion defines itself by what it's against. Liberation defines itself by what it's for.

When Religion Becomes Captivity

I need to be careful here because this is tender territory for a lot of people. But it needs to be said.

Religion can become captivity.

Not religion itself. Not faith itself. Not God Himself. But the systems we build, the rules we create, the expectations we enforce, the traditions we maintain, the performances we demand—those things can become chains.

And the most dangerous part is that we don't always recognize it's happening. Because it's dressed in spiritual language. It's wrapped in biblical terminology. It's enforced by people who genuinely believe they're protecting you, helping you, keeping you on the right path.

But captivity is captivity, even when it's dressed in religious robes.

You know you're in religious captivity when:

- Your relationship with God feels like a contract with fine print
- Your worth is tied to your performance rather than His love
- You're more concerned with appearing righteous than actually being transformed
- You're afraid to ask questions or express doubts
- You feel like you're constantly on probation, one mistake away from losing everything
- Your faith produces anxiety instead of peace
- You're performing for an audience of critics rather than resting in the love of a Father

That's not what God intended. That's not the Spirit's work. That's not liberty.

That's the law without grace. That's the letter that kills without the Spirit that gives life.

False Freedom

But here's where it gets complicated: not all freedom is from God.

There's a counterfeit freedom that looks like liberation but leads to another kind of bondage. And we need to talk about it honestly because the enemy is subtle, and deception doesn't announce itself.

License vs. Liberty

License says, "I can do whatever I want." Liberty says, "I'm free to become who I was created to be."

License is about the absence of restraint. Liberty is about the presence of purpose.

License asks, "What do I want?" Liberty asks, "Who am I called to be?"

License focuses on what you're free from. Liberty focuses on what you're free for.

And here's the critical distinction: license eventually leads to bondage. Because when you remove all boundaries, when you reject all authority, when you pursue whatever feels good in the moment—you don't find freedom. You find chaos. And chaos is its own kind of captivity.

I've seen this play out too many times. Someone breaks free from religious legalism, and in their pursuit of freedom, they run straight into self-destruction. They trade one set of chains for another.

They're still not free. They've just changed captors.

The Markers of False Freedom

False freedom promises liberation but delivers isolation.

It tells you that you don't need anyone, that you're complete on your own, that community and accountability are just more attempts to control you. And you end up alone.

Cut off. Disconnected from the very relationships that could have supported your growth.

False freedom produces chaos, not peace.

It feels exciting at first. Liberating. Like you're finally living without limits. But over time, the chaos becomes exhausting. The lack of structure becomes destabilizing. What felt like freedom starts to feel like drowning.

False freedom leads to stagnation, not growth.

Because real growth requires discipline. It requires commitment. It requires staying with something even when it's uncomfortable. False freedom tells you to run from discomfort, to avoid anything that feels constraining, to keep moving whenever things get hard.

And you never grow. You just keep running.

False freedom produces pride, not humility.

It tells you that you've figured it out, that you're enlightened, that you see what others are too blind or too bound to see. And that pride becomes its own prison.

True liberty produces humility because you recognize you didn't free yourself. God freed you. His Spirit produced the liberation you're experiencing. You're not the hero of this story. You're the recipient of grace.

The Liberty Test In Practice

So how do you actually apply this test? How do you know, in the moment, whether you're moving toward liberty or captivity?

Let me give you some real-world scenarios.

When Making Career Decisions

You're offered a promotion. More money. More prestige. More responsibility. On paper, it looks like a blessing. But when you think about accepting it, something feels off. Not fear of change. Not imposter syndrome. Something deeper.

Apply the liberty test: Does this move you toward freedom or captivity?

If taking this position would require you to compromise your values, to sacrifice your peace, to become someone you're not—that's captivity, no matter how good it looks on paper.

But if it aligns with who you're called to be, if it creates space for growth, if it produces peace even in the midst of challenge—that might be liberty calling you forward.

When Navigating Relationships

There's someone in your life who keeps pulling you back into old patterns. Old versions of yourself. Old behaviors you've been trying to leave behind. They say they love you. They say they're just trying to help. But every interaction leaves you feeling smaller. Confused. Less yourself.

Apply the liberty test: Does this relationship produce freedom or captivity?

True love produces freedom. It gives you room to grow. It celebrates your becoming. It doesn't require you to stay small so someone else can feel big.

If a relationship consistently makes you feel like you need to shrink, to hide, to perform—that's captivity, regardless of what it calls itself.

When Questioning Your Faith

You have questions. Doubts. Things that don't make sense anymore. And you're afraid that asking these questions makes you a bad Christian. That doubt disqualifies you. That wrestling with God means you've lost your faith.

Apply the liberty test: Does exploring your questions produce freedom or captivity?

If your faith community tells you that questions are dangerous, that doubt is sin, that you need to just believe harder and stop thinking so much—that's captivity.

But if you can bring your questions into the light, if you can wrestle with God like Jacob did, if you can say "*help my unbelief*" and trust that God won't abandon you—that's liberty.

God is not afraid of your questions. The Spirit doesn't produce fear of intellectual honesty. Real faith has room for doubt because real faith is built on relationship, not rigid certainty.

When Evaluating Your Identity

You've spent years performing. Being who others needed you to be. And now you're discovering who you actually are underneath all those layers. But it's different from what you thought. Different from what others expect. Different from the version of yourself you've been presenting.

Apply the liberty test: Does becoming who you actually are produce freedom or captivity?

If stepping into your authentic self produces peace, if it allows you to breathe deeply for the first time, if it feels like coming home—that's liberty.

If it produces constant anxiety, if you're trading one performance for another, if you're just swapping masks—

that might not be liberation. That might be a different kind of captivity.

The key question isn't "What will people think?" or "How will this look?" The key question is: "Where is the Spirit leading me?"

And where the Spirit leads, there is liberty.

Your Identity As Free

Let me tell you who you are.

Not who you've been told you are. Not who you've been performing as. Not who you think you need to be to earn love or approval or acceptance.

Who you actually are.

You are favored. Not because you've earned it, but because God chose to love you. His favor is the foundation. Everything else builds on that.

You are free. Not because you've escaped every constraint, but because the Spirit of the Lord lives in you. And where the Spirit is, there is liberty.

You are becoming. Not stuck in who you were, not anxious about who you'll be, but actively growing into who you were created to be.

This is your identity. Not captive. Not bound. Not chained to performance or fear or the expectations of others.

Free.

Who You Are When You're Not Performing

The truest version of yourself shows up when you stop trying to be impressive.

It's who you are at 3 a.m. when you can't sleep and you're wrestling with questions nobody else sees. It's who you are when you're alone and there's no audience to perform for. It's who you are when you forget to be who you think you should be.

That person, the one underneath all the layers, the one you've been afraid to let anyone see—that's who God created. That's who He loves. That's who He's been waiting for you to discover.

And here's the beautiful, terrifying, liberating truth: you don't have to be anyone else.

You can stop performing. Stop pretending. Stop managing everyone's perception of you.

You can just be.

And being yourself, your actual self, is enough.

The Freedom to Be Imperfect and Still Beloved

This might be the hardest part of liberty to accept.

You don't have to be perfect to be loved. You don't have to have it all figured out. You don't have to hide your flaws or edit your struggles or present a polished version of yourself.

You can be a mess and still be favored. You can have doubts and still be faithful. You can struggle and still be growing. You can fail and still be beloved.

Because God's favor isn't based on your performance. It's based on His character.

He doesn't love you because you're perfect. He loves you because He's good. He doesn't favor you because you've earned it. He favors you because that's who He is.

And that means your imperfection doesn't disqualify you. Your questions don't disqualify you. Your struggles don't disqualify you.

You are free to be exactly who you are, flaws and all, and trust that you're still held. Still loved. Still favored.

That's liberty.

Living from Favor, Not for Favor

There's a massive difference between living from favor and living for favor.

Living for favor means you're constantly trying to earn what you already have. You're performing, striving, proving yourself worthy. You're exhausted because you're carrying a weight you were never meant to carry.

Living from favor means you start with the knowledge that you're already loved. Already chosen. Already held. And from that place of security, you move forward. Not to earn anything. Not to prove anything. Just to become who you were created to be.

One produces captivity. The other produces liberty.

One leaves you anxious and striving. The other gives you peace and purpose.

One keeps you performing. The other sets you free to simply be.

This is the test of liberty. The way you distinguish God's voice from every counterfeit. The litmus test that helps you know whether you're moving toward freedom or just trading one set of chains for another.

Does it produce liberty in your spirit? Does it give you room to breathe, to grow, to become? Does it produce peace, even in difficulty? Does it align with who you were created to be?

If yes, that's the Spirit's work. That's God's voice. That's the path forward.

If no, if it produces captivity, if it makes you smaller, if it fills you with fear—that's not God. That's something else. And you have permission to walk away from it.

Because you were created for liberty. Not captivity.

And where the Spirit of the Lord is, there is freedom.

CHAPTER THREE
THE DEMONS WITHIN

I've got something to tell you: the demons don't disappear just because you close your eyes.

I learned that the hard way. For years, I thought if I kept busy enough, distracted enough, moving fast enough, the past would just... fade. Stay in motion, stay ahead of the pain. That was the strategy. Don't look back. Don't dig too deep. Don't ask questions you're not ready to answer.

I'm a Libra, which means I'm hardwired to avoid confrontation in any form. Give me peace over conflict every single time. If I can sidestep an uncomfortable conversation, I will. If I can smooth things over without addressing the actual issue, even better. It's not that I can't handle confrontation when it's forced on me—I will, and I do—but it's never my first choice. Balance, harmony, avoidance dressed up as peacekeeping. That's the playbook.

And for a long time, I thought that approach worked. I thought I was being mature, choosing my battles, not sweating the small stuff. But here's what nobody tells you about avoidance: it's exhausting. You think you're choosing the easier path by not confronting what hurts, but you're actually choosing the longer one. Every day you spend running from your demons is a day they're running right alongside you, matching you stride for stride, breath for breath. They're not chasing you. They're with you.

When we choose not to directly confront our inner demons, we're not avoiding confrontation at all. We're just opting for a different kind—a passive one. The kind that happens in the background of our lives, quietly sabotaging our relationships, our decisions, our peace. Ignoring them doesn't make them less real. It just makes them more comfortable.

And here's the kicker: that passive strategy eventually collides with reality. It has to.

You can only outrun yourself for so long before something forces you to stop. A relationship falls apart. A pattern repeats one too many times. Someone you trust points out something you've been refusing to see. Or maybe, like me, you just wake up one day exhausted from carrying weight you've been pretending isn't there.

That collision hurts. The unresolved issues we've been sidestepping come crashing to the surface, demanding the attention we've been withholding. It's painful. I won't lie to you about that. But here's what else it is: an opportunity. A chance to finally stop running and start healing. A moment where growth becomes possible because you're finally present for it.

This is what it means to chase your demons instead of letting them chase you.

Self-Inflicted Wounds

Let me be clear about something: the wounds I'm talking about weren't self-inflicted when they happened to you.

The abuse wasn't your fault. The betrayal wasn't your doing. The loss that shattered you wasn't something you caused. The rejection that made you question your worth wasn't warranted. Those things were done to you, or happened around you, or fell on you like stones from the sky. You were wounded. And in that moment, you were the victim of circumstance, cruelty, or just the brutal randomness of life.

But here's where it gets complicated. Here's where we need to talk about what happens next.

What you do with those wounds now, in the present—that's where the self-inflicted part comes in. Every day you refuse to look at them, you're reopening them yourself. Every time you pretend they're not there, you're preventing them from healing. Every moment you spend building walls around the pain instead of dealing with it, you're choosing to stay wounded.

That's the wound on top of the wound. That's the injury you're giving yourself.

I know it sounds harsh. Trust me, I wrestled with this truth for longer than I care to admit.

I was pre-med at Xavier University of Louisiana, on the path to becoming a doctor. Not just any doctor—a cardiothoracic surgeon. I wanted to hold a human heart in my hands. I wanted to be in the OR, doing the kind of work that meant life or death with every decision. That was the dream. That was the calling I felt pulling me forward.

I had the grades. I had the drive. I had mapped it all out in my head—residency, fellowship, the whole thing. But even with all the scholarships I'd earned, Xavier came with a cost. My mother was making sacrifices I didn't fully understand at first. Sacrifices that, when I finally learned about them, stopped me cold.

She let her truck be repossessed so she could cover the unmet portion of my cost of attendance. Let me say that again: my mother lost her truck so I could stay comfortable at college, pursuing my dream of becoming a surgeon.

When I found out, I felt horrible. Guilty. Grateful. Angry at myself for not realizing sooner what it was costing her. I knew immediately that I couldn't keep asking her to carry that weight. I had to go somewhere that didn't present such a financial burden. So I transferred to Bethune-Cookman University.

That's where I met the professor who convinced me I'd never make it.

Organic chemistry. Every time I asked for help, I got negativity. Every time I tried to engage, I got dismissiveness. He wasn't any more helpful than the textbook, and honestly, the textbook at least didn't make me feel like an idiot for trying. He had made up his mind that my ambitions were pointless, that I'd never make it past state licensure examinations. And here's the part that still stings: I believed him.

I walked away from medicine. Just turned around and left that dream on the table—the dream my mother had sacrificed her truck for—because one grumpy man convinced me I wasn't good enough. I eventually became a different kind of doctor, a Doctor of Business Administration. And don't get me wrong, I'm grateful for the path my life took. I love what I do. But that doesn't change the fact that I let someone else's pessimism define the boundaries of my capabilities.

Much of that medical calling still resides in me to this day. I can't shake it completely, and maybe I'm not supposed to. Maybe it shaped me in ways I needed to be shaped. But I also can't ignore that I walked away from cardiothoracic surgery—from the very specific thing I was called to do—because one person said I couldn't. I walked away from the dream my mother had believed in enough to sacrifice for.

For years, I avoided anything that even resembled a licensure examination. Didn't matter what field or what certification. The moment I saw that type of testing ahead of me, something in me would tense up. I'd find reasons to go a different route. I'd convince myself it wasn't necessary. I was living beyond the question mark on the surface, writing about breaking free and chasing dreams, while that professor's voice was still running the show behind the scenes.

It took years before I realized what I was doing. Years before I could name the wound and see how I'd been keeping it open, letting it bleed into decision after decision. That professor wounded me, yes. But I was the one who kept picking at the scab. I was the one who let his assessment become my identity.

That's what self-inflicted wounds look like in real time.

Maybe for you it's not a professor. Maybe it's childhood trauma—a parent who couldn't love you the way you needed, an environment that taught you to shrink instead of grow, something that happened once but echoed through every year that followed. Whatever it was, it left a mark. That mark is real. Valid. It shaped you.

But if you're still making decisions based on what your younger self learned just to survive, that's not the trauma anymore. That's you refusing to update the programming. That's you keeping yourself in that wound because examining it feels too overwhelming.

Or maybe it's failed relationships. A breakup that gutted you. Betrayal that made you question everything you thought you knew about trust, about love, about your own judgment. The pain of watching someone walk away, or having to walk away yourself—that's legitimate suffering. You're allowed to grieve that. You should grieve that.

But when you're three relationships deep and still blaming the first one for why you can't commit now? When you're sabotaging something good because you're terrified of being hurt again? When you're so busy protecting yourself from potential pain that you're guaranteeing your own loneliness? That's self-inflicted. That's you holding onto a wound that's begging to be released.

Or maybe it's loss. Grief. Death, distance, the end of a season, the closing of a door you wanted to stay open forever. Grief is not something you get over. It's something you learn to carry. And anyone who tells you different hasn't really lost anything that mattered.

But there's a difference between carrying grief and being buried by it. There's a difference between honoring what you lost and using that loss as a reason to stop living. When grief becomes your identity instead of your teacher, when you can't imagine yourself without the weight of it, when you won't let anyone in because you're still holding space for what's gone—that's when the wound becomes self-inflicted.

I'm not saying any of this is easy. I'm not saying you should just "get over it" or "move on" or any of those useless platitudes people throw around like they're helpful. What I'm saying is this: you have a choice. The original wound wasn't your fault, but your healing is your responsibility.

And yes, that's unfair. It's absolutely unfair that you have to do the work to heal from something you didn't cause. But fair or not, it's the truth. You can spend the rest of your life resenting that unfairness, or you can acknowledge it and start healing anyway.

The wounds are real. The pain is valid. But the question is: are you going to let what happened to you define what happens next? Or are you going to take back your power and do the uncomfortable, exhausting, absolutely necessary work of healing?

Because every day you avoid that question is another day the wound stays open. Another day you're bleeding out while pretending you're fine. Another day you're inflicting pain on yourself that doesn't have to continue.

This is what I mean by self-inflicted wounds. Not the original injury, but what we do—or refuse to do—with it now. It took me years to acknowledge the deep wounds that professor left, wounds that altered the course of my life. But acknowledging them was the first step toward taking back my power. Toward realizing that his assessment wasn't truth, it was just his opinion. And I had given it way too much authority for way too long.

The Demons We Inherit

One thing I need you to understand is that not all demons come from what people do to us. Some come from what people show us.

My grandfather on my dad's side—we called him Papa—taught me a lot. How to work hard. How to stand firm. How to carry myself with dignity. He was a man of principle, a man of strength, a man who commanded respect. I learned valuable things from watching him navigate the world.

But I also learned something else. Something I didn't recognize as a demon until much later.

Papa wasn't big on affection. Not with my dad, not with his children. There was love, I'm sure of that, but it was the kind that stayed locked up inside, never quite making it to the surface. No hugs. No "I love yous." No softness that would let you know you were cherished and not just tolerated. It was a coldness that felt normal because it was all I knew on that side of the family.

I watched my father carry that same template into his own life. The same emotional distance. The same inability to express what he felt. The same walls that kept affection at arm's length. And then I started to notice it in myself. That same coldness. That same struggle to show what I felt, even when I felt it deeply.

To an extent, I had inherited it. Not because I chose it, but because it was modeled for me. It was the water I swam in, the air I breathed. It was normal until I realized it wasn't.

I remember the first time I ever saw my dad cry. It was at Papa's funeral. And it scared me. I didn't know what was happening. I'd never seen him show that kind of emotion, never seen him break like that. The man who had been stoic and controlled my entire life was suddenly vulnerable, grief-stricken, human. And instead of it bringing us closer, it terrified me because I had no framework for understanding that level of feeling.

That's what generational demons do. They rob you of the ability to recognize healthy emotion when you finally see it.

My mother was the balance. She struck the equilibrium between feeling and expressing, between strength and softness. She would point out to my dad when he was being cold, when he was acting just like Papa. She'd call it out, gently but firmly, because she recognized what it was doing to him and to us. She saw the demon that had been passed down and refused to let it go unchallenged.

I'm grateful for that. Because without her voice, I might never have questioned it. I might have just accepted that this is how men in my family operate, and passed it on to the next generation like it was some kind of inheritance worth keeping.

But here's the thing about inherited demons: you don't have to keep them.

Just because your father struggled to show affection doesn't mean you have to. Just because your mother carried anxiety like a second skin doesn't mean you have to wear it. Just because your family operated in dysfunction doesn't mean that's your only blueprint for relationships. Just because rage or silence or control or perfectionism or emotional unavailability was modeled for you doesn't mean you're sentenced to repeat it.

You get to choose.

That's the power you have that previous generations might not have had. You can see the pattern. You can name the demon. You can recognize where it came from and decide it stops with you.

But first, you have to be willing to look at the people who raised you—not with judgment, but with honesty. You have to ask yourself the hard questions. What did I learn by watching them? What behaviors did I absorb without realizing it? What wounds did they carry that I've now picked up and carried forward?

Maybe it's anger. Maybe you watched a parent explode over small things and now you find yourself doing the same. Maybe it's withdrawal. Maybe you watched someone shut down emotionally every time things got hard, and now you disappear when conversations get uncomfortable. Maybe it's perfectionism. Maybe you watched someone never feel good enough, always striving, always falling short in their own eyes, and now you can't rest because rest feels like failure.

Maybe it's addiction. Maybe it's workaholism. Maybe it's the inability to trust. Maybe it's the need to control everything because chaos feels dangerous. Maybe it's people-pleasing because conflict was never safe. Maybe it's emotional unavailability because vulnerability was punished.

Whatever it is, it's not entirely yours. It was handed to you. You inherited it. And that's not your fault.

But what you do with it now? That is your responsibility.

You can break the cycle. You can be the one who says, "This pattern ends here." You can be the one who chooses differently, feels differently, responds differently. You can be the one who refuses to pass the demon on.

It won't be easy. Generational patterns have deep roots. They feel like identity because they've been there so long. Changing them means going against everything that feels familiar, everything that was normalized for you. It means being different from the people who raised you, and that can feel like betrayal even when it's actually freedom.

I'm learning to show affection even when it feels awkward. I'm learning to express what I feel even when the words don't come naturally. I'm learning that softness isn't weakness, that vulnerability isn't dangerous, that letting people in doesn't mean losing myself.

But it's possible. I've seen it. I've lived it. I'm still living it.

I'm learning to be different than what was modeled for me. Not because Papa or my father were bad men—they weren't. They were doing the best they could with what they had. But I have something they might not have had: awareness. The ability to see the pattern and choose a different path.

You have that too.

So I'm asking you: what demons did you inherit? What patterns are you repeating without questioning them? What emotional templates were you given that maybe don't actually serve you?

Look at them. Name them. And then decide—are you keeping them, or are you finally putting them down?

Because the demons you inherit don't have to become the demons you pass on.

Identifying The Demons Within

So now that you're thinking about both the demons inflicted on you and the ones you inherited, let's talk about how you actually identify them. Because guess what: you already know what they are.

You might be pretending you don't. You might be telling yourself you need more therapy, more self-help books, more time to "figure it out." But deep down, in that place you don't like to visit too often, you know exactly what's haunting you. The question isn't what are your demons. The question is: are you ready to name them?

Because naming them changes everything.

When I finally admitted to myself that I was still carrying that professor's assessment like it was gospel truth, something shifted. Not immediately. Not dramatically. But acknowledging it out loud—even just to myself—took away some of its power. It's like when you turn on the light in a room you thought had monsters in it. The monsters don't disappear, but you can finally see what you're actually dealing with.

My preferred method for identifying personal demons is genuine self-reflection. And I don't mean the kind where you sit around thinking positive thoughts and affirming yourself in the mirror. I mean the uncomfortable kind. The kind where you look at your habitual behaviors and ask yourself the hard questions. Why do I always do this? Why does this situation trigger me every single time? What am I actually afraid of?

This requires honesty that doesn't come naturally to most of us. We're experts at lying to ourselves, at creating narratives that make us look better, at blaming circumstances instead of confronting patterns. Self-reflection that matters is the kind that makes you squirm a little. If you're completely comfortable with everything you're discovering about yourself, you're probably not digging deep enough.

Pay attention to what multiple people have pointed out about you. If three different people in your life have mentioned the same behavior, the same reaction, the same pattern—they're probably onto something. I used to get defensive when people pointed out things about me. Now I listen. Not because they're always right, but because they're seeing something I can't see from where I'm standing. Good, bad, or otherwise, there is love in honesty.

That's why I surround myself with people who don't tell me what I want to hear but what I need to hear. The friends who will say, "You know you do this every time, right?" The family members who will call out your patterns even when it's uncomfortable. The colleagues who will ask the questions you've been avoiding. These people are gifts, even when their honesty stings.

I am a firm believer that therapy and counseling can help form a connected understanding of these patterns and help devise a plan to conquer them. I'm not going to pretend therapy is a magic cure, because it's not. But a good therapist can help you see the connections you've been missing, can point out the stories you've been telling yourself that aren't actually true. They can help you reduce the influence these demons have on your life by giving you tools to challenge them when they show up.

Another effective approach is mindfulness and meditation. And before you roll your eyes and think I'm about to tell you to sit cross-legged and chant, hear me out. These practices allow you to quiet your mind enough to actually hear what's going on inside. Most of us are so loud in our own heads—constantly moving, constantly distracted, constantly filling the silence with noise—that we can't hear what we need to hear.

Mindfulness isn't about achieving some Zen state of enlightenment. It's about being present enough to notice when a demon shows up. To recognize, "Oh, there's that fear again. There's that old wound talking. There's that pattern I keep repeating." You can't change what you can't see. These practices help you see clearly.

But if I'm being honest, the most powerful tool I've found personally is journaling.

I cannot stress enough the significance of writing things down. There's something about seeing your thoughts stare back at you in your own handwriting that forces a reckoning. The lies can't hide there. The excuses sound flimsy when you read them on paper. The patterns become obvious when you see them written out week after week.

When I wrote "I'm afraid everyone will leave," I had to confront what that said about me, about my past, about the wounds I'd been carrying. The page doesn't let you lie to yourself. You can spin stories in your head all day long, but when you put pen to paper, the truth has a way of bleeding through.

Write about what triggers you. Write about the moments you felt small. Write about the person who wounded you and why it still hurts. Write about the decision you made that altered your path. Write about the fear that keeps showing up uninvited. Write about the patterns you see but don't want to admit.

You don't have to show anyone. This isn't for publication. This is for you. This is you talking to yourself honestly, maybe for the first time in a long time. And as you write, you'll start to see the threads connecting everything. You'll start to understand why you react the way you do, why certain situations feel impossible, why some wounds never seem to heal.

Journaling helps you identify your demons, but it also helps you track your progress as you work toward resolving them. You can look back and see how far you've come. You can see where you're still stuck. You can catch yourself repeating old patterns before they take root again.

I won't lie to you and say there is a one-size fits all method that works for everyone. Maybe you need therapy to guide you through the process. Maybe you need meditation to quiet your mind enough to hear the truth. Maybe you need trusted friends to hold up the mirror. Maybe you need to write until your hand cramps and your heart hurts.

Most likely, you need some combination of all of it.

The point is this: you have to be willing to look. You have to be willing to name what you find. You have to be willing to sit with the discomfort of acknowledging that yes, these are your demons, and yes, they've been running parts of your life without your permission.

That acknowledgment is where the real work begins.

Self-love Over Self-Hate

I need you to understand something crucial: chasing your demons is not about self-hate. It's not about tearing yourself down or punishing yourself for past mistakes. It's not about drowning in shame or beating yourself up for not being further along than you are.

This is about self-love. Real self-love. Not the Instagram version where everything is filtered and perfect. Not the kind that avoids hard truths in the name of positivity. I'm talking about the kind of self-love that says, "I care about myself enough to do the hard work of healing."

There's a difference between constructive evaluation and destructive criticism. One leads to growth. The other leads to paralysis.

Destructive criticism sounds like this: "I'm worthless. I'll never change. I always mess everything up. Why do I even try?" That's self-hate dressed up as self-awareness. That's the demon speaking, not the truth.

Constructive evaluation sounds different. It sounds like this: "I see this pattern. I understand why I do this. It makes sense given what I've been through. But it's not serving me anymore, and I'm ready to work on changing it." That's self-love in action. That's you taking responsibility without taking on shame.

When I finally looked at how that professor's words had shaped my life, I had a choice in how I processed it. I could have spiraled into self-hate: "I was so stupid. I let one man destroy my dream. I'm weak. I'm a failure." But that wouldn't have helped me heal. That would have just created another wound on top of the existing one.

Instead, I chose constructive evaluation: "I was young. I was vulnerable. I believed someone who had authority but not truth. I made a decision based on limited perspective. And now, years later, I can see it clearly and make different choices moving forward." That's the difference. That's self-love.

The same applies to the generational patterns I inherited from Papa and my father. I could hate myself for the times I've been emotionally unavailable, for the moments I've struggled to show affection, for the coldness that sometimes surfaces when I'm not paying attention. But self-hate wouldn't change the pattern. It would just make me avoid looking at it.

Self-love says: "I see this in me. I understand where it came from. And I'm choosing, consciously and intentionally, to be different. Not because there's something wrong with me, but because I want to grow."

Scripture tells us something important about our nature. The Bible says,

"Human beings are born to have trouble, just as sure as sparks fly up"

Job 5:7 (NIrV)

We are born into trouble. We are born flawed. From the moment we enter this world, we are full of potential and full of brokenness at the same time. That's not a judgment. That's just reality. We are human. And being human means being imperfect.

But here's what self-love understands that self-hate doesn't: imperfection is not the same as worthlessness. Being flawed doesn't mean being broken beyond repair. Needing growth doesn't mean being fundamentally defective.

You are allowed to be both a masterpiece and a work in progress. You are allowed to acknowledge your demons while still believing in your worth. You are allowed to recognize your patterns while still extending grace to yourself for the journey it's taking to change them.

This is about understanding what triggers you. About recognizing how past hurt informs present behavior. About being kind to yourself because, after all, you're human. And humans are complicated. We carry wounds. We develop coping mechanisms. We learn survival strategies that made sense once but don't anymore. We inherit patterns we didn't choose. We make decisions based on information we had at the time, even when we later wish we'd chosen differently.

All of that is part of being human. None of it makes you less worthy of love, especially your own.

In our journey through life, we must consciously acknowledge our imperfections and shortcomings. Not to wallow in them. Not to use them as evidence that we're beyond help. But to learn from them. To improve. To grow. This is about embracing the journey of self-discovery and using it as a tool for personal transformation.

This process is challenging. Sometimes it's downright painful. But it ultimately leads to a stronger, more resilient version of yourself. A version that knows its demons by name. A version that isn't controlled by past wounds. A version that can look in the mirror and say, "I see you. I know you. And I'm committed to your healing."

As we navigate this journey, we learn to forgive ourselves for past mistakes. We let go of guilt and regret that serves no purpose except to keep us stuck. We move forward with wisdom and understanding. We cultivate resilience, not just to bounce back from setbacks, but to thrive despite them. To turn challenges into opportunities for growth.

This is the true nature of personal growth. It's a continuous process of learning, unlearning, and relearning.

Of constantly evolving. Of constantly improving. Not because you're not good enough as you are, but because you're committed to becoming the fullest version of yourself.

The name of the game is self-love, not self-hate.

Self-love means looking at your demons without flinching. It means calling them by name without being destroyed by the naming. It means acknowledging the wounds, both inflicted and inherited, and choosing to heal them rather than hide from them.

Self-love means being patient with yourself when the work is slow. It means celebrating small victories even when the big transformation hasn't happened yet. It means recognizing that healing isn't linear, that progress isn't always visible, and that simply showing up to do the work is worthy of honor.

Self-love means surrounding yourself with people who tell you what you need to hear, not just what you want to hear. It means accepting feedback even when it stings. It means being humble enough to admit when you're wrong and courageous enough to change.

Self-love means writing in your journal even when it hurts. It means going to therapy even when you'd rather pretend everything is fine. It means sitting in meditation even when your mind won't quiet. It means doing the uncomfortable work because you believe you're worth the discomfort.

And most importantly, self-love means remembering that chasing your demons is an act of courage, not weakness. It's a commitment to living free rather than staying captive. It's a refusal to let your past dictate your future.

You are not defined by what happened to you. You are not sentenced to repeat what was modeled for you. You are not doomed to stay stuck in patterns that no longer serve you.

You have the power to choose differently. To heal intentionally. To grow purposefully. To love yourself enough to do the hard work.

That's what this chapter has been about. Not self-hatred. Not self-destruction. Not shame or blame or endless guilt.

Self-love. The kind that says, "I see my demons, and I'm chasing them down—not to destroy myself, but to free myself."

CHAPTER FOUR
THEY HAVE NAMES

If you've made it this far, then you should remember that I previously said recognizing your demons is an act of self-love, not self-destruction. That naming what's chasing you is the first step toward freedom. But here's what I didn't tell you: I'm not talking about vague shadows or nameless anxieties that keep you up at night.

I'm talking about specific adversaries with specific assignments against your life.

And if we're going to chase these demons down instead of letting them chase us, we need to stop being polite about it. We need to stop speaking in generalities and start getting specific. Because everything that has power in your life has a name, and your demons are no different.

It would be a disservice to you if I danced around this. If I let you keep fighting blind, swinging at darkness without knowing what you're actually up against. So let me be clear about the ones I've encountered most often, the ones that have destroyed marriages, separated families, ended friendships, and stolen destinies.

Their names are Guilt, Greed, Envy, Selfishness, and Rejection.

You might have expected a different list. Maybe you thought I'd talk about anger or addiction or depression. And listen, those are real battles too. But what I've learned, both from my own journey and from watching others fight theirs, is that these five demons are often the architects behind those more visible struggles. They're the invisible chains that tether you to your past mistakes and prevent you from reaching your place of destiny.

If they're not addressed, they don't just make life difficult. They consume it. They create cycles of negativity that get passed down like inheritance, generational patterns that nobody questions because "that's just how we are." They breed self-doubt so convincing that you stop believing you were meant for anything more than survival.

So yes, we're going to confront these feelings head-on. We're going to break free from their grip. We're going to learn to walk worthy of our vocations, filled with confidence and hope rather than shame and hesitation.

But first, we have to call them by name.

Why Naming Matters

In the beginning, God brought every creature to Adam to see what he would name them. And whatever Adam called each living creature, that became its name. This wasn't busywork. This was an act of authority. Naming something means you recognize its existence. It means you understand its nature. It means you have power over it.

When you can't name what you're fighting, you can't fight it effectively. You just flail in the dark, exhausted and confused, wondering why you keep losing ground. But when you can look your demon in the eye and call it by name, something shifts. The battle becomes clearer. The strategy becomes possible.

Naming your demons is a crucial step in the journey toward self-improvement and personal growth. It allows you to confront them directly, to understand their impact, and to devise strategies to overcome them. By doing so, you reclaim control over your life and begin the journey toward your destined place.

But let me be clear about something: this process is not about demonizing parts of yourself. I'm not asking you to hate yourself or to believe that you're fundamentally broken or beyond repair. That's the lie the demons want you to believe, that you *are* the problem rather than that you *have* a problem.

What we're doing here is understanding the negative influences at work and learning how to transform them. We're turning weaknesses into strengths, fears into courage. Above all else, we're separating who you are from what's been attacking you.

Because there's a difference.

You are not your guilt. Guilt is something that has attached itself to you. You are not your greed. Greed is a force that has influenced your decisions. You are not your envy. Envy is a demon that has whispered lies about your worth.

When you understand this distinction, when you can name the demon without naming yourself as the demon, you can finally do the work of freedom.

The Origins

So where do these demons come from? How did they get their hooks in you?

When we analyze our inner demons, we often find they're rooted in past trauma, the fear of being hurt again, or inherited patterns whose origins we've never questioned. These are the generational curses that get passed down like recipes or surnames, patterns so embedded in family culture that nobody thinks to ask where they started or why they continue.

Have you ever found yourself acting in a certain way without understanding why? Have you ever heard yourself say something and thought, "I sound exactly like my mother," or watched yourself make a decision and realized you're following in the footsteps of your parents and their parents before them?

That's an inherited pattern. A path worn smooth by generations of feet walking the same direction without ever asking if it's the right direction.

Maybe it's the way your family handles conflict by shutting down and going silent. Maybe it's the way money creates anxiety no matter how much you have because poverty was a demon that haunted your grandmother and she taught your mother to fear it and your mother taught you. Maybe it's the way you apologize for taking up space because women in your family learned to make themselves small to survive.

These patterns don't announce themselves. They don't come with warning labels or instruction manuals. They just *are*, woven into the fabric of your identity so tightly that you can't tell where family history ends and your own story begins.

Unraveling inherited patterns can be a challenging task, but it's a crucial step toward self-awareness and personal growth. This process requires introspection, bravery, and sometimes professional help. A good therapist can help you see the patterns you've been blind to your whole life. A trusted friend can point out behaviors you didn't know you had. Prayer can reveal truths you've been afraid to face.

And here's the truth about healing inherited patterns: sometimes you have to break something before you can fix it properly.

A doctor will tell you that if a bone healed crooked, the only way to set it right is to re-break it and set it so that it can heal correctly. It sounds brutal. Because it *is* brutal. But leaving it crooked means living with pain and limitation for the rest of your life. The temporary agony of breaking and resetting is nothing compared to the permanent damage of leaving it broken.

That's what we're doing with these generational patterns. They've been set wrong for so long that they feel normal.

But normal doesn't mean healthy. Normal doesn't mean right. And if we want to heal correctly, we have to be willing to break what was set crooked and endure the pain of letting it heal the way it was meant to.

Only then can we liberate ourselves from these patterns and chart our own path.

By recognizing and addressing these patterns, we can deconstruct them gradually. I want you to understand that this process will be difficult. It will be unsettling. You'll feel disloyal to your family. You'll question whether you have the right to do things differently. You'll wonder if breaking the pattern means rejecting the people you love.

But here's what I need you to understand: breaking a generational curse is not betraying your family. It's freeing them too. When you refuse to pass the demon forward, you don't just save yourself. You save your children and their children. You become the generation that says, "It stops here. This doesn't go any further."

That's not betrayal. That's liberation.

As we undertake this journey of self-discovery, we learn to identify the triggers that set off these patterns. We begin to comprehend the underlying emotions and reactions that influence our behavior. This understanding provides us with the tools to consciously choose our responses rather than being controlled by inherited patterns.

And that's when the real work begins.

The Power Of Past Hurt

There's no shortage of books about how past pain affects our present functioning. Therapists build entire practices around it. Self-help sections overflow with titles promising to help you heal your inner child, process your trauma, overcome your past.

But here's the question that matters: how and why does past hurt continue to have so much power over our beliefs, behaviors, and relationships?

Because it does have power. Real power. The kind that makes you sabotage good relationships because bad ones taught you that love always ends in pain. The kind that keeps you small and quiet because speaking up once got you hurt. The kind that convinces you to settle for less because reaching for more feels dangerous.

If not addressed and healed, past pain perpetuates cycles of suffering and self-destructive behavior. It becomes the lens through which you see everything, distorting the present until it looks just like the past. You start assuming outcomes before they happen. You protect yourself from wounds that haven't occurred yet. You build walls so high that nothing can hurt you, but nothing can reach you either.

And here's the thing: often, without our awareness and in the absence of honest feedback from others, we miss crucial moments of reflection. We don't realize we're doing it. We think we're being wise, being careful, being realistic. We don't see that we're being held hostage by something that already happened and can't be changed.

I've watched people destroy their marriages defending against hurts from previous relationships. I've seen talented individuals refuse opportunities because failure once felt unbearable, myself included. I've even known parents who damaged their children trying to protect them from the pain the parents experienced, not realizing they were just creating a different pain, different demons for the next generation to fight.

This is where therapy and self-awareness exercises become essential. They provide us with the tools to confront our past hurts, understand their impact on our present lives, and ultimately break the cycle of pain. It's a journey of self-discovery and healing that can lead to profound personal growth and improved relationships.

But you have to be willing to look at it. I mean really look at it. Not just acknowledge that something bad happened, but examine how it changed you, what beliefs it installed, what fears it activated, what patterns it created.

By acknowledging and addressing our past hurts, we can rewrite our narrative and redefine our beliefs and behaviors. This process not only fosters resilience but also empowers us to establish healthier relationships. It's a transformative journey that requires courage, patience, and commitment.

Did I forget to mention that it also requires grace? Grace for yourself when you realize how long you've been carrying weight that wasn't yours to carry. Grace for others when you understand that they were probably carrying their own pain when they hurt you. Grace for the process when healing doesn't happen on your timeline.

Remember, progress is not linear. There will be setbacks. There will be moments when you think you've dealt with something only to have it resurface when you're triggered. There will be days when you feel like you're back at square one, fighting battles you thought you'd already won.

But each step, no matter how small, brings you closer to healing and freedom. It's about embracing the process, learning from each experience, and persisting despite the challenges. It's about refusing to let your past write your future.

Guilt

Guilt is a destroyer.

These five letters have ended marriages, separated families, destroyed friendships, and taken lives. Guilt has turned otherwise strong people into enablers of others' addictions. It has kept victims silent about abuse. It has made parents sacrifice their own well-being to appease children who learned to weaponize it. It has convinced good people that they deserve bad treatment.

As a chief demon, guilt is multifaceted, possessing both beneficial and detrimental aspects. There's healthy guilt, the kind that alerts you when you've genuinely done something wrong, when you've hurt someone and need to make it right. That guilt serves a purpose. It's your conscience doing its job.

But then there's toxic guilt. The kind that attaches itself to things that aren't your fault. The kind that makes you responsible for other people's feelings, other people's choices, other people's pain. The kind that whispers you should have known better, done more, been different, even when you did everything you possibly could.

Toxic guilt will convince you that your happiness causes others' sadness. That your success means someone else's failure. That taking care of yourself is selfish. That setting boundaries is cruel. That saying no is abandonment.

This is the guilt that keeps you trapped in toxic relationships because leaving would hurt them. The guilt that makes you sacrifice your dreams because pursuing them might disappoint someone. The guilt that turns every good thing in your life into a source of shame because someone else doesn't have it.

By recognizing guilt's influence and utilizing effective coping strategies, we can transform it into a driving force for personal growth and positive change instead of letting it control and characterize us. We can learn to distinguish between conviction that leads to correction and condemnation that leads to captivity.

Depending on how we handle it, guilt can either propel us forward or drag us down. The question is: are you going to let guilt drive your decisions, or are you going to examine where it's coming from and whether it's even yours to carry?

Because sometimes, the guilt you feel isn't about what you did wrong. It's about what someone else needed you to feel so they could control you.

Greed

At what point do we say enough?

When do we stop chasing more and admit that our cup is full? When do we look at what we have and declare ourselves satisfied? This isn't just about money or possessions, though it certainly includes those things. This is about the insatiable appetite for more that lives in all of us if we're not careful.

Greed is an insidious demon that breeds self-centered actions, ultimately causing us to sacrifice what genuinely holds value in our lives. It convinces us that happiness is always one more purchase away, one more promotion away, one more achievement away. It whispers that we deserve more, that we've earned it, that everyone else is getting theirs so why shouldn't we get ours?

And before we know it, we're working sixty-hour weeks and missing our children's childhood. We're accumulating things we don't need with money we don't have to impress people we don't like. We're climbing ladders only to discover they were leaning against the wrong wall the entire time.

In the pursuit of more, we lose sight of the beauty of enough. The constant yearning for excess blinds us to the simple pleasures and profound peace that contentment can bring. It is in recognizing the sufficiency of what we already have that we can truly find fulfillment.

I've watched greed destroy relationships when one partner always needed a bigger house, a nicer car, a better lifestyle, while the other just wanted time together. I've seen it tear apart families fighting over inheritances, siblings who grew up together becoming strangers over money that wouldn't matter in eternity. I've known people who sacrificed their integrity for financial gain, only to discover that the cost was far higher than the profit.

The key to satisfaction is not to acquire more but to desire less. This isn't about becoming apathetic or unmotivated. It's not about settling or refusing to pursue excellence. It's about understanding that happiness does not lie in the abundance of possessions but in the richness of the soul.

By embracing simplicity and gratitude, we can cultivate a sense of fulfillment that is not dependent on external factors. We can learn to distinguish between wants and needs, between what we desire and what we require, between what culture tells us we must have and what God says is already ours.

Because here's the truth that greed doesn't want you to know: you already have enough. Not because you've acquired everything, but because enough is not a number. It's a decision.

Envy

Envy is the demon that makes you hate your own life while staring at someone else's.

It's the voice that whispers, "If only I had what they have, then I'd be happy. If only I'd made the choices they made, taken the path they took, been given the opportunities they were given." Envy sows seeds of insufficiency within us, convincing us that we're perpetually lacking, perpetually behind, perpetually less than.

At its core, envy is yearning for what was never meant for you. It's looking at someone else's blessing and calling it theft. It's believing that their gain is somehow your loss, that God's provision for them means He's forgotten about you.

We convince ourselves that if only we had walked their road, we would possess those things we observe them having. We replay our own stories with alternate endings, imagining different choices, different circumstances, different outcomes. And in doing so, we miss the entire point of our own journey.

Because here's what envy doesn't tell you: you're comparing your behind-the-scenes to everyone else's highlight reel. You're looking at the harvest they're celebrating while ignoring the seeds they planted in tears. You're coveting the crown without knowing the weight of it, the promotion without understanding the sacrifice, the relationship without seeing the work it required.

I've watched envy poison friendships when one person's success became unbearable for the other to witness. I've seen it destroy families when one sibling's achievement was treated as another's failure. This isn't new. Envy has been destroying brothers since Cain decided that if God accepted Abel's offering, it meant God rejected him. Rather than examining his own heart or improving his own offering, Cain let envy convince him that Abel's blessing was his curse. And we know how that story ended.

Envy instills within us feelings of inadequacy. We start to believe that if our journey mirrored that of others, we would be in possession of all the things we see them blessed with. But this thinking is fundamentally flawed because it ignores a crucial truth: each individual's journey is unique and tailored to their own experiences and lessons.

The possessions and achievements of others are the fruits of their own paths, not ours. What was meant for them was prepared specifically for them. And what's meant for you is being prepared specifically for you, in ways you can't see yet, on a timeline that isn't subject to your impatience.

Instead of succumbing to envy, we should strive to appreciate our own journey and the blessings it brings. We should focus on cultivating gratitude for what we have and the progress we've made. This shift in perspective can help us combat the feelings of inadequacy that envy breeds.

Remember, the only journey you need to compare yourself to is the one you were on yesterday. The only person you need to be better than is the person you were last week, last month, last year. Because envy keeps you so focused on someone else's lane that you swerve out of your own.

And when you're busy watching where they're going, you miss where you're supposed to be headed.

Selfishness

We are designed to have the mind of Christ. And when we have the mind of Christ, we are able to put the needs of others before our own. Call this perfect love.

Selfishness is the antithesis of perfect love.

It's the demon that whispers, "What about me? What do I get out of this? How does this serve my interests?" It's the voice that calculates cost before considering compassion, that measures investment before offering love, that asks "What's in it for me?" before asking "How can I help?"

If Jesus had been selfish, He would have finished praying in the garden of Gethsemane, walked away from what was coming, and gone into hiding. He had every reason to. He knew the betrayal, the beating, the mockery, the cross. He felt the weight of it so heavily that He sweat drops of blood asking if there was another way.

But perfect love stayed.

Perfect love ensured that by the stripes and bruises He took, we could be liberated. Without these acts of selfless love, we could never be healed and restored to our birthright, which is eternal life with the Father.

Selfishness would have saved Jesus from the cross. But it would have condemned the rest of us to death.

Here's what selfishness does: it makes you the center of your own universe and shrinks that universe down until nothing else fits. It convinces you that your comfort is more important than someone else's crisis. That your convenience matters more than someone else's need. That protecting yourself from inconvenience is worth leaving others in desperation.

I've watched selfishness destroy marriages when one partner consistently prioritized their own desires over the relationship. I've seen it damage children raised by parents who treated them as accessories to their own lives rather than souls to nurture. I've known friendships that ended because one person only showed up when they needed something, never when they were needed.

But understand that perfect love does something else for us that selfishness never can. Perfect love casts out all fear. When we embrace the love of Christ and learn to love like Christ, we stop operating from a place of scarcity and start operating from abundance. We stop being afraid that giving means losing. We stop believing that serving others diminishes us.

When we stop chasing our own comfort and start chasing what is trying to apprehend us, which is God Almighty, everything changes. We discover that the more we give, the more we have. That the more we serve, the more fulfilled we become. That the path to finding your life is losing it for the sake of something greater than yourself.

Selfishness tells you to protect what's yours. Perfect love teaches you that nothing was ever yours to begin with. It was all given to you so you could give it away.

Rejection

Now we arrive at the final spirit. The spirit of rejection. The spirit of rejection gives birth to a host of emotions that drive us to make life choices that are not for our good. It's one of the most devastating demons because it doesn't just wound you once. It teaches you to wound yourself repeatedly, to reject yourself before anyone else gets the chance.

Feeling rejected by a parent leads you to look for love in someone just like the parent who rejected you, hoping that this time, with this person, you'll finally be chosen. You keep going back to the same type of relationship, the same dynamic, the same pain, because some part of you believes that if you can just get it right this time, you can retroactively heal the original wound.

But it doesn't work that way.

The rejection of a potential mate leads you to never attempt dating again, or worse, to carry baggage from one relationship into the next. You punish the new person for the old person's sins. You build walls before they can. You leave before they get the chance to. You sabotage good things because you're so convinced that rejection is inevitable that you'd rather control when it happens than risk being blindsided again. I know this all too well because I've done it, and ever since, I have avoided dating because the last experience left me scarred.

Rejection leaves us fundamentally broken. It rewires how we see ourselves, how we interpret others' actions, how we move through the world. Every slight becomes proof of our unworthiness. Every disappointment becomes confirmation that we were right to expect the worst. Every relationship becomes a waiting game to see when they'll finally see what we believe about ourselves and leave.

And until we break free from rejection's hold, we can never chase that which we are meant to chase in life. We can't pursue our purpose because we're convinced we don't have one. We can't build healthy relationships because we don't believe we deserve them. We can't step into our calling because the fear of being rejected for who we really are keeps us performing a version of ourselves that we think will be acceptable.

But here's what rejection doesn't want you to know: the person who rejected you didn't have the authority to define your worth. Their opinion, their choice, their abandonment says more about them than it does about you. And the rejection you experienced, as painful as it was, does not get to write the rest of your story.

You have to separate the act of rejection from your identity. You were rejected. That's a fact. But you are not rejection. You are not defined by who didn't choose you. You are defined by who you are and whose you are.

And the God who created you never once looked at you and thought, "I made a mistake." Let that sink in.

What Now?

So now you know their names. Guilt, Greed, Envy, Selfishness, and Rejection. Five demons, five different strategies, but one common goal: to keep you from your place of destiny.

These aren't abstract concepts or philosophical ideas to discuss over coffee. These are real forces with real assignments against your life. They work together, they reinforce each other, they build on one another's lies. Guilt makes you feel unworthy. Envy makes you resent others' blessings. Greed makes you chase what won't satisfy. Selfishness isolates you. Rejection convinces you that you deserve all of it.

But here's what I need you to understand: naming them is only the first step. Recognition without action is just informed captivity. You can know the name of every demon chasing you and still let them catch you if you don't do the work of confronting them.

In the chapters ahead, we're going to dig deeper into each of these demons. We're going to examine their tactics, expose their lies, and develop strategies to defeat them. We're going to learn how to distinguish their voices from God's voice, how to recognize when they're operating, and how to shut them down when they attack.

But for now, I want you to sit with what you've read. I want you to be honest with yourself about which of these demons you've been wrestling with. Maybe it's one. Maybe it's all five. Maybe you're realizing for the first time that what you thought was just your personality or your circumstances is actually a demon that's been lying to you for years.

That realization might hurt. It might make you angry. It might make you grieve for the time you've lost, the relationships you've damaged, the opportunities you've missed while under their influence.

Feel that. Don't run from it.

Because that pain is the beginning of your liberation. That anger can be channeled into action. That grief can become the fuel for your transformation.

You're not reading this book by accident. You picked it up, or someone who loves you put it in your hands, because somewhere deep inside, you knew it was time to stop running and start chasing. Time to stop being hunted and start hunting. Time to call these demons by name and command them to leave.

They have names. You know them now.

The question is: what are you going to do about it?

CHAPTER FIVE
DEMONS THAT CHAIN YOU TO THE PAST

The Weight Of Yesterday

There's a difference between remembering your past and being imprisoned by it.

Memory is meant to be a teacher, not a warden. It should inform your present without dictating it, shape your wisdom without stealing your peace. But somehow, some memories don't stay where they belong. They become anchors, heavy chains wrapped around your ankles, holding you in place while the rest of the world moves forward.

You know the ones I'm talking about. The memories that show up uninvited at 2 a.m. The regrets that color every decision you make today. The shame that whispers you'll never be free from what you've done. These aren't just memories anymore. They've become prisons, and you've been serving a sentence for years without realizing the cell door was never actually locked.

I've carried that weight. After my mother passed from COVID-19, I didn't just grieve her loss. I grieved every conversation we never had, every moment I took for granted, every time I chose work over visiting her. Those weren't just sad thoughts. They were chains, each link forged from a different regret, each one heavier than the last.

What makes yesterday's weight so crushing is that it's always about things you can't change. You can't go back. You can't redo. You can't unsay those words or reclaim that moment. The past is fixed, immovable, set in stone. And yet we keep trying to lift it, to shift it, to somehow make it different than it was.

And there lies the trap.

The demons that chain you to your past don't need to be particularly creative. They don't have to invent new lies or craft elaborate schemes. All they have to do is keep your focus backward, keep you replaying what's already been played, keep you imprisoned by what you cannot change. While you're stuck there, you miss what's happening now. You miss who you could become. You miss the destiny that's waiting for you to finally let go and take the next step forward.

Some people carry trauma from what was done to them. Others carry guilt from what they did. Some carry both. But here's what I've learned about the weight of yesterday, regardless of how it got placed on your shoulders—it only has the power you give it. The past happened. That's a fact. But the past defining your present and determining your future? That's a choice, even when it doesn't feel like one.

Not every memory deserves equal weight in your life. Some need to be honored, learned from, and then released. Others need to be examined, understood for what they were, and deliberately set down. But too often, we treat every yesterday like it has the same claim on today, giving moments that have exceeded their expiration date the same authority as the ground you're standing on right now.

The question isn't whether you remember your past. The question is whether your past remembers you—whether it still has a grip on how you see yourself, how you move through the world, how you receive love, and how you pursue your purpose.

Bottomline, if yesterday still dictates today, you're not free. And freedom is your birthright.

Guilt's Greatest Lie

If the weight of yesterday is the anchor, then guilt is the chain that connects you to it.

In Chapter 4, we named guilt as one of the five chief demons. We acknowledged its power to destroy marriages, separate families, and take lives. But now we need to understand its specific assignment when it comes to your past—the lie it tells that keeps you imprisoned long after you've served your time.

Here's guilt's greatest lie: *You can never be free from what you've done.*

Not just that you did something wrong. Not just that you hurt someone or made a mistake. But that what you did has permanently defined who you are, and no amount of time, growth, change, or redemption can ever alter that reality. Guilt whispers that your past mistakes aren't just part of your story, they are your story. They're the headline, the title, the summary of your entire existence.

This is where guilt shifts from being a moral compass to becoming a prison warden.

In Revelation 12:10, we read about the accuser who stands before God day and night, bringing charges against believers.

"Then I heard a loud voice in heaven. It said, 'Now the salvation and the power and the kingdom of our God have come. The authority of his Messiah has come. The one who brings charges against our brothers and sisters has been thrown down. He brings charges against them in front of our God day and night."

Revelation 12:10 (NIrV)

The accuser's job is relentless accusation. Day and night. Without rest. Without mercy. It doesn't matter if you've repented, if you've changed, if you've made amends. The accuser isn't interested in your transformation. It's interested in your condemnation.

This is the spirit of guilt operating at its most destructive level. It takes genuine failures, real mistakes, actual sins, and weaponizes them against you. It replays them endlessly, distorts them to seem worse than they were, and convinces you that they define your entire worth as a human being.

I know this demon all too well. Felt like he and I are old acquaintances. After my mother died, guilt didn't attack me where I was actually vulnerable. My mother was like my best friend. We spent time together. We talked all the time. We had a relationship I treasured. But the crazy thing about guilt is that it doesn't need truth to build its case. It just needs an opening.

So guilt told me that if I had been a doctor, I could have saved her. That if I had been smarter, more successful, more accomplished, I could have bought her the house she always dreamed of. It convinced me that her dreams died unfulfilled because I wasn't enough. That she passed away before I could give her what she deserved. That my failures as a son weren't about absence but about inadequacy.

None of that was true. But guilt isn't interested in truth. It's interested in condemnation.

The insidious part is that guilt often starts with something real. Maybe you did hurt someone. Maybe you did make a selfish choice. Maybe you did fail when someone was counting on you. Healthy guilt, the conviction that comes from the Holy Spirit, would lead you to acknowledge that, make amends where possible, learn from it, and change your behavior going forward.

But toxic guilt, the kind wielded by the accuser, doesn't want your growth. It wants your destruction. It wants you stuck in the past, rehearsing your failures, unable to move forward because you're convinced you don't deserve to.

Here's how you can tell the difference between conviction and condemnation:

Conviction says, *"You made a mistake, and here's how to make it right."* Condemnation says, *"You are a mistake, and nothing can make you right."*

Conviction leads to specific action and then to peace. Condemnation leads to vague shame and endless self-punishment.

Conviction reminds you once and then releases you when you respond. Condemnation reminds you constantly, even after you've repented.

Conviction comes with a path forward. Condemnation comes with a life sentence.

The greatest lie guilt tells isn't just that you did something wrong. It's that you can never be free from what you've done. That your mistake is permanent. That your failure is final. That there's no statute of limitations on your shame.

But here's what guilt doesn't want you to know: the accuser has already been defeated. The charges have already been dropped. The sentence has already been served, not by you, but for you.

The same passage in Revelation that names the accuser also declares his defeat. He's been thrown down. His accusations, while loud, carry no legal weight in the courtroom of heaven. The debt has been paid. The record has been cleared.

You don't have to keep paying for what's already been purchased. You don't have to keep serving time for a sentence that's already been completed.

Guilt wants you to believe that freedom requires you to somehow earn your way out of your past. That if you just punish yourself enough, feel bad enough, sacrifice enough, maybe eventually you'll deserve to be free.

And that's the lie.

Freedom doesn't come from self-punishment. It comes from accepting that the punishment has already been borne, the price has already been paid, and you are invited to walk out of the prison cell whose door has been standing open the whole time.

So the question isn't whether you can be free from what you've done. The question is whether you're finally ready to believe you already are.

Unforgiveness As Chains

If guilt chains you to what you've done, unforgiveness chains you to what's been done to you.

It's a different kind of imprisonment, but equally binding. Guilt says you can't move forward because of your failures. Unforgiveness says you can't move forward because of theirs. Both keep you locked in the past, rehearsing old wounds, carrying weight that was never meant to be permanent.

Here's the cruel irony about unforgiveness: the person who hurt you has probably moved on. They're living their life, building their future, free from the burden of what they did to you. Meanwhile, you're still carrying the debt. You're still replaying the conversation. You're still nursing the wound. You're still building your life around the hurt they caused.

The difference is they're free while you're chained.

The sad thing is the chain isn't even real. It's a choice you're making every day, sometimes without even realizing it. A choice to hold on to what happened, to keep the offense alive, to make them pay by making yourself suffer. Because that's what unforgiveness does. It convinces you that holding on to the hurt is somehow holding them accountable.

But accountability and imprisonment aren't the same thing. Sure, they may owe you something, but the irony is you're the one serving time.

I used to believe that forgiveness was about them. That if I forgave someone who hurt me, I was letting them off the hook, giving them permission to walk away unpunished for what they'd done. I even used to say, "God is the God of Second Chances, Not Me." I wore that statement like a badge of honor, proof that I had standards, that I wouldn't be a doormat, that I knew my worth.

What I didn't realize was that I was building a prison and calling it protection. I was creating walls to keep hurt out, but those same walls were keeping me in. I was carrying baggage from old hurts into every new relationship, every new opportunity, every new season, wondering why nothing felt light anymore.

The reality I had to face was this: forgiveness isn't about the other person. It's about you. It's about taking back the power that pain has in your life and refusing to let it rent space in your head anymore. It's about releasing the debt they'll never pay so that you can finally stop being a collection agent for a bill that's bankrupting you.

Scripture makes this clear. In Colossians 3:13, we're given a direct instruction about how to handle the hurts we carry:

"Put up with one another. Forgive one another if you are holding something against someone. Forgive, just as the Lord forgave you."

Colossians 3:13 (NIrV)

Notice the instruction isn't conditional. It doesn't say forgive if they apologize. It doesn't say forgive if they deserve it. It doesn't say forgive if they've changed or proven themselves worthy of your grace. It says forgive as you have been forgiven.

That's the standard. And it's not about them. It's about modeling the grace you've received.

Now let me be clear about what forgiveness is not. Forgiveness is not pretending the hurt didn't happen. It's not excusing their behavior or minimizing the damage they caused. It's not inviting them back into your life to hurt you again. It's not even about reconciliation, though sometimes that happens.

Forgiveness is the decision to release them from the debt they owe you. It's acknowledging that something or someone caused a shift in your once positive outlook, turning it into a negative one, and then choosing not to let that shift define the rest of your story.

You can forgive someone and still maintain boundaries. You can forgive someone and never trust them again. You can forgive someone and choose not to have them in your life anymore. Forgiveness doesn't require you to be foolish. It requires you to be free.

The weight of unforgiveness shows up in ways we don't always recognize. Medical professionals have documented how emotions manifest themselves physically. People who can't forgive develop heart disease. They carry chronic pain. They age faster than they should because of the stress and anxiety lodged in their bodies. Unforgiveness isn't just a spiritual problem or an emotional problem. It's a whole-body problem.

I've watched people destroy their marriages defending against hurts from previous relationships. I've seen talented individuals refuse opportunities because betrayal once felt unbearable. I've known parents who damaged their children trying to protect them from the pain the parents experienced, not realizing they were just creating a different kind of pain for the next generation to fight.

That's the generational curse of unforgiveness. It doesn't just chain you to your past. It chains everyone around you to it too.

The process of forgiving isn't a one-time event. It's an ongoing journey that challenges your perceptions and the very essence of your relationships. It demands that you confront the pain inflicted upon you by those who managed to breach your walls of trust. And some days, you'll have to choose forgiveness again, even for the same offense, because the hurt keeps trying to reassert itself.

But each time you choose it, the chain gets weaker. Each time you release them from the debt, you take another step toward freedom. Each time you refuse to rehearse the offense, you reclaim a piece of your peace.

Whether they accept your forgiveness or not is irrelevant to your liberation. Whether they apologize or acknowledge what they did is none of your concern. You're not forgiving them for their sake. You're forgiving them for yours.

You're reclaiming the power you gave to pain. You're rendering it powerless over you. You're firmly placing yourself in the driver's seat of your own life and beginning the true journey toward your place of destiny.

The person who hurt you might never know you forgave them. They might never care. They might never change. But you'll know. You'll care. And you'll be different because you refused to let their actions continue to dictate your story.

That's not weakness. That's power. That's freedom. That's choosing to be unchained.

The Mythology Of "If Only"

"If only I had taken that job."

"If only I had stayed in that relationship."

"If only I had been there that day."

"If only I had said yes instead of no, or no instead of yes."

These two words together form one of the most seductive lies the past can tell you. They create a mythology, a fantasy version of your life where everything would have worked out perfectly if you had just made one different choice at one critical moment.

The mythology of "*if only*" convinces you that there's a parallel universe somewhere where you made the right call, and in that universe, everything is better. Your relationships are healthier. Your bank account is fuller. Your regrets don't exist. And if you could just go back and change that one thing, you could step into that better life.

But here's the problem with that mythology: it's built on an impossible premise. It assumes that changing one variable wouldn't change anything else. That you could alter one decision without a cascade of consequences rippling through every moment that followed. That you could rewrite one chapter without affecting the rest of the story.

If only life were that simple and worked that way but it doesn't.

If you had taken that job, you don't know what you would have encountered there. You don't know if the company would have downsized six months later or if the work environment would have been toxic or if you would have been miserable in ways you can't imagine. You're comparing your actual life, with all its visible struggles and disappointments, to a fantasy life where only the good things happen.

If you had stayed in that relationship, you don't know if it would have gotten better or worse. You don't know if the problems you saw on the surface were masking deeper issues. You don't know if staying would have meant sacrificing more of yourself than leaving did. You're romanticizing a past that may never have existed the way you remember it.

The "*if only*" game is infinite regression. You can trace it back endlessly. If only you had chosen a different major. If only you had moved to a different city. If only you had met different people. If only, if only, if only. Each one leading to another, creating a chain that stretches all the way back to decisions you made as a teenager, as a child, decisions your parents made before you were born.

But at what point do you stop? At what point do you accept that the life you have is the only one you can actually live?

The demons love "*if only*" because it keeps you stuck in an impossible past. Not just any past, but a past that never existed and never could have existed the way you imagine it. It's a prison made of fantasies, and you're serving time for crimes you never committed in a world that was never real.

I've watched people spend decades trapped in this mythology. They make every decision based on the ghost of a choice they didn't make twenty years ago. They sabotage present opportunities because they're too busy mourning the imaginary life they could have had. They refuse to embrace where they are because they're convinced they should be somewhere else.

And here's the cold hard truth: while you're living in the land of "*if only*," real opportunities are passing you by. Real relationships are being neglected. Real growth is being postponed. The present moment, the only moment where you actually have power, is being sacrificed on the altar of an unchangeable past.

Living with regrets is like living in a house without walls. It's constant exposure, constant vulnerability, constant inability to find solace. But living in "if only" is worse. It's living in a house that doesn't exist, trying to furnish rooms that were never built, arranging your life around a floor plan you can never walk through.

I am sorry to be the bearer of bad news, but you can't live in two places at once. You can't be in the present while dwelling in an alternate past. And you certainly can't build a future while your foundation is nothing but speculation about roads not taken.

The truth you need to hear is this: you don't know what would have happened if you had made a different choice. You can't know. And spending your life trying to figure it out is a waste of the life you actually have.

Maybe that job would have been worse. Maybe that relationship would have destroyed you. Maybe that different path would have led to different pain, just dressed up in different clothes. Or maybe it would have been better in some ways and worse in others, because that's how life works. There's no perfect path. There's only the path you're on and what you choose to do with it.

The antidote to "if only" isn't pretending you made all the right choices. It's accepting that the choices you made, right or wrong, led you to where you are. And where you are is the only place you can start from. The only place you have any actual power. The only place where your decisions matter.

You can't undo the past. You can't rewrite history. You can't step into the parallel universe where you made different choices. But you can stop letting "if only" rob you of today.

You can make peace with the fact that you did the best you could with the information you had at the time. You can choose to learn from your mistakes without being enslaved by them. You can acknowledge regret without letting it become your identity.

The question isn't "what if I had done things differently?" The question is "what am I going to do now that I'm here?"

Because "here" is the only place you actually exist. And "now" is the only time you have power to act.

Stop living in the mythology of "*if only*." Start living in the reality of "right now." That's where your destiny is. Not in some fantasy past you can never access, but in the present moment you keep missing while you're busy looking backward.

Replaying The Tape

Your mind has a rewind button. And sometimes, it gets stuck.

You know the feeling just as well as I do. It's 2 a.m. and you're rehearsing a conversation from five years ago. You're rewriting your responses, coming up with the perfect comeback, imagining what you should have said instead of what you actually said. Or you're replaying a failure, watching it unfold frame by frame, zooming in on every mistake, every misstep, every moment where things went wrong.

The demons love this. They thrive on repetition. Because every time you replay the tape, you're not just remembering what happened. You're re-traumatizing yourself by constantly re-engaging with the pain. You're preventing the wound from healing properly, keeping it open and sharp, so the pain remains as intense today as it was when you first experienced it.

This is one of the most insidious ways the past keeps its grip on you. Not through dramatic flashbacks or obvious triggers, but through quiet, constant rehearsal. The mental loop that plays in the background of your daily life, reminding you of what went wrong, who hurt you, what you lost, what you should have done differently.

And here's the thing: the tape never tells the full story. It only shows the highlight reel of your worst moments. It edits out the context, the circumstances, the fact that you were doing the best you could with what you had. It magnifies your failures and minimizes your efforts. It turns a mistake into a character flaw, a bad decision into permanent evidence of your inadequacy.

I've replayed tapes I wish I could burn. Conversations where I said the wrong thing. Moments where I let someone down. Decisions that altered the course of my life in ways I didn't want. And every time I hit rewind, it felt like I was solving something, like if I just analyzed it enough, replayed it enough, I could somehow change what happened or at least make sense of it.

But replaying isn't solving. It's suffering. It's choosing to live in the worst moments of your past over and over again instead of in the present moment where you actually have power.

The re-traumatization loop works like this: something happens that hurts you. Your brain records it because pain is important, pain means danger, pain means pay attention. But instead of processing it and filing it away as something that happened, you keep pulling it back out. You replay it when you're trying to sleep. You replay it when something in the present reminds you of it. You replay it when you're anxious or stressed or feeling vulnerable.

Each time you replay it, the neural pathway gets stronger. The memory becomes more ingrained. The emotional response becomes more automatic. What started as one painful moment becomes a pattern, a groove worn deep in your mind that your thoughts fall into without you even realizing it.

This is how trauma stays alive long after the original event is over. This is how a single betrayal becomes a lifetime of trust issues. This is how one failure becomes a permanent belief that you're not good enough. Not because the original event was so powerful, but because you've replayed it so many times that it's become more real than your actual present reality.

The demons use this against you. They know that if they can get you to replay your worst moments on a loop, they don't have to do anything else. You'll imprison yourself. You'll keep your own wounds fresh. You'll make sure the past never loses its power over you.

And often, without your awareness and in the absence of honest feedback from others, you miss crucial moments of reflection. You don't realize you're doing it. You think you're processing, working through it, trying to understand. You don't see that you're being held hostage by something that already happened and can't be changed.

If you really want to break the replay loop then that requires conscious interruption. It requires you to recognize and stop yourself when you start to rewind and choosing not to press play. It means recognizing when you're rehearsing old pain and deliberately redirecting your thoughts to the present moment.

None of this means you start pretending the past didn't happen. It's about refusing to give it more airtime than it deserves. It's about acknowledging that yes, that happened, and no, replaying it won't change it, and yes, it hurt, but staying in that hurt serves no purpose except to keep you stuck.

Sometimes the tape plays automatically. You can't always control when a memory surfaces or when something triggers you. But you can control what you do once it starts. You can choose to watch the whole thing again, or you can choose to turn it off. You can choose to let it pull you back into the past, or you can choose to acknowledge it and return to the present.

I found that journaling helped me with this. What I discovered by doing this is that when I wrote about what kept replaying, I was externalizing it. In doing this, you get it out of your head and onto paper where you can see it for what it is. And often, when you write the same story for the third or fourth time, you start to notice something: you're not discovering anything new. You're just rehearsing. And that's your signal that it's time to stop pressing rewind.

I am a firm believer in therapy. A good therapist can help you process what happened so you can finally file it away instead of keeping it on constant replay. They can help you identify the lies embedded in the tape, the distortions your mind has added over time, the ways you're making the past worse than it was or taking on responsibility that wasn't yours to carry.

But ultimately, you have to be the one who chooses to stop pressing play. You have to be the one who says, "I've seen this tape enough times. I know what happened. Watching it again won't change anything. It's time to let it rest."

The past happened. You can't rewrite it. But you can stop giving it a prime-time slot in your present. You can stop letting demons use repetition to keep you chained to moments that are long gone.

You can choose to be here, now, instead of trapped in there, then.

The Past As False Safety

Here's something nobody wants to admit: sometimes we cannot be free because we don't really want to be free.

At least not consciously, anyway. Not in the part of our mind that says we're ready to move forward, ready to heal, ready to leave the past behind. But in that deeper place, the place where fear makes decisions before logic can intervene, freedom feels dangerous. The unknown is a very scary place because you have never been there and don't know what to expect. It makes that familiar pain, as much as it hurts, feels safer than the unfamiliar peace we've never experienced.

This is one of the hardest truths about breaking chains. The chains hurt. They limit you. They keep you imprisoned in moments that are long gone. But they're also predictable. You know how they feel. You know how to live with them. You've built your entire identity around carrying this weight, and the thought of setting it down raises a terrifying question: who are you without it?

I've watched people sabotage their own liberation over and over again. They do the work. They make progress. They get right to the edge of a breakthrough and then something shifts. They pick up an old habit. They revisit an old wound. They start replaying tapes they'd finally stopped watching. They reach back for the chains they'd almost broken free from.

And when you ask them why, they can't always tell you. Because it's not rational. It's not a conscious choice. It's the part of them that's terrified of who they might become if they're not defined by their past anymore.

The devil you know feels safer than the God you're learning to trust. Familiar suffering feels more manageable than unfamiliar joy. The prison cell you've lived in for years feels like home, and stepping out into freedom feels like walking off a cliff into nothing.

This is why people stay in toxic relationships long after they should leave. This is why talented individuals refuse opportunities that could change their lives. This is why some people keep choosing the same pain over and over, even when better options are available. Not because they're weak or foolish, but because the alternative requires them to step into unknown territory where the old rules don't apply anymore.

Your past, as painful as it is, has become your comfort zone. You know how to navigate it. You know what to expect. You've developed coping mechanisms that work, even if they're unhealthy. You've built walls that keep certain things out, even if they also keep you in. You've created a version of yourself that can survive in this pain, and you're not sure if that version of yourself can survive anywhere else.

But here's what you need to understand: that's not safety. That's just familiarity. And familiarity is not the same thing as security.

A bone that heals crooked might feel normal after a while. You adjust to it. You learn to live with the limitation. You convince yourself it's fine because the pain has become predictable. But normal doesn't mean healthy. And the longer you leave it crooked, the more damage it does, not just to that bone but to everything connected to it.

Sometimes the only way to heal correctly is to re-break what was set wrong. And yes, that sounds brutal. Because it is brutal. The temporary agony of breaking and resetting feels worse than the chronic ache of living with dysfunction. But leaving it crooked means living with pain and limitation for the rest of your life. The permanent damage of leaving it broken is worse than the temporary pain of fixing it.

The same is true for your chains. Breaking them feels dangerous. It feels destabilizing. It feels like you're losing something, even though what you're losing is what's been hurting you. Because it's yours. It's familiar. It's the pain you know, and the human brain is wired to prefer known danger over unknown safety.

But breakthrough often feels like breakdown at first. Liberation can be disorienting when you've spent years in captivity. Freedom feels strange when you've gotten used to the weight.

The question isn't whether letting go feels scary. Because it most certainly will. The question is whether you're willing to feel that fear and step forward anyway. Whether you're willing to risk the unknown peace instead of clinging to the familiar pain.

Because the past isn't protecting you. It's imprisoning you. And no matter how safe that prison feels, it's still a prison. The door is open. The chains are breakable. The question is whether you're finally ready to walk out, even if you don't know exactly what's waiting on the other side.

God is not asking you to leap blindly. He's asking you to trust that He's already on the other side of your chains, waiting to show you who you were meant to be without them. That the person you become in freedom is stronger than the person you've been in bondage. That unfamiliar peace is better than familiar pain, even when your body tells you otherwise.

The past as false safety is one of the demons' favorite tactics. Because if they can convince you that you need your chains, they don't have to fight to keep them on you. You'll do it yourself. You'll sabotage your own liberation and call it wisdom. You'll choose predictable suffering and call it stability.

But you were not created for captivity, no matter how comfortable you've tried to make it. You were created for freedom. And that freedom is waiting for you to choose it, even when everything in you wants to retreat back to what's familiar.

The devil you know is still the devil. And the God you're learning to trust has already proven He's faithful.

CHAPTER SIX
DEMONS THAT STEAL YOUR PRESENT

The Thief Of Now

You know that feeling when you're physically present but mentally somewhere else? When your body is sitting at dinner with people you love, but your mind is replaying an argument from last week or rehearsing one you're convinced is coming tomorrow? When you're at your child's recital, phone in hand, scrolling through other people's lives while missing your own?

That's precisely what I mean when I say demons steal your present.

Chapter 4 was about the chains that keep you tethered to your past. This chapter is about something equally deceptive but harder to recognize because it's happening right now, in real-time, while you're too distracted to notice. These demons don't just haunt your history or threaten your future. They rob you blind in the only moment you're actually guaranteed to live.

Right now.

This moment is where life happens. Not yesterday. Not tomorrow. But here. And while you've been worrying about what's coming or obsessing over what's already gone, these demons have been pickpocketing your joy, your peace, your connection, and your contentment. They've been teaching you to be anywhere but where you are, to want anything but what you have, to be anyone but who you actually are.

And you're so busy chasing or running that you don't even realize what you're missing.

Let me tell you what it cost me before I understood this. I lost years, not all at once, but in a thousand stolen moments. Conversations I was physically present for but mentally absent from. Celebrations where I showed up but never actually arrived. Quiet evenings I could have enjoyed but spent worrying about problems that never materialized. Achievements I worked toward for years but couldn't celebrate because I was already focused on the next thing, convinced that contentment was always just one more accomplishment away.

The demons that steal your present are clever. They don't announce themselves the way guilt does, dragging chains behind them. They don't make dramatic entrances like rejection, slamming doors and declaring you unwanted. They whisper. They distract. They redirect your attention so skillfully that you don't realize you've been robbed until the moment has already passed.

And by then, it's too late to get it back.

Here's the truth that I am ashamed to say took me too long to learn: you can't live in a moment you're refusing to inhabit. You can't experience joy if you're constantly looking over your shoulder at what you lost or straining your eyes trying to see what's around the next corner. You can't build genuine connection with people when you're comparing your life to everyone else's insta-life. You can't find peace when you're running on a hamster wheel, chasing satisfaction that keeps moving just out of reach.

The cost of not being present in your own life is everything. It's the relationships that withered because you were there but not really there. It's the moments you can never recreate because you missed them the first time. It's the joy you traded for anxiety, the contentment you sacrificed for comparison, the connection you forfeited for self-protection.

And the worst part? You can't get those moments back. You can heal from your past. You can prepare for your future. But once now is gone, it's gone. The things you could have done and didn't in the moment become about as useful as a drinking cup with a hole in it.

So before we dive into the specific demons operating in this space, before we name Envy, Greed, and Selfishness, I need you to understand what's at stake here. This isn't just about feeling better or being more mindful or practicing gratitude like it's another item on your self-improvement checklist.

This is about learning to actually live your life instead of just surviving it. This is about being fully present for the people you love and the moments that matter. This is about reclaiming the gift of now before these demons convince you that life is something that happens somewhere else, to someone else, in some other time.

Those demons are lying to you. Life is happening right here. Right now. While you read these words.

So the question is: are you going to be here for it?

Envy's Present-Tense Poison

What if the life you're living is the one someone else is praying for?

Sit with that for a moment. Because Envy never will.

You already know this demon's name. We met it in Chapter 4, where we learned it makes you hate your own life while staring at someone else's. We talked about how it sows seeds of insufficiency, how it convinces you that their gain is your loss, how it keeps you so focused on someone else's lane that you swerve out of your own.

But here's what I need you to understand now: Envy doesn't just distort your perspective. It steals your present by making it impossible for you to actually be *here*—in your own life, in your own moment, in your own blessing.

Think about it. How can you be grateful for your life when you're constantly measuring it against everyone else's? How can you celebrate your wins when you're too busy cataloging their victories? How can you be present in your own story when you're obsessed with the plot of someone else's?

You can't. And Envy knows it.

I know this demon intimately because I fed it for years. I used to scroll through Instagram and see everyone's fabulous life—big houses and nice cars, always traveling the world—and I wanted to trade places with them. I started to think, what did I do wrong in life that I was not on the other side of the equation? Don't get me wrong, I do alright and have established a name for myself, especially in the education space, but I didn't have all the glitz and glamour that I saw on Instagram.

And that's when Envy had me. Right there. In that moment of comparison, in that question of "what did I do wrong," the demon convinced me that my life wasn't enough because it didn't look like someone else's carefully curated feed.

But here's what I didn't see. Here's what Envy made sure I couldn't see.

I wasn't comparing reality to reality. I was comparing my ordinary Tuesday—the messy kitchen, the unfinished projects, the bills on the counter, the mundane moments that make up an actual life—to someone else's carefully edited greatest hits. I was declaring myself the loser in a competition that was rigged from the start, judged by rules that nobody actually lives by.

That big house in the photo? I didn't know about the crippling mortgage strangling them every month. I didn't see the marriage falling apart inside those beautiful walls. I didn't hear the arguments echoing through those rooms that looked so peaceful in pictures.

Those exotic vacations? I didn't see the credit card debt piling up with every trip. I didn't know they were running from problems back home that would still be waiting when they landed. I didn't understand that sometimes people travel to escape lives they can't stand living.

That perfect family photo? I couldn't see the fight that happened thirty seconds before the shutter clicked. I couldn't feel the tension that returned thirty seconds after everyone stopped smiling for the camera. I didn't know that the perfection I envied was a performance that exhausted everyone in it.

But Envy doesn't deal in full stories. It deals in half-truths and carefully edited lies. It shows you the highlight reel and hides the blooper footage. It shows you the trophy and hides the cost of winning it. It shows you the destination and hides the journey that broke people to get there.

And while I was scrolling—while I was comparing, resenting, coveting—I was missing my own life.

I want you to hear that. Really hear it.

While I was busy wishing I had someone else's house, I wasn't enjoying the one I was sitting in. While I was envying someone else's career, I wasn't present for the work that was actually in front of me. While I was staring at someone else's relationship, I wasn't showing up for the people who were actually in my life.

I was physically present in moments I was mentally absent from. I was surrounded by blessings I couldn't see because my eyes were fixed on someone else's. I was living a life I couldn't appreciate because Envy had convinced me it wasn't enough.

That's how this demon steals your present. Not by taking anything from you directly, but by making you incapable of receiving what's already yours. Not by removing blessings from your life, but by blinding you to the ones already there. Not by giving someone else what should have been yours, but by convincing you that what you have doesn't count.

I've watched this demon steal years of joy from people who had every reason to celebrate. They had homes—real homes, with roofs and warmth and safety—but they couldn't enjoy them because someone else's home was bigger. They had relationships—people who loved them, who showed up for them, who chose them—but they couldn't appreciate them because someone else's seemed easier. They had careers—meaningful work, steady income, opportunities to grow—but they couldn't find satisfaction because someone else's seemed more glamorous.

They had everything they needed to be content. And Envy convinced them it wasn't enough. So they spent their present longing for a life they didn't have instead of living the one they did.

The problem is that Envy robs you of the capacity for gratitude. And without gratitude, you cannot be present. It's impossible. You can't enjoy what you have because you're too busy wanting what you don't. You can't celebrate where you are because you're too focused on where you're not. You can't rest in God's provision for you because you're questioning why He provided differently for someone else.

Envy makes you a tourist in your own life—always looking elsewhere, always convinced that happiness exists somewhere you're not, always believing that contentment is one comparison away.

But here's the truth Envy will never tell you: what was meant for them was prepared specifically for them. Their journey required their preparation. Their blessings came with their responsibilities. Their highlight reel was purchased with struggles you never saw and sacrifices you wouldn't want to make.

And what's meant for you? It's being prepared specifically for you. In ways you can't see yet. On a timeline that isn't subject to your impatience or their Instagram feed. With blessings tailored to your journey, your growth, your purpose.

Your story is not their story. Your lane is not their lane. Your blessings are not their blessings. And their success—real or performed—does not diminish your worth or delay your future.

So here's my question: are you going to let Envy keep stealing your present by making you resent everyone else's? Or are you going to put down the phone, look around at your actual life, and choose to be grateful for what's right in front of you?

Because here's what I've learned: gratitude is the antidote to Envy. You cannot be envious and grateful at the same time. You cannot resent someone else's blessings while genuinely appreciating your own. You cannot scroll through someone else's life and be present in yours.

One of them has to go.

So put down the phone. Close the app. Stop the scroll.

Look around. Not at what you wish you had. At what you actually have. The people. The moments. The ordinary blessings you've been too distracted to notice.

And choose to be here. Really here. Present in your own life instead of spectating someone else's.

Because this life—your life, the one you're actually living—is the only one you get. And every moment you spend wishing it looked like someone else's is a moment of your own you'll never get back.

Don't let Envy steal another one.

Greed's Hamster Wheel

At what point do we say enough?

Not in theory. Not someday. Right now, in this moment, with what you already have—when do you stop chasing and start living?

You already know Greed's name. We met this demon in Chapter 4, and you understand what it does: it breeds self-centered actions, sacrifices what genuinely matters, and convinces you that happiness is always one more acquisition away. But knowing a demon exists and recognizing when it's robbing you blind are two different things.

And Greed is robbing you right now. In real-time. While you're reading this sentence, it's whispering about something you don't have yet.

Here's how it works.

You finally get the promotion you've been chasing for five years. The one you stayed late for, sacrificed weekends for, lost sleep over. It's yours. You did it. But instead of celebrating—instead of being present in that accomplishment, instead of letting it sink into your bones that *you made it*—Greed whispers, "Great. Now you need to aim for the next level."

The celebration lasts thirty seconds. The hunger returns immediately.

You buy the house you've been dreaming about. The one you drove past a hundred times imagining yourself living there. The keys are finally in your hand. But instead of enjoying it—instead of sitting on the porch and breathing in the fact that this is *yours*—you're already scrolling through listings in better neighborhoods, convinced that satisfaction lives somewhere else. Somewhere bigger. Somewhere more impressive.

You start to operate from a space where you're never where you are. You're always where you're going next. Always reaching for the next rung while standing on a ladder you never stopped to appreciate.

This is Greed's hamster wheel. And once you're on it, you don't know how to get off.

I lived on this wheel for years without recognizing it. Every goal I hit became a starting line for the next race. Every blessing I received became a baseline for what I expected next. I couldn't rest in any accomplishment because Greed had trained me to see arrival as just another departure. There was always something else. Always something more. Always somewhere I hadn't reached yet.

And while I was running—while I was chasing, accumulating, striving—I was missing everything that was actually happening around me.

Moments with people I loved. Milestones I should have savored. Quiet blessings I was too distracted to receive. I was so focused on building the future that I forgot to live in the present. So busy chasing "more" that I couldn't see "enough" was already standing right in front of me, waiting to be noticed.

That's what makes Greed a thief of your present. It doesn't just make you want more. It makes you incapable of enjoying what you have. It robs you of contentment, of gratitude, of the ability to actually be *here*—fully present in your own life. You could have everything you ever said you wanted and still feel empty because Greed has trained you to always be hungry. Always reaching. Always dissatisfied.

Jesus warned about this.

He said, "Watch out! Be on your guard against wanting to have more and more things. Life is not made up of how much a person has."

Luke 12:15 (NIrV)

I want you to read that again and let it settle. Your life—the quality of it, the meaning of it, the joy of it—has nothing to do with the abundance of your possessions. But Greed will convince you otherwise. It will enlist its siblings to keep you distracted. It will whisper that if you just had a little more, *then* you'd finally be happy. *Then* you'd finally be satisfied. *Then* you'd finally arrive.

It's a lie. And every lap around that wheel is a present moment you'll never get back.

I've watched this demon steal years from people who had every reason to celebrate but couldn't because they were too busy reaching for the next thing. I've seen it hollow out relationships when one partner was always chasing a bigger house, a nicer car, a better lifestyle, while the other just wanted time together. I've watched it convince people that rest is laziness, that contentment is complacency, that being satisfied with what you have means you've stopped growing.

But here's the truth Greed will never tell you: the wheel doesn't have to keep spinning.

You can step off. Not by rejecting ambition or abandoning goals—those things aren't the enemy. But by refusing to let Greed convince you that satisfaction lives in the next thing instead of this moment. By choosing to be present with what you have rather than perpetually distracted by what you don't.

The pursuit of more will blind you to the beauty of enough if you let it. And enough—real enough, soul-deep enough—isn't a number you reach. It's a decision you make.

Greed will never tell you to stop running. That's not its nature. It will keep you on that wheel until you die, convinced that satisfaction was always just one more thing away.

So you have to tell yourself.

Stop. Look around. Realize you've been blessed all along.

Then do something radical: *stay here*. In this moment. With these people. In this life. In this blessing you've been too busy chasing to actually receive.

Because this moment—right now—is the only one you're guaranteed.

Don't let Greed steal it too.

Selfishness As Isolation

The walls you built to protect yourself have become the prison that contains you.

I need you to sit with that. Because Selfishness won't let you see it on your own.

In Chapter 4, we named Selfishness as the antithesis of perfect love—the demon that whispers "What about me?" before considering anyone else's needs. We talked about how it calculates cost before compassion, how it measures investment before offering love.

But here's what makes Selfishness particularly devastating when it comes to stealing your present: it doesn't just make you self-centered. It isolates you. And in that isolation, it robs you of the very thing that makes life worth living—genuine connection with other people.

Remember the man in scripture who lived among the tombs? The one cutting himself with stones, so tormented that no chain could hold him, so isolated that he lived among the dead instead of the living? When Jesus asked the demon's name, the response was chilling:

"My name is Legion, for we are many."

Not a single spirit. A multitude. A chaotic crowd of voices working together to keep that man naked, wounded, and utterly alone in his suffering.

That's what Selfishness does. It multiplies. It brings friends. And together, they build walls around you so high that nobody can get in—and you can't get out.

Let me show you how it steals your present, moment by moment, relationship by relationship.

You're at dinner with someone who wants to connect with you—really connect—but you're calculating what you're getting out of the conversation. Your body is at the table, but your mind is running cost-benefit analysis. Is this worth my time? What do I gain from this? How does this serve my interests?

And while you're calculating, you're missing them. Missing the story they're trying to tell you. Missing the vulnerability they're offering. Missing the moment of connection that could have deepened into something meaningful.

You're in a relationship where vulnerability would create intimacy, but you're protecting yourself instead of opening up. Every time they reach for you emotionally, you pull back. Every time they ask for more of you, you give them less. You've decided that letting someone truly know you is too dangerous, too costly, too risky.

So you keep them at arm's length. Close enough to say you have someone. Far enough that they can never really hurt you.

And you wonder why the relationship feels hollow.

You're surrounded by people who want to know you—really know you—but you've built walls so effective that knowing you has become impossible. You've mastered the art of surface-level connection. You can talk for hours without saying anything real. You can be in a room full of people and remain completely alone.

Those walls you built? They were supposed to keep hurt out. But here's what Selfishness didn't tell you: they keep love out too.

Every wall that protects you from potential pain also blocks you from potential connection. Every barrier that shields you from rejection also prevents you from being truly known. Every defense mechanism that keeps you safe also keeps you isolated.

And isolation is its own kind of suffering.

I've watched Selfishness hollow out relationships that should have been life-giving. Marriages where every conversation became a negotiation, where self-interest trumped partnership, where "What do I get out of this?" mattered more than "How can we grow together?" I watched love slowly starve because neither person was willing to give more than they received.

I've seen friendships that felt more transactional than transformational. Every interaction had to serve a purpose or it wasn't worth the investment. Every request for support was weighed against what had been given before. Scorekeeping replaced genuine care until the friendship became nothing more than a ledger of debts and credits.

I've known families where children learned early that their needs were inconvenient, their emotions were burdensome, and their very existence was supposed to revolve around making someone else comfortable. Those children grew into adults who didn't know how to receive love because they'd never been taught they were worth it.

That's the fruit of Selfishness. Not just self-centeredness, but profound isolation. Not just putting yourself first, but ending up utterly alone.

And here's the tragic irony that Selfishness will never admit: it promises you security but delivers loneliness. It promises you control but delivers isolation. It promises you protection but delivers a prison where you're both the guard and the inmate.

You're safe, maybe. But you're also alone.

You're protected from being hurt. But you're also cut off from being loved.

You've secured yourself from rejection. But you've also eliminated the possibility of being truly known and chosen.

While you're busy protecting yourself, while you're calculating costs and measuring investments and guarding your walls, you're missing the present moment you could be sharing with someone else. You're missing the conversation that could have become a lifelong friendship. You're missing the moment of connection with your child because you were too focused on your own comfort. You're missing the opportunity to love someone deeply because you were too afraid of what it might cost you.

Those moments don't wait. They don't come back. They happen once, and if you're too busy protecting yourself to be present for them, they're gone forever.

Jesus could have chosen Selfishness in the garden of Gethsemane.

Think about it. He knew what was coming—the betrayal by someone He'd loved, the abandonment by people He'd poured into for years, the mockery, the beating, the crown of thorns pressed into His skull, the nails driven through His hands, the cross. He felt the weight of it so heavily that He sweat drops of blood asking if there was another way.

Every reason to walk away. Every justification to protect Himself. Every argument for self-preservation that Selfishness could whisper.

But He stayed.

Perfect love stayed. Perfect love chose the cross over comfort. Perfect love prioritized our liberation over His protection. Perfect love demonstrated that giving—even when giving costs you everything—is the only path to life that actually matters.

Scripture tells us something that Selfishness doesn't want you to hear:

"There is no fear in love. Instead, perfect love drives away fear."

1 John 4:18, NIrV

Read that again. Let it sink in.

Fear is what builds the walls. Fear of rejection. Fear of being hurt. Fear of giving more than you get. Fear of being truly known and found wanting.

But perfect love—the kind of love that stays, that gives, that opens itself to potential pain for the sake of genuine connection—that love casts out fear. It dismantles the walls. It tears down the barriers. It makes real relationship possible.

When we learn to love like that—to stop operating from scarcity and start operating from abundance—everything changes. We stop being afraid that giving means losing. We stop believing that serving others diminishes us. We discover that vulnerability isn't weakness but the gateway to the very connection we've been craving.

The walls have to come down.

Not all at once, maybe. Not recklessly or foolishly. You don't have to tear them down for people who have proven they can't be trusted with your heart. But brick by brick, in relationships that have earned it, with people who have shown up for you, the walls have to come down.

Because here's what Selfishness doesn't want you to know: you were never meant to live in isolation. You were created for connection, for community, for the kind of love that only happens when you're willing to be fully known. You were designed for relationships that require vulnerability, that demand presence, that cost something.

And every moment you spend behind those walls—protecting yourself from potential pain, calculating costs instead of offering love, guarding yourself instead of giving yourself—is a moment of genuine connection you'll never get back.

So here's my question: are you going to keep building walls? Or are you going to risk being present—really present—with the people right in front of you?

Because you can't do both. You can't be isolated and connected at the same time. You can't protect yourself from everyone and still be known by anyone. You can't hoard yourself and experience the fullness of love.

One of them has to go.

So lower the walls. Not for everyone. But for someone. Start somewhere.

Risk being known. Risk being present. Risk loving someone without calculating what you'll get in return.

Because this moment—with these people, in this relationship, right now—is the only one you're guaranteed.

Don't let Selfishness steal it too.

The Interconnected Web

Here's what you need to understand about demons: they don't work alone.

I've been talking about Envy, Greed, and Selfishness as separate forces, and in one sense they are. Each has its own voice, its own tactics, its own way of stealing your present. But the truth is far more complicated and dangerous than that.

These demons collaborate.

They reinforce each other. They build on one another's lies. They create a web so intricate that by the time you realize you're caught in it, you can't tell where one strand ends and another begins.

Let me show you how this works in real time.

It starts with Envy. You're scrolling through social media and you see someone's vacation photos, their new house, their promotion, their seemingly perfect life. Envy whispers, *"Why don't you have that? What did they do to deserve it that you didn't?"* That seed of resentment takes root, and suddenly you're not present in your own life anymore. You're mentally cataloging everything you don't have, everything you think you deserve, everything that feels unfair about your circumstances compared to theirs.

That's when Greed shows up. Envy made you want what they have. Now Greed tells you how to get it. *"You need to work harder. Earn more. Buy bigger. Achieve more. Then you'll finally be happy. Then you'll finally measure up."* So you start chasing. You take the extra shifts. You sacrifice time with your family. You accumulate things you don't need because having them makes you feel like you're keeping up, like you're not falling behind in the race Envy convinced you that you were losing.

And then Selfishness arrives to justify it all. When your partner asks for more time together, Selfishness whispers, *"You deserve to pursue your goals. You've earned this. Don't let anyone make you feel guilty for wanting more."* When your kids need you but you're exhausted from working sixty-hour weeks, Selfishness says, *"You're doing this for them. They'll understand later."* When a friend needs help but you're too busy climbing your ladder, Selfishness assures you, *"You have to take care of yourself first. You can't pour from an empty cup."*

And let me tell you about that last line! That's where Selfishness gets particularly clever. Because there's a difference between self-care and selfishness, and this demon knows how to blur that line until you can't tell which one you're practicing.

Self-care is recognizing your limits and setting healthy boundaries. Selfishness is making everything about you and calling it boundaries.

Self-care is taking time to recharge so you can show up for others. Selfishness is always taking and never giving, then justifying it with therapy language.

Self-care is protecting your peace. Selfishness is avoiding anything that requires sacrifice, then calling it protecting your peace.

The demons know this. They know how to take something healthy and twist it just enough that you can't see what's happening. So you end up isolated, exhausted from chasing what you don't have, resentful of people who seem to have it easier, and convinced that you're just practicing self-care when really you're building walls that are keeping everyone out.

This is the web. Envy feeds Greed. Greed justifies Selfishness. Selfishness creates isolation. And isolation invites another demon we haven't fully explored yet in this chapter—Rejection.

Because when you're isolated long enough, when you've built walls high enough, when you've prioritized yourself to the point where nobody can reach you anymore, you start to believe that nobody wants to. You interpret your self-imposed loneliness as evidence that you're unlovable. You see the natural consequences of your choices as proof that you were right to protect yourself all along.

And the cycle continues. The web tightens. And your present keeps slipping away while you're tangled in lies that work together so seamlessly you think they're truth.

I've lived in this web. I've felt the way these demons pass you back and forth between them like a hot potato, each one taking their turn stealing a piece of your present until you look up one day and realize years have passed and you weren't really present for any of it.

You were envying. You were chasing. You were protecting. You were isolating.

But you weren't living. Not really.

Here's what breaks the web: recognition. When you can see how these demons work together, when you can trace the thread from Envy's whisper to Greed's promise to Selfishness's justification, you can start to untangle yourself.

But it requires honesty. It requires looking at your life and asking hard questions. Where did this start? Which demon spoke first? How did I end up here, exhausted and isolated, chasing things I don't even want anymore?

And it requires humility. Because you have to admit that what you've been calling self-care might actually be selfishness. That what you've been calling ambition might actually be greed. That what you've been calling awareness might actually be envy.

The demons work together. But freedom requires you to separate the threads, name each one, and refuse to let them continue weaving their web around your life.

What Now?

The demons that steal your present are relentless, but they're not invincible. Now that you know their names, now that you understand how they work together to rob you of the only moment you're actually guaranteed to live, you have a choice to make.

You can keep letting Envy poison your contentment, Greed drive you toward exhaustion, and Selfishness isolate you behind walls of self-protection. You can keep feeding the web they've woven around your life, moment by stolen moment.

Or you can start being here. Actually here. Not scrolling through someone else's life while yours passes by. Not chasing the next thing while missing what you already have. Not protecting yourself so completely that nobody can reach you.

Right now, in this moment, you have everything you need to begin. Not tomorrow. Not when circumstances change. Not when you finally achieve enough or acquire enough or become enough.

Now.

Life is happening right here. The people you love are right here. The blessings you've been too distracted to notice are right here.

The question I asked you at the beginning of this chapter still stands: are you going to be here for it?

Because your present is still yours to claim. But only if you stop running, stop chasing, stop comparing long enough to actually inhabit the life you're living.

The demons want to keep you everywhere but here.

Don't let them.

CHAPTER SEVEN
THE BATTLE FOR YOUR FUTURE

The Infinite Realities

I need you to understand something about the future: it doesn't exist yet.

I know that sounds obvious. Maybe even too simple. But here's what I mean—the future isn't a fixed destination you're traveling toward. It's not a place you can map out with perfect precision, no matter how hard you try. The future is potential, possibility, a thousand different paths that branch out from every decision you make today.

And that alone should be liberating.

But for people like me, it's paralyzing.

Because somewhere along the way, I convinced myself that if I could just think hard enough, plan thoroughly enough, control carefully enough, I could predict every possible outcome and prepare for it. That if I could master every level, anticipate every obstacle, mitigate every risk, I could guarantee the future I wanted.

I created entire realities in my mind. Not just one version of tomorrow, but dozens. Hundreds. An infinite number of timelines branching off from every choice, every conversation, every decision I might make today. And in my head, I lived through all of them. The good ones. The bad ones. The catastrophic ones.

My mind became a battleground where I fought wars that hadn't started yet, solved problems that didn't exist yet, defended myself against criticism I hadn't received yet. I rehearsed conversations I'd never have. I prepared for disasters that would never come. I built contingency plans for scenarios that existed only in the anxious corners of my imagination.

And all of it was an attempt to control what cannot be controlled.

This is what the demons do when they can't chain you to your past and they can't steal your present. They wage war on your future. They turn tomorrow into a weapon against today. They take your dreams, your ambitions, your hopes for what could be, and they twist them into instruments of torture.

Do you want to see what this looks like?

The Dream Of College Presidency

I've known for years that I wanted to rise to college presidency. It wasn't a casual thought or a passing ambition. It was a vision, clear and compelling. I could see it. I could feel it. I believed it was part of my destiny. I revered college presidents like Dr. Oswald P. Bronson (4th president of Bethune-Cookman College), Dr. Frederick S. Humphries (8th president of Florida Agricultural & Mechanical University), Dr. Norman C. Francis (5th president of Xavier University of Louisiana), Dr. Dwaun J. Warmack (9th president of Claflin University) and countless others.

And there was nothing wrong with that dream. Nothing wrong with aspiring to leadership, with wanting to make a difference at that level, with pursuing excellence in higher education. The dream itself was good.

But here's where the demons got involved.

I didn't just want to be a college president. I wanted to be worthy of it. I wanted to master every level that came before it, to learn everything I needed to know, to become the kind of person who deserved that position. And that meant I needed to model myself after the college presidents I admired—the ones who led with integrity, who transformed their institutions, who maintained their compassion even as they made difficult decisions.

So I studied them. I watched how they moved through the world. I noted what they valued, how they carried themselves, what they prioritized. And then I tried to live up to what I imagined their standards would be.

Do you see what started to happen here? Without realizing it, I had taken a dream and turned it into a prison.

I started controlling every aspect of my life to fit inside what I believed were the expectations of someone destined for college presidency. Not what college presidents actually expected, mind you. What I imagined they would expect if they were watching me. Every decision had to be measured against this invisible standard. Every choice had to align with this future version of myself that didn't exist yet.

Would a college president handle it this way? Would someone in that position make this choice? Is this behavior consistent with the integrity I'd need to demonstrate at that level?

The questions were relentless. And they weren't coming from a place of wisdom or discernment. They were coming from Fear.

Fear that if I didn't start living like a president now, I'd never become one. Fear that any misstep today would disqualify me from tomorrow. Fear that I wasn't preparing enough, learning enough, growing enough, becoming enough. Fear that the future I wanted required a version of myself I might never be able to become.

And beneath all of that was the deepest fear—that if I ever did reach that position, I wouldn't be able to sustain it. That the weight of it would crush me. That I'd fail spectacularly and publicly. That everyone would see what I secretly believed about myself: that I was never qualified for it in the first place.

So I tried to control everything. My schedule. My relationships. My reactions. My reputation. My growth. My learning. Every variable I could identify, I tried to manage. Because if I could just control enough of the present, maybe I could guarantee the future.

But doing all of this didn't change the things I was trying so hard to control.

When Control Becomes Captivity

The anxiety didn't decrease as I gained more control. It increased.

Every new thing I managed to control revealed ten more things I couldn't. Every scenario I prepared for spawned three more I hadn't considered. Every risk I mitigated made me aware of five others I'd overlooked. The more I tried to secure my future, the more unstable it felt.

And my mind—my brilliant, beautiful, exhausting mind— became a simulation machine.

I wasn't living in reality anymore. I was living in projections. I'd run through every possible version of a conversation before it happened. I'd anticipate every potential problem before it arose. I'd game out every scenario, weighing the probabilities, calculating the risks, trying to determine the optimal path forward.

If I make this choice, then this might happen, which could lead to that, which would require me to do this, unless they respond with that, in which case I'd need to pivot to this other approach, but what if they don't respond at all, what if I misjudged the situation, what if there's something I'm not seeing, what if, what if, what if...

You see what was happening? I wasn't preparing for the future. I was trying to live every possible version of it simultaneously.

And that's not wisdom. That's not strategic thinking. That's not even anxiety in its normal form.

That's a demon.

Actually, that's multiple demons working together, using your ambition against you, turning your dreams into chains, transforming tomorrow into today's prison.

Let me show you how they do it.

The Demonic Collaboration

If you recall, I previously talked about how the demons work together. How Envy feeds Greed, Greed justifies Selfishness, and Selfishness invites Rejection? Well, they don't just collaborate to steal your present. They collaborate to weaponize your future.

So how exactly does that work you ask?

Well, its simple, fear starts by whispering that you need to control tomorrow to survive it. That if you don't anticipate every problem, you'll be destroyed by the ones you missed. That uncertainty is dangerous and control is safety. Fear creates the foundation—the belief that your future is something to be managed rather than something to be trusted.

Then Greed steps in. Not the greed for money or possessions—the greed for certainty. The insatiable appetite for knowing what comes next, for having guarantees, for eliminating all variables. Greed says you need more information, more preparation, more control. It's never satisfied because there's always another scenario to consider, another contingency to plan for, another unknown to wrestle with.

Selfishness joins the party by convincing you that you have to do this alone. That trusting others means losing control. That vulnerability is weakness and asking for help is admission of inadequacy. Selfishness isolates you behind walls of self-sufficiency, cutting you off from the very people who could speak truth into your spiraling thoughts.

Guilt appears next, reminding you of every time you've failed to control outcomes in the past. Every mistake you made because you didn't see something coming. Every opportunity you lost because you weren't prepared enough. Guilt says if you'd been better at anticipating problems, you wouldn't have those regrets. So you'd better not make that mistake again.

Envy whispers that everyone else seems to have their future figured out. They're not drowning in possibilities. They're not paralyzed by uncertainty. They're moving forward with confidence while you're stuck in analysis paralysis. Envy makes you resent people who seem to trust the process more easily than you can.

And finally, Rejection shows up with its most devastating message: if you can't master your future, if you can't guarantee the outcomes, if you can't live up to the imagined standards you've set for yourself, then you don't deserve the dream. You'll be rejected by the opportunity. Disqualified by your inability to control what needs to be controlled. Exposed as unworthy of the destiny you thought was yours.

You see how they work together? Each demon building on the others, creating a web of anxiety so tight that you can't move without triggering another strand. And the target isn't just your present—it's your future. Your dreams. Your destiny.

They don't want you to stop dreaming. That would be too obvious. Instead, they want to turn your dreams into burdens. They want your aspirations to become the source of your anxiety rather than your motivation. They want tomorrow to terrorize you so completely that you can't function in today.

And that's exactly what happened to me.

The Tyranny Of "What If"

There's a phrase that has probably done more damage to my peace than any other combination of words in the English language.

What if.

What if I'm not ready? What if I fail? What if they reject me? What if I'm making the wrong choice? What if I miss something important? What if I let people down? What if I succeed and then can't sustain it? What if, what if, what if...

These two words have the power to turn possibility into prison. They take the future, which should be a source of hope and anticipation, and transform it into a minefield of anxiety where every step could trigger disaster.

But here's what I've learned about "what if" thinking—it's not actually about the future. It's about stealing the present.

Because when you're living in "what if," you're not living in "what is." You're not present to the moment you're actually in. You're not experiencing the reality right in front of you. You're somewhere else entirely, trapped in a timeline that doesn't exist, wrestling with problems that aren't real, fighting battles that haven't started.

And while you're doing that, life is happening. Real life. The life you're supposed to be living, the moments you're supposed to be experiencing, the people you're supposed to be connecting with—all of it is passing you by while you're busy preparing for scenarios that will never come to pass.

Let me tell you what this looked like for me.

I'd be sitting in a meeting, but I wasn't really there. I was running simulations of future meetings. I'd be having dinner with friends, but my mind was already three steps ahead, planning conversations I might need to have, preparing defenses for criticism I hadn't received, calculating how every current interaction might affect future opportunities.

I'd be achieving things I'd worked hard for, but I couldn't enjoy them because I was already worried about the next level. The promotion didn't bring satisfaction because I was immediately anxious about whether I could perform at that level. The accomplishment didn't bring joy because I was already calculating the next goal and all the ways I might fail to reach it.

The present became nothing more than a waiting room for the future. And the future became a threat I had to constantly prepare for.

This is how demons steal your present by weaponizing your future. They don't need to chain you to yesterday if they can make you terrified of tomorrow. They don't need to destroy what you have if they can make you so anxious about what you might lose that you can't enjoy it in the first place.

But there's a theology that confronts this tyranny head-on. And it's found in one of the most familiar prayers ever prayed.

Give Us This Day Our Daily Bread

When Jesus taught His disciples to pray, He included a line that most of us recite without thinking too deeply about what it actually means.

"Give us this day our daily bread."

Not next week's bread. Not next year's bread. Not a stockpile that will last us the rest of our lives.

But daily bread.

Just enough for today.

There's something radical about that request when you really sit with it. Because what Jesus is teaching us to ask for is provision for right now, not insurance for forever. He's teaching us to trust God for today's needs, not to demand guarantees about tomorrow's.

"So do not worry. Don't say, 'What will we eat?' Or, 'What will we drink?' Or, 'What will we wear?' People who are ungodly run after all those things. Your Father who is in heaven knows that you need them. But put God's kingdom first. Do what he wants you to do. Then all those things will also be given to you. So don't worry about tomorrow. Tomorrow will worry about itself. Each day has enough trouble of its own."

Matthew 6:31-34 (NIrV)

Read that last line again. Each day has enough trouble of its own.

Jesus isn't saying that life won't have difficulties. He's not promising that tomorrow will be easy or that the future holds no challenges. What He's saying is that you don't need to carry tomorrow's troubles today. You don't need to borrow anxiety from a future that hasn't arrived yet.

Trust me, today has more than enough. Deal with today.

But thats easier said than done, right? Because we are still collecting tomorrow's worries and adding them to today's load. We are still carrying next week's anxieties on our backs while we're trying to navigate this moment. We are consumed with stockpiling future fears like we're preparing for some kind of emotional apocalypse.

And we do it because we don't trust the promise of daily bread.

We want the whole bakery. We want guarantees. We want to know exactly how God will provide not just for today, but for next month, next year, the next decade. We want the security of certainty, the comfort of knowing exactly how everything will work out.

But that's not how faith works. And it's not how trust works.

Trust means believing that the God who provided for you today will provide for you tomorrow. Faith means stepping forward even when you can't see the whole path. Daily bread means you don't need to figure out the entire menu— you just need to trust that today's provision will be enough.

And here's what I had to learn the hard way: trying to secure tomorrow is actually an act of control masquerading as responsibility.

The Illusion Of Control

I told myself I was being wise. Strategic. Prepared. Responsible.

I convinced myself that I was thinking ahead, anticipating obstacles, planning for contingencies. That's what good leaders do, right? That's what responsible adults do. That's what you have to do if you want to achieve anything meaningful.

And there's truth in that. Planning isn't wrong. Preparation isn't a sin. Wisdom includes thinking about consequences and considering the future.

But there's a line between preparation and control. And I had crossed it a long time ago.

I wasn't preparing for the future. I was trying to control it. I wasn't being strategic. I was being afraid. And I was calling my fear wisdom to avoid admitting what was really happening.

Because the reality is that if I admitted I was afraid, I'd have to confront what I was actually afraid of—that God might not come through. That if I didn't figure it all out, it wouldn't get figured out. That trusting Him with tomorrow meant risking disappointment, failure, or worse.

So instead, I tried to be my own provision. My own security. My own guarantee.

And it nearly broke me.

Take it from me, the weight of trying to secure your own future is crushing. Because its an impossible task. No matter how much you plan, how thoroughly you prepare, how carefully you control every variable you can identify, you cannot guarantee tomorrow.

What you have to realize is that life is full of things beyond your control. People will make choices you can't predict. Circumstances will shift in ways you can't anticipate. Doors will close that you thought were open. Paths will appear that you didn't know existed.

Don't get me wrong, you can prepare. You can be wise. You can make good decisions based on available information.

But you cannot control the outcome. Trying to will do nothing more than steal every moment you have right now.

The Cost Of Living Nowhere

So let me ask you something, and I want you to be honest with yourself: Where do you actually live?

I don't mean your address. I mean where does your mind spend most of its time? Are you here, in this moment, or are you somewhere else? Are you present in your actual life, or are you living in simulations, projections, memories, fantasies, comparisons, and possibilities?

Because here's what I've learned: you can't simultaneously live in the future you're trying to control and the present you're supposed to be experiencing. You have to choose. And most of us, without even realizing it, have chosen to live nowhere.

We're not fully in today because we're too anxious about tomorrow. We're not fully in the moment because we're replaying yesterday. We're not present with the people in front of us because we're comparing our lives to people we don't actually know. We're not enjoying what we have because we're obsessing over what we don't have yet.

We've become people who are always somewhere else. Always planning the next thing. Always worried about the future thing. Always distracted by the other thing. And in the process, we've lost the ability to simply be where we are.

The cost of this is staggering, even though we rarely sit down and count up the cost.

It's the dinner conversation you missed because you were checking your phone. It's the sunset you didn't see because you were worried about tomorrow's presentation. It's the child who needed your attention but got your physical presence without your mental engagement. It's the achievement you worked years to accomplish but couldn't celebrate because you immediately started worrying about maintaining it.

It's every moment stolen by anxiety about a future that hasn't happened yet. Every experience diminished by comparison to someone else's insta-life. Every relationship that suffered because you were there but not really there.

And here's the cruelest irony: while you're busy trying to secure your future by controlling every variable, you're actually destroying it. Because the future you're building is made up of the moments you're living right now. If you're not present for these moments, if you're not investing in the relationships and opportunities right in front of you, then what future are you actually creating?

You're trying to build tomorrow while ignoring today. And that doesn't work. It can't work.

Because today is the only raw material you have to construct your future with.

Breaking The Cycle

So how do you stop? How do you break free from the tyranny of "what if" and reclaim the gift of "what is"? How do you learn to trust God with tomorrow while living faithfully in today?

I will not lie to you and tell you it's easy. It's not. In fact it will be one of the hardest things you will ever do in life other than living it. When you've spent years, maybe decades, training your mind to live anywhere but the present, retraining it takes intentional work. It takes practice. It takes catching yourself every time you start to drift into future anxiety or past regret and gently, firmly, pulling yourself back to now.

But I am a living witness that it is possible. And it starts with a decision.

You have to decide that being present is more important than being in control. You have to choose to believe that God's provision for today is enough, even when you can't see tomorrow's provision yet. You have to accept that some things are beyond your control and that trying to control them is costing you everything.

This isn't about becoming passive or irresponsible. This isn't about abandoning planning or preparation. This is about recognizing the difference between wisdom and worry, between preparation and control, between faith and fear.

Wisdom plans. Worry obsesses. Preparation acts on what you can control. Control tries to manipulate what you can't. Faith trusts God with the unknown. Fear demands guarantees.

So here's what I had to learn, and what I'm still learning every single day.

First: Practice presence through awareness.

You can't change what you don't notice. Start paying attention to where your mind goes. When you're having a conversation, notice if you're actually listening or if you're already formulating your response. God gave us two ears and one mouth for a reason. Think about the moment when you're working on a task, notice if you're focused on it or if you're worried about ten other things. When you're eating a meal, notice if you're tasting the food or if you're scrolling through your phone.

Don't judge yourself for being distracted. Just notice it. Awareness is the first step toward change.

I started setting reminders on my phone with a simple question: "Where are you right now?" Not physically, but mentally. Every time the reminder went off, I'd stop and honestly assess where my mind was. Was I here? Or was I living in some future scenario or past regret?

Most of the time, I wasn't here. But noticing that was the beginning of learning how to come back.

Second: Choose gratitude over comparison.

Envy steals your present by making you focus on what you don't have instead of what you do. The antidote is gratitude. Not the superficial "be thankful" platitude, but the deep, intentional practice of acknowledging what's actually in front of you.

Every morning, before I let myself start planning the day or worrying about what needed to get done, I made myself name three specific things I was grateful for. Not generic things like "my health" or "my family," but specific, concrete things. "The way the morning light comes through my bedroom window." "The conversation I had with my friend yesterday that made me laugh." "The fact that I have hot water for my shower."

Small things. Present things. Real things.

This practice doesn't erase your problems. It doesn't make your challenges disappear. But it does something powerful: it reminds you that even in the midst of difficulty, there are gifts. There is provision. There is grace. You just have to train yourself to see it instead of looking past it while you chase what's next.

Third: Release the illusion of control.

Now this is the hardest one. Because control feels like safety. Letting go feels like free fall.

But here's the stone cold truth: you were never in control anyway. You were just exhausting yourself trying to be. And all that effort wasn't giving you security. It was stealing your peace.

So you have to make a daily, sometimes moment-by-moment choice to release what you cannot control. To stop trying to anticipate every possible problem. To stop running through endless scenarios of things that might happen. To stop treating your mind like a simulation machine for potential disasters.

When I catch myself spiraling into future anxiety, I've learned to pray a very simple prayer: "God, I'm doing it again. I'm trying to carry tomorrow's weight today. Help me trust You with what I can't see."

Sometimes I have to pray it multiple times in an hour. Sometimes I have to pray it in the middle of a meeting when I feel that familiar tightness in my chest that means I'm trying to control things beyond my reach. Sometimes I join this prayer with the Serenity Prayer.

But every time I pray it and choose to release the control, I find a little more space to breathe. A little more room to be present. A little more peace in the not-knowing.

The Fear That Identity Would Limit Destiny

There's something I haven't told you yet. A layer beneath all the anxiety about control, beneath all the simulations and scenarios, beneath all the attempts to prove I was worthy of a college presidency someday.

I was terrified that being gay would disqualify me from ever getting there.

I know what you're thinking. We live in a world that's supposedly more accepting now. We've made progress. There are LGBTQ+ leaders in every field. Things are better than they were.

And all of that is true. But it's also true that higher education, particularly at the presidential level, is still a deeply conservative space in many ways. That board rooms and donor meetings and community relations all come with unspoken expectations. That there are institutions where being openly gay would absolutely limit your opportunities, no matter how qualified you are.

So I convinced myself that I had to manage this variable too. Control this part of my identity. Navigate it carefully. Time the disclosure perfectly. Calculate the risk at every level.

I told myself I shouldn't have to come out to the world as a gay man because straight people don't have to announce their heterosexuality to the world. And that's true. The asymmetry is real and it's unjust. But the demons didn't care about justice. They cared about fear. And they used that very real asymmetry to keep me trapped in anxiety about how and when and if I should be open about who I am.

Because here's what the demons whispered: Your dreams are unattainable because of who you are.

They pointed to societal norms. The expectation that a college president should be married to someone of the opposite sex, have 2.3 kids, a house with a white picket fence, the whole traditional package. And by those very norms, I was abnormal. Outside the template. A risk factor that boards would have to "consider."

The demons convinced me that while I could control my education, my experience, my performance, my reputation, I couldn't control this. And this one uncontrollable variable could undo everything else.

So I added it to the infinite list of things to manage. How much to reveal and when. How to navigate professional spaces without lying but without being "too open." How to let people get to know my competence before they knew my identity, as if the two were somehow separate. As if I could partition myself into acceptable parts and unacceptable parts, revealing only what wouldn't threaten my future.

I was exhausting myself trying to be authentic enough to have integrity but not so authentic that I'd be disqualified. Trying to be honest enough to sleep at night but not so honest that I'd derail my career. Trying to be true to myself while also being palatable to everyone else.

And the weight of it was crushing.

Because here's what I was really doing: I was treating my identity as a problem to be managed. A risk to be mitigated. A variable to be controlled. I was living like who I am at my core was incompatible with the destiny I believed I was called to.

And that lie—that fundamental lie that your authentic self is your biggest obstacle—is one of the demons' most effective weapons.

It kept me performing instead of being. Calculating instead of connecting. Hiding instead of living. And all of it was in service of a future that I was convinced required me to be less than fully myself.

But here's the thing about trying to control how people perceive your identity: you can't do it. No matter how carefully you navigate it, no matter how strategic you are about disclosure, you can't control what people think or how they'll respond. Some will accept you. Some won't. Some will surprise you in both directions.

And spending your present trying to engineer their future responses is another form of living nowhere.

I was so focused on whether being gay would limit my destiny that I didn't stop to ask a more fundamental question: What is a future worth if it requires me to hide my truth?

What's the point of achieving a position if I have to perform a version of myself that isn't real to maintain it? What kind of destiny is it if it demands I live in fear of being fully known? What kind of leadership can I actually offer if I'm too afraid to be authentic?

Because here's what I've learned, and I'm still learning it every day: a future built on hiding who you are is not a future worth having. It's just a more elaborate prison. It's captivity disguised as success.

And if you remember from Chapter 2, where the Spirit of the Lord is, there is liberty. If your identity feels like captivity, that's not God. If your dream requires you to hide your truth, that's not your destiny. If the future you're chasing demands that you live in fear of being fully seen, then you're not chasing freedom—you're chasing another chain.

The demons want you to believe that authenticity and destiny are incompatible. That you have to choose between being true to yourself and achieving your calling. That who you are at your core will disqualify you from what you're meant to do.

But that's a lie.

The truth is harder and more beautiful: your calling includes your identity. Your destiny doesn't require you to hide who you are. Your purpose isn't something separate from your authentic self—it's woven into it.

And yes, being open about who you are might close some doors. It might limit some opportunities. Some people might reject you specifically because of your identity.

But here's what I had to accept: those weren't my doors anyway. Those weren't my opportunities. And those people's acceptance was never mine to control.

The only thing I could control was whether I would live in integrity. Whether I would trust God with my truth instead of trying to manage everyone else's perception of it. Whether I would be present in my actual life or continue performing in the simulation I'd created.

And I had to decide, just like you have to decide: was I going to spend my future hiding who I am, or was I going to trust that the God who made me knew exactly what He was doing?

I chose trust. Not perfectly. Not all at once. Not without fear or doubt or moments of wanting to retreat back into the safety of hiding.

But I chose it. I choose it. Every day, I'm still choosing it.

And here's what happened when I did.

The Irony Of Presence

When I chose trust over control, when I chose authenticity over performance, something I hadn't noticed became clear: while I was busy trying to prove I was worthy of rising to college presidency someday, I was already doing the work.

On my journey through higher education, I brought lasting change that continues to operate at the core of institutional operations. I established practices and processes that outlived my tenure in those positions. I created systems that improved how things functioned. I mentored people who went on to lead in their own right in both the public and private sectors. I solved problems that needed solving. I built things that needed building.

I was making presidential-level impact while obsessing about whether I'd ever be presidential-level material.

Do you see the irony?

I was so consumed with becoming worthy of the future that I missed the fact that I was already creating value in the present. I was so focused on the destination that I didn't notice the meaningful work I was doing along the journey. I was so anxious about whether I was enough that I couldn't see the evidence right in front of me that I was already making a difference.

And here's what's even more painful to admit: I can't fully enjoy those accomplishments even now because I wasn't present for them when they happened. I was already three steps ahead, already worried about the next thing, already calculating the next move. I achieved things I'd worked hard for, but I robbed myself of the satisfaction because I couldn't be where I was.

The demons had convinced me that the future was what mattered. That today was just preparation for tomorrow. That the present moment was only valuable insofar as it positioned me for the next opportunity.

And in believing that lie, I missed the point entirely.

The point is this: faithful presence in today builds tomorrow better than anxious control ever could.

Think about it. The lasting changes I brought to those institutions didn't come from obsessing about my future presidency. They came from showing up fully in the roles I had, seeing what needed to be done, and doing it with excellence. They came from being present enough to notice problems others missed. From being invested enough in the moment to care about solving them properly.

The future I was trying so hard to engineer was actually being built by the moments I was too distracted to fully inhabit.

And that's true for all of us.

Your destiny isn't just waiting for you somewhere in the future. It's being constructed in the decisions you make today. The relationships you invest in right now. The work you do with integrity in this moment. The character you develop through today's challenges.

You can't build a meaningful future while ignoring a meaningful present. They're not separate. Today is the building block of tomorrow. This moment is the foundation of what's next.

So when you're anxious about the future, when you're trying to control outcomes that haven't happened yet, when you're simulating scenarios instead of living your actual life —you're not securing tomorrow. You're sabotaging it.

Because you're too busy planning to actually build.

What Becomes Available

When I finally started learning to be present, when I started releasing the illusion of control and trusting God with what I couldn't see, when I chose authenticity over the exhausting performance of trying to be palatable— something unexpected happened.

I got better at my job.

Not because I was trying harder or planning more thoroughly. Not because I was hiding less or managing perceptions more carefully. But because I was actually paying attention. I was present enough to notice opportunities others missed. I was engaged enough to have genuine conversations instead of strategic ones. I was calm enough to think clearly instead of reacting from anxiety. I was authentic enough to connect with people instead of calculating how they might perceive me.

The very things I thought I needed to control in order to succeed—including how people saw my identity—were actually blocking my success. And releasing them created space for me to do the work I was actually called to do.

But more than that, I started experiencing something I hadn't felt in years.

Peace.

Not the absence of challenges. Not the elimination of uncertainty. Not even the guarantee that everyone would accept me. But the deep, sustaining peace that comes from knowing you're where you're supposed to be, doing what you're supposed to do, being who you're supposed to be, and trusting the One who holds tomorrow.

There's a specific kind of peace that comes from not hiding. From not having to monitor every word, calculate every interaction, or maintain a performance. It's the peace of integrity—when who you are in private matches who you are in public. When you're not carrying the weight of a secret or the exhaustion of code-switching between your authentic self and your professional self.

That peace isn't about everyone accepting you. Some people won't. Some doors will close. Some opportunities will pass you by specifically because of who you are.

But here's what I discovered: the peace of living authentically is worth more than the anxiety of living strategically. The freedom of being fully known is worth more than the prison of being carefully managed. The joy of showing up as yourself is worth more than the exhaustion of performing a version you think people will accept.

I started enjoying moments I would have rushed through before. Started having conversations I would have been too distracted to appreciate. Started celebrating accomplishments I would have been too anxious to acknowledge. Started showing up as myself instead of as a carefully curated version designed to minimize risk.

I started living my actual life instead of the simulated version in my head.

And here's what I discovered: the present moment, when you're actually in it, when you're actually being yourself in it, is rich. It's textured. It's full of things you miss when you're living three steps ahead or hiding behind a performance. There's wisdom in it. Connection in it. Joy in it. Purpose in it.

Everything you need for today is available in today. But only if you're actually here to receive it. And only if you're actually you when you receive it.

The demons want you to believe that tomorrow is where everything important happens. That today is just a hurdle to get through on your way to what really matters. That the future is where your real life begins. And they especially want you to believe that authenticity is a luxury you can afford only after you've achieved enough success to withstand the risk.

But that's backwards.

Authenticity isn't what you get to do after you succeed. It's how you succeed in ways that actually matter. Presence isn't what's available once you've controlled all the variables. It's what allows you to stop trying to control them in the first place.

And as long as you believe that you have to earn the right to be yourself, that you have to prove your worth before you can show your truth, that you have to secure your future before you can live authentically in your present—you'll spend your entire life waiting to live instead of actually living.

So let me ask you again: where do you live?

Are you here, in this moment, present to what's actually in front of you? Are you being who you actually are, or are you performing who you think you need to be? Are you building a future on the foundation of your authentic self, or are you trying to construct a destiny that requires you to hide your truth?

Because right now—this moment, this breath, this choice —is the only time you're actually alive. Yesterday is gone. Tomorrow isn't promised. But right now is yours.

And the only version of you that can truly inhabit this moment is the real one.

What are you going to do with it?

The Choice Before You

So now you know what the battle for your future really looks like.

It's not about achieving more or planning better or securing guarantees. It's about learning to be present. Learning to trust God with tomorrow while living faithfully in today. Learning that authenticity and presence build better futures than anxiety and control ever could.

But knowing isn't the same as doing. Understanding the problem isn't the same as breaking free from it.

And that's where the real work begins.

Because here's the inconvenient truth: the demons that wage war on your future don't just disappear because you've recognized their tactics. Fear doesn't stop whispering just because you've named it. The habit of living three steps ahead doesn't break itself just because you understand how it's sabotaging you. The performance of trying to be palatable doesn't end just because you've decided authenticity matters more.

These patterns have been built over years, maybe decades. They're woven into how you think, how you react, how you move through the world. They've become so familiar that they feel like part of who you are.

But the reality is they're not.

They're nothing more than chains. And chains can be broken.

The anxiety about your future that steals your present. The control that masquerades as responsibility. The performance that pretends to be strategy. The fear that your authentic self will disqualify you from your destiny. The exhausting attempt to live in infinite realities instead of the one that's actually in front of you.

All of it. Chains.

And you don't have to keep carrying them.

If you have made it this far then you will remember that we have talked about the demons that chain you to your past. We have also talked about the demons that steal your present. And now, in this chapter, you've seen how the demons weaponize your future against you.

Past. Present. Future.

The demons want you imprisoned in all three. Chained to what was. Robbed of what is. Terrorized by what might be. Never fully free. Never fully here. Never fully alive.

But here's what I need you to understand: you don't have to stay in bondage.

Sure, the chains are real. The patterns are deep. The demons are persistent.

But the chains are also breakable. The patterns can be interrupted. The demons can be defeated.

And that's exactly where we are going to focus our energy.

Because recognizing the battle isn't enough. Understanding the tactics isn't enough. Even choosing to trust and be present and live authentically isn't enough if you don't know how to actually break the chains that have been holding you captive.

You need tools. Strategies. Practical steps. You need to understand how these chains were built so you can understand how to dismantle them. You need to know what forgiveness looks like, what liberation requires, what freedom costs.

You need to know how to break the chains.

Not just understand that they can be broken. Not just hope that they'll break on their own. But actually do the work of breaking them.

So ensure your seatbelt is securely fastened, because that's where we're going next. Into the hard work. The uncomfortable work. The necessary work of liberation.

You've been carrying these chains long enough. You've let fear dictate your future, steal your present, and keep you performing instead of being long enough.

It's time to break free.

CHAPTER EIGHT
BREAK THE CHAINS

You've been carrying them long enough.

The chains that tether you to past mistakes. The ones that lock you in patterns you inherited but never questioned. The weight you've grown so accustomed to that you've forgotten what it feels like to move freely.

In the last chapter, we talked about how the demons wage war on your future, how they weaponize tomorrow against you, how they keep you performing instead of being. We named the anxiety that steals your present while pretending to protect your future. We exposed the fear that makes you live in infinite possible realities instead of the one that's actually in front of you.

And maybe as you read it, something shifted. Maybe you recognized yourself in those pages. Maybe you saw how much energy you've been spending trying to control outcomes you can't control, anticipating problems that haven't happened, preparing for disasters that may never come.

That recognition matters. Naming the demons matters. Understanding their tactics matters.

But recognition without action is just informed captivity.

You can know the name of every demon chasing you and still let them catch you if you don't do the work of confronting them. You can understand exactly how the chains were forged and still wear them every single day if you don't learn how to break them.

And here's what I need you to understand before we go any further: breaking chains is hard work. It's uncomfortable work. It's the kind of work that makes you want to quit halfway through because staying chained starts to feel easier than doing what it takes to get free.

The demons know this. In fact, they're counting on it. They're betting that you'll get tired, that you'll convince yourself the chains aren't that heavy, that you'll decide familiar bondage is better than the unknown territory of liberation.

But you didn't make it this far to stay in captivity. You didn't pick up this book, didn't read about the demons that chain you to your past and steal your present and weaponize your future, just to acknowledge the problem and do nothing about it.

You're here because somewhere deep inside, you're ready to be free.

So let's get to work.

The Architecture Of Bondage

Before you can break chains, you need to understand how they were built.

Because chains don't appear overnight. They're not forged in a single moment of trauma or failure or rejection. They're built link by link, slowly, over time, until one day you wake up and realize you can't remember what it felt like to move without their weight.

Think about how a chain actually works. Each link connects to the next. One piece of metal looped through another, and another, and another, until you have something strong enough to hold a ship to shore or keep a prisoner locked in place. No single link creates the bondage. It's the accumulation, the connection, the way each piece reinforces the others.

Your chains work the same way.

The first link might have been forged when you were young. Maybe it was the first time someone made you feel like you weren't enough, like love was conditional, like you had to perform to be accepted. That moment created a belief, and that belief became a link.

Then came another moment. Another wound. Another time you were rejected or abandoned or hurt. Another belief was formed and connected to the first. The chain grew longer.

Over time, more links were added. Every betrayal, every disappointment, every time you reached out and got hurt, every time you tried and failed, every time you were told you weren't smart enough or good enough or worthy enough— each experience became another link in the chain.

And here's the thing about chains built over years: they become part of how you see the world. They shape your expectations. They inform your decisions. They tell you what's possible and what isn't, who you are and who you'll never be.

The chain that started with one rejection becomes a belief system that says you're fundamentally unlovable. The chain that began with one failure becomes a conviction that you'll never succeed at anything meaningful. The chain forged in one moment of abandonment becomes a certainty that everyone leaves eventually, so why bother getting close?

Some chains feel heavier than others, and there's a reason for that. It's not just about how many links you've accumulated. It's about what those links are made of and where they're anchored.

A chain made of guilt weighs differently than a chain made of fear. A chain anchored in childhood trauma has a different grip than one attached to more recent wounds. A chain you inherited from generational patterns has been reinforced by decades of repetition before you were even born.

This is why two people can experience similar pain but carry it so differently. Why one person's rejection becomes a brief setback while another's becomes a defining identity. Why some people can forgive quickly while others hold onto hurt for years.

The architecture of your bondage is unique to you. Your chains were custom-made by your specific experiences, your particular wounds, your individual responses to pain.

But here's what's crucial to understand: there's a difference between being chained and choosing chains.

Being chained means someone or something bound you against your will. It means the links were forged by circumstances beyond your control, by people who hurt you, by systems that failed you, by traumas you didn't ask for and couldn't prevent.

Choosing chains is different. That's what happens when you keep picking them up even after they've been loosened. When you refuse to step out of bondage because it's familiar. When you hold onto the weight because letting go feels more terrifying than staying bound.

Most of us are dealing with both. We were chained by things that weren't our fault, and then we chose to keep wearing those chains long after we had the key to unlock them.

Maybe you were chained by abuse that taught you love always comes with violence. That wasn't your choice. But continuing to pursue relationships with people who hurt you, convincing yourself that's all you deserve—that's choosing chains.

Maybe you were chained by poverty that made you believe you'd never have enough. That wasn't your fault. But refusing opportunities because you're convinced you'll just lose everything anyway, sabotaging your own success because failure feels more predictable—that's choosing chains.

Maybe you were chained by rejection that convinced you you're fundamentally flawed. That wasn't your doing. But performing constantly to be acceptable, hiding who you really are because authenticity feels too risky, settling for surface-level connections because vulnerability might lead to more rejection—that's choosing chains.

The chains that were forced on you are not your fault. You didn't ask for them. You didn't deserve them. You were a victim of circumstances, of other people's brokenness, of systems and patterns and pain that existed long before you arrived on the scene.

But the chains you're still wearing today? Some of those are your responsibility now.

Not because you're weak. Not because you're broken beyond repair. Not because there's something wrong with you for struggling to break free.

But because at some point, if you want to be liberated, you have to stop being defined solely by what was done to you and start making choices about who you're becoming. You have to move from victim to survivor to warrior. You have to examine the chains you're still carrying and ask yourself honestly: which of these am I ready to put down?

Because here's the truth that might be hard to hear: some people get so used to their chains that they start to need them. The weight becomes familiar. The limitation becomes predictable. The bondage becomes a convenient excuse for why they can't move forward, why they can't change, why they can't be held accountable for their own liberation.

And the demons love that. They love it when you confuse your chains with your identity, when you can't imagine who you'd be without them, when you're more afraid of freedom than you are tired of bondage.

But I don't believe that's you. I don't think you'd still be reading if you were content in captivity. I think you're here because you're tired of the weight. Because you're ready to understand how the chains were built so you can figure out how to dismantle them.

So let's start with the truth: your chains are real, but they're not permanent. They were built link by link, and they can be broken link by link. Some will come off easier than others. Some will require help. Some will require tools you don't have yet.

But they can be broken.

And that's exactly what we're going to learn how to do.

Forgiveness As Bolt Cutters

If I told you there was one tool powerful enough to break chains that have held you for years, would you use it?

Well, what if I told you that tool was forgiveness?

I know. You might have just rolled your eyes. Or felt your jaw clench. Or thought about closing this book because you've heard the forgiveness speech before and you're tired of being told to just let it go, to be the bigger person, to forgive and forget like it's that simple.

But stay with me. Because I'm not here to give you the sanitized church version of forgiveness, the one that pretends it's easy or quick or that it means pretending nothing happened. I'm here to tell you the truth about forgiveness, the kind of truth that might set you free if you're willing to hear it.

Before we go anywhere else, I need you to understand that forgiveness is not about the person who hurt you.

Let me say that again, because it's the most important thing you need to understand: forgiveness is not about them. It's not for them. It's not even primarily about them.

Forgiveness is about you. It's about reclaiming the power you gave to your pain. It's about refusing to let what happened to you continue to define what happens in you. It's about cutting the chain that tethers you to someone who might have moved on with their life while you're still carrying the weight of what they did.

Think about how a chain works. One end is attached to you. The other end is attached to the person or event or trauma that hurt you. As long as that chain exists, you're connected. You can't move forward without dragging them with you. Every step you take, you feel the pull of that connection. Every time you try to build something new, you're reminded of what they took.

Forgiveness is the bolt cutter that severs that connection.

It doesn't erase what happened. It doesn't make the hurt disappear. It doesn't mean you trust them again or let them back into your life or pretend the damage wasn't real.

What it does is free you from being permanently anchored to your worst moment.

I learned this the hard way. For years, I carried unforgiveness like a badge of honor. I told myself I was justified in my anger, entitled to my bitterness, right to hold onto the hurt. And I was justified. I was entitled. I was right about what had been done to me.

But I was also still in chains.

The people who hurt me had moved on. They were living their lives, making their choices, probably not thinking about me at all. And there I was, rehearsing the offense, reliving the pain, letting what they did continue to control my present even though they were long gone from my life.

That's when I realized something crucial: unforgiveness doesn't punish the person who hurt you. It punishes you. It's like drinking poison and expecting them to die. It's like carrying a burning coal in your hand, hoping they'll feel the heat.

Medical professionals will tell you what I learned through experience: unforgiveness shows up in your body. It manifests as chronic pain, heart disease, high blood pressure, digestive issues. It ages you faster than you should age. It steals your peace, your joy, your ability to be present in the moments that matter.

I've watched people destroy their marriages defending against hurts from previous relationships. I've seen talented individuals refuse opportunities because betrayal once felt unbearable. I've known parents who damaged their children trying to protect them from the pain the parents experienced, not realizing they were just creating a different kind of pain for the next generation to fight.

That's the generational curse of unforgiveness. It doesn't just chain you to your past. It chains everyone connected to you to it, too.

Your children learn to hold grudges because you modeled it. Your spouse suffers because you can't trust them for what someone else did. Your friends walk on eggshells because you're still triggered by wounds they didn't inflict. The unforgiveness that was supposed to protect you ends up isolating you, keeping everyone at a distance because getting close means risking being hurt again.

But here's what forgiveness actually looks like, stripped of all the religious platitudes and oversimplified advice.

Forgiveness is acknowledging that something or someone caused a shift in your once positive outlook, turning it into a negative one, and then choosing not to let that shift define the rest of your story. It's looking at the hurt honestly, calling it what it is, and then deciding that the person who hurt you no longer gets to write your narrative.

It's the decision to release them from the debt they owe you. And yes, they do owe you. If someone betrayed you, they owe you loyalty. If someone abandoned you, they owe you presence. If someone abused you, they owe you safety. The debt is real, and acknowledging it is part of the process.

But here's the thing about debts that can never be repaid: holding onto them doesn't collect what you're owed. It just keeps you bound to the debtor.

Forgiveness is deciding that you'd rather be free than right. That you'd rather have peace than revenge. That you'd rather move forward than stay stuck demanding payment from someone who either can't or won't give it.

I want to be absolutely clear, you can forgive someone and still maintain boundaries. You can forgive someone and never trust them again. You can forgive someone and choose not to have them in your life anymore. Forgiveness doesn't require you to be foolish. It requires you to be free.

Let me be even clearer about what forgiveness is not, because the church has done a lot of damage here with its oversimplified teachings.

Forgiveness is not pretending the hurt didn't happen. If someone asks you to forgive and forget, they're asking you to lie. You can forgive fully and still remember clearly. In fact, remembering is often necessary to maintain healthy boundaries and avoid repeating patterns.

Forgiveness is not minimizing the damage. It's not saying, "It wasn't that bad" or "They did the best they could" or "I probably overreacted." Sometimes it was that bad. Sometimes they didn't do their best. Sometimes your reaction was completely appropriate to the harm inflicted.

Forgiveness is not reconciliation. Reconciliation requires two people, both willing to do the work of rebuilding trust.

Forgiveness only requires one, you, willing to do the work of releasing resentment. You can forgive someone and never speak to them again. You can forgive someone who never apologizes, never acknowledges what they did, never changes their behavior.

Because forgiveness isn't contingent on their response. It's independent of whether they deserve it or earn it or even want it. It's about your liberation, not their redemption.

Now, here's the part people never tell you about forgiveness: it's not a one-time event. It's a process. It's a decision you make over and over again, sometimes daily, sometimes hourly, until one day you realize the chain has finally broken and you're free.

There will be days when you think you've forgiven, and then something triggers the memory and all the anger comes flooding back. There will be moments when you have to choose forgiveness again for the same offense because the hurt keeps trying to reassert itself.

Understand that this is normal. This is part of the process. Forgiveness is not failure just because you have to do it more than once.

Think of it like this: when you're cutting through a heavy chain with bolt cutters, you don't slice through it in one motion. You apply pressure, make a dent, apply more pressure, make a deeper cut, keep working at it until finally the chain breaks. Each time you choose forgiveness, you're applying more pressure to that chain. Each time you refuse to rehearse the offense, you're making a deeper cut. Each time you release them from the debt, you're closer to freedom.

And here's what makes this even harder: sometimes the person you need to forgive is yourself.

Sometimes the chain that's holding you isn't attached to someone else. It's attached to your own past, your own choices, your own failures. You're bound not by what was done to you but by what you did, what you didn't do, who you were when you didn't know better.

I realized a long time ago that guilt is a master chain-maker. It will forge links out of every mistake you've made, every opportunity you've missed, every time you fell short of who you wanted to be. And it will convince you that you deserve to stay bound, that forgiveness is for other people, that what you did is somehow beyond the reach of grace.

But if you can extend forgiveness to others, you have to learn to extend it to yourself too. You have to look at the person you were, acknowledge the hurt you caused or the mistakes you made, and then decide that you're not going to spend the rest of your life paying for something that's already been covered by grace.

"God is faithful and just and will forgive us our sins and purify us from all unrighteousness."

1 John 1:9 (NIrV)

If God can forgive you, who are you to withhold forgiveness from yourself? If the Creator of everything can look at your worst moment and offer redemption, why are you still insisting you're beyond repair?

Self-forgiveness doesn't mean you're excusing what you did. It means you're refusing to let your past mistakes be the chains that keep you from your future purpose. It means you're acknowledging that you were hurt and broken and operating from pain, and you're choosing to extend to yourself the same grace you're learning to extend to others.

Because here's the truth: until you forgive yourself, you'll keep punishing everyone around you for what you can't let go of. You'll project your self-hatred onto others. You'll sabotage good things because you don't believe you deserve them. You'll keep choosing chains because bondage feels like the penance you owe.

But you don't owe penance. You owe yourself freedom.

So pick up the bolt cutters. Look at the chains that have been holding you, the ones attached to people who hurt you and the ones attached to your own past. And start cutting.

One link at a time. One choice at a time. One act of forgiveness at a time.

It won't be easy. Some chains will fight back, and we'll talk about that in a moment. Some will require help, support, professional guidance to break. Some will take longer than you want them to take.

But every chain can be broken. Every single one.

Letting Go Of What Never Was

There's a particular kind of chain that's harder to break than all the others. It's not attached to something that happened. It's attached to something that didn't.

It's the chain of "*if only*."

If only I had made a different choice. If only they had stayed. If only I had been smarter, stronger, more careful. If only that opportunity hadn't passed me by. If only things had gone the way they were supposed to go.

This chain is connected to a phantom, a version of reality that exists only in your mind. A life you were supposed to have. A relationship that should have worked. A future that got stolen before it could arrive. A version of yourself you were meant to become but somehow never did.

And because this chain isn't attached to something real, you can't cut it the way you cut the others. You can't forgive a relationship that never existed. You can't release a future that never came. You can't make peace with a version of yourself you never got to be.

What you have to do instead is grieve.

You have to mourn what never was. You have to acknowledge the loss of the fantasy, the death of the dream, the ending of the story you thought you were writing. And that grief is real, even though the thing you're grieving isn't.

I spent years chained to a version of my life that existed only in my imagination. The career that was supposed to take off. The relationship that was supposed to last. The family dynamics that were supposed to heal. I had written the story in my head, cast all the characters, planned all the scenes. I knew exactly how it was supposed to unfold.

And then it didn't.

Reality showed up and refused to follow my script. People made choices I didn't anticipate. Circumstances shifted in ways I couldn't control. The future I had counted on evaporated like morning fog, leaving me standing in a present I never wanted, grieving a past that never actually existed.

Because that's the thing about "if only" thinking. It doesn't just keep you stuck in the past. It keeps you stuck in a past that's partially fiction. You're not mourning what actually was. You're mourning your idealized version of what could have been if everything had gone differently.

You remember the relationship as better than it was. You imagine the opportunity as bigger than it would have been. You picture yourself handling things perfectly in a way you never could have managed with the information and resources you had at the time.

This is what I call the mythology of "if only." It's the belief that changing one thing, just one single variable, would have fixed everything. That if you had just said the right words, made the right choice, been in the right place at the right time, your entire life would be different.

But life doesn't work like that. Life is not a series of isolated moments where one different choice creates a completely different trajectory. Life is complex, interconnected, influenced by thousands of variables most of which you don't control and can't even see.

That relationship that ended? Changing one thing wouldn't have saved it. There were fundamental incompatibilities, patterns that would have shown up eventually, issues that existed beneath the surface long before the breaking point.

That opportunity you missed? Taking it might not have been the miracle you think it would have been. You don't know what problems came with it, what sacrifices it would have required, what you would have lost in gaining it.

That version of yourself you think you should have become? You're comparing your real, messy, human journey to a fantasy version that never had to deal with actual obstacles, real pain, or genuine limitations.

The "*if only*" chain keeps you imprisoned in an impossible past. It asks you to fix something that can't be fixed because it never existed in the first place. It demands that you grieve not just what you lost, but what you never had, what was never real, what was always just a story you told yourself about how things were supposed to go.

And the demons love this chain. They love it when you're stuck comparing your actual life to an imaginary one. They love it when you're so busy mourning what never was that you can't see what is. They love it when you're chained to a fantasy because it means you're not free to engage with reality.

So how do you break this chain? How do you let go of what never was?

First, you have to get honest about the difference between memory and mythology.

Memory is what actually happened. Mythology is the story you've told yourself about what happened, complete with embellishments, omissions, and reinterpretations that make it fit the narrative you need it to fit.

That relationship you're still mourning? Try to remember it honestly. Not just the good moments, but all of it. The fights you ignored. The red flags you dismissed. The times you felt small or unheard or like you were performing instead of being. The ways you weren't compatible that you convinced yourself didn't matter. The reality of who they actually were, not who you needed them to be.

That opportunity you think you missed? Consider it realistically. What would it have actually cost you? What would you have had to sacrifice? What problems would it have created? What do you know now about that path that you didn't know then?

That version of yourself you think you should have become? Acknowledge that person was never real. You're comparing your actual journey, complete with trauma and obstacles and limitations, to an idealized version that never had to overcome what you've overcome. That's not a fair comparison. That's not even a real comparison.

Second, you have to make peace with reality as it actually is, not as you wish it were.

This is harder than it sounds. Making peace with reality means accepting that some things are over, some doors are closed, some versions of your life are never going to happen. It means releasing the fantasy of what could have been and dealing with what is.

It means saying out loud: "That relationship is over, and it's not coming back." Not "maybe someday" or "if they change" or "if I change." Just over.

It means acknowledging: "That opportunity has passed, and I'm not going to get another chance at it." Not "maybe something similar will come along" or "maybe I can recreate it." Just passed.

It means accepting: "That version of my life I planned is not the version I'm living, and wishing won't change that." Not "maybe I can still fix it" or "maybe it's not too late." Just accepting.

This feels like death because, in a way, it is death. You're killing the fantasy. You're letting the dream die. You're burying the version of your life that exists only in your imagination.

And that requires grief.

Real grief. The kind that acknowledges loss even when what you lost was never yours to begin with. The kind that honors the pain of disappointed hope even when the hope was unrealistic. The kind that lets you cry for what never was without pretending it was.

I need you to understand that grief is not weakness. Grief is how you process loss. And you can grieve the loss of something that never existed. You can mourn the ending of a fantasy. You can feel the pain of a future that didn't arrive.

What you can't do is stay there forever.

At some point, after you've grieved what never was, you have to turn your attention to what is. You have to look at the life you're actually living, the relationships you actually have, the opportunities that are actually in front of you, the version of yourself you're actually becoming.

And you have to decide: am I going to keep mourning what isn't, or am I going to start building what can be?

Because here's what the "if only" chain steals from you: it steals your present. While you're mourning what never was, you're missing what is. While you're replaying the past looking for the moment where everything went wrong, you're not showing up for the moments that are happening right now.

Your children are growing up while you're grieving the family dynamics that never healed. Your opportunities are passing while you're stuck on the one that got away. Your actual relationships are suffering while you're comparing them to an idealized one that existed only in your head.

The life you could be living is waiting for you to stop mourning the life you'll never live.

I'm not saying this to be harsh. I'm saying it because I've been there. I've spent years chained to "if only," so convinced that my real life was somewhere in the past I missed that I couldn't see the one unfolding in front of me.

And I finally had to make a choice. I had to decide whether I was going to keep living in the fantasy or start living in the reality. Whether I was going to keep grieving what never was or start building what could be.

That choice required me to do something that felt impossible: I had to let go of the story I had written about how my life was supposed to go. I had to release my grip on the script I had created, the plans I had made, the future I had counted on. I had to accept that life had other ideas, that God had a different path, that the story being written was not the one I would have chosen.

And in that letting go, I found something unexpected. Freedom.

Not the freedom to go back and fix what went wrong. Not the freedom to change the past or reclaim what was lost. But the freedom to be present in my actual life instead of imprisoned in an imaginary one.

The freedom to say, "Yes, that hurt. Yes, I wish it had been different. Yes, I grieve what never was. And also, I'm here now. In this life. With these people. Facing these challenges. Building this future."

Two things can be true at the same time. You can acknowledge the loss and engage with the present. You can grieve what never was and hope for what might be. You can accept that the past didn't go the way you wanted and still believe your future can be good.

But you can't do that while you're chained to "if only."

So here's what I want you to do. I want you to identify the fantasy you're still holding onto. The relationship that was supposed to work. The opportunity that was supposed to come. The version of yourself you were supposed to become. The life that was supposed to unfold.

Name it. Be specific. Don't just say "things were supposed to be different." Say exactly what you thought was supposed to happen that didn't.

And then, when you've named it, I want you to grieve it. I mean actually grieve it. Let yourself feel the loss of it, the disappointment, the anger, the sadness. Don't rush this part. Don't spiritualize it away with platitudes about God's plan. Just let yourself feel what you feel about what never was.

And then, when you're ready, when you've honored the grief and felt the loss, I want you to release it.

Say it out loud if you need to: "I release this fantasy. I let go of this version of my life that never existed. I accept reality as it is, not as I wish it were."

And then, after you've released it, I want you to look around at your actual life. Not the life you planned. Not the life you think you deserve. Not the life you would have chosen. Your actual life, with all its imperfections and disappointments and unexpected turns.

And I want you to ask yourself: what can I build here? In this reality, not the fantasy? With these resources, not the ones I wish I had? As this version of myself, not the one I thought I'd be?

Because that's where freedom lives. Not in the past that never was. But in the present that actually is.

And you can't get there while you're still holding onto the chain of "if only."

So let it go. Grieve it, honor it, acknowledge it, and then let it go.

The life you're actually living is waiting for you to show up for it.

The Healing Paradox & Building Your Support Network

Here's something nobody tells you about breaking chains: sometimes it gets worse before it gets better.

Sometimes the act of breaking free hurts more than staying bound. Sometimes liberation feels like destruction. Sometimes freedom looks an awful lot like falling apart.

I call this the healing paradox, and if you don't understand it, you'll quit right when you're on the verge of breakthrough.

Think about what happens when you break a bone that healed wrong. The bone feels normal because you've adjusted to it. You've learned to compensate for the limitation. You've built your life around the dysfunction. It's not right, but it's familiar.

Then a doctor tells you the only way to heal correctly is to re-break it. To intentionally cause the pain again. To go backward before you can go forward. To make it worse so it can get better.

And everything in you screams that this is wrong. That more pain can't be the answer. That breaking what's already broken makes no sense.

But it's the only way to heal properly.

The same is true for breaking chains. When you start doing the work of forgiveness, of letting go, of releasing what never was, you're essentially re-breaking bones that healed crooked. You're disrupting patterns that feel normal even though they're dysfunctional. You're destabilizing a system that, while painful, at least had the benefit of being predictable.

And it hurts.

It hurts to forgive when you've been wearing unforgiveness like armor. It hurts to let go of fantasies when they've been your comfort in disappointment. It hurts to face reality when you've been hiding in imagination. It hurts to acknowledge that the chains you've been carrying aren't just something that happened to you but something you've been choosing to keep.

When I first started doing this work, really doing it and not just talking about it, I felt worse than I had in years. Memories I thought I'd dealt with came flooding back. Emotions I'd successfully numbed suddenly demanded attention. Pain I'd managed to avoid by staying busy or distracted or addicted to forward motion caught up with me all at once.

I remember thinking I had made a mistake. That I should have left well enough alone. That poking at old wounds was only making them bleed again.

What I didn't understand then was that those wounds had never actually healed. They'd just scabbed over. And scabs aren't healing, they're just covering. Real healing requires getting underneath the surface, cleaning out what's infected, letting air and light reach what's been hidden in darkness.

That process is brutal. There's no way around that truth. Breaking chains, real liberation, actual freedom requires you to feel things you've been avoiding, face things you've been running from, acknowledge things you've been denying.

And you can't do it alone.

This is where most people fail. Not because they're weak or uncommitted or lack faith. They fail because they try to break chains in isolation, believing that healing is a solo journey, that asking for help is weakness, that if they just try harder or pray more or have enough willpower, they can do it themselves.

But chains that were forged over years, reinforced by trauma, built link by link through pain and disappointment and betrayal, those chains don't break just because you've decided you're ready to be free. They break when you have the right tools, the right support, the right people helping you do what you can't do alone.

You need a support network. Not eventually. Not when things get really bad. But now. Before you start the deep work, before you begin breaking the chains that have been holding you longest, you need to know who's going to be there when it gets hard.

Let me be specific about what I mean by support network, because I'm not talking about your social media friends or your casual acquaintances or the people who like your posts but don't actually know what you're going through.

I'm talking about people who can handle your truth. People who won't run when you stop performing. People who can sit with you in the mess without trying to fix it or spiritualize it away or tell you to just have more faith.

First, you need a professional. A therapist, a counselor, someone trained in the art of helping people navigate trauma and break destructive patterns. This is not optional. This is not something you do only if you can afford it or only if things get really bad. This is essential.

The church has done incredible damage by suggesting that prayer and Bible reading should be enough, that if you need therapy, you must not have enough faith, and that psychological help is somehow less spiritual than pastoral counseling. That's not just wrong, it's reckless and malpractice.

God created therapists the same way He created doctors. Using their expertise isn't a failure of faith any more than going to a hospital when you break your leg is admitting God can't heal you. It's wisdom. It's stewardship of the resources He's provided. It's acknowledging that sometimes we need help to access the healing He's already made available.

A good therapist can help you see patterns you've been blind to. They can provide tools you don't have. They can create a safe space for you to process pain you've never felt safe enough to feel. They can guide you through the re-breaking process without letting you quit when it gets hard.

If you're thinking you can't afford therapy, I want you to consider what you're already paying for in terms of dysfunction. What is your unforgiveness costing you in terms of relationships, opportunities, peace, physical health? What is staying chained worth compared to the investment in your liberation?

Most communities have sliding scale options, community mental health centers, pastoral counselors who work on donation basis. The resources exist. You have to be willing to seek them out and use them.

Second, you need accountability partners. People who know what you're working through and can check in, not to judge but to support. People who will ask the hard questions: Are you doing the work? Are you showing up for your therapy appointments? Are you practicing forgiveness or just talking about it?

These can't be people who enable your dysfunction or reinforce your chains. They can't be people who join you in blaming everyone else for your bondage, or who agree that you're right to hold onto unforgiveness, or who validate every feeling without challenging any behavior.

You need people who love you enough to tell you the truth even if the truth hurts. People who will call you out when you're choosing chains. People who will remind you why you started this journey when you want to quit.

Third, you need safe people who can just be with you. Not everyone in your support network needs to be actively helping you break chains. Some people just need to be present, to remind you that you're not alone, to sit with you in the pain without trying to make it go away.

These are the friends who show up with food when you're too exhausted from the work to cook. The family members who let you cry without telling you to be strong. The people who can handle your silence without filling it with platitudes.

Now here's something I need you to understand: not everyone in your life belongs in your healing journey.

Some people need to be kept at a distance while you're doing this work. Not because they're bad people, but because they can't handle your process, or they benefit from your bondage, or they're so triggered by your healing that they'll sabotage it without even meaning to.

Family members who need you to stay small might not support your growth. Friends who bonded with you over shared victimhood might not know how to relate to you as a survivor. People who are still chained themselves might resent your liberation because it confronts their own captivity.

You have to be strategic about who you let into the room when you're doing the deep work. You have to protect your process from people who, intentionally or not, would derail it.

This might mean having some hard conversations. It might mean setting boundaries you've never set before. It might mean disappointing people who are used to you being available for their needs while you focus on your own healing for a season.

That's okay. It's not selfish. It's survival.

You cannot heal in the same environment that made you sick. You cannot break chains while people who benefit from your bondage are holding onto them. You cannot do the hard work of transformation while managing other people's reactions to your change.

Your healing has to matter more than their comfort. Your freedom has to take priority over their expectations. Your liberation has to be worth the cost of their disappointment.

And here's the thing: the right people will understand. The people who genuinely love you, who want you to be free more than they want you to stay familiar, those people will give you space to do what you need to do. They'll adjust to your boundaries. They'll support your process even when it's uncomfortable for them.

The people who fight your healing, who resist your boundaries, who make your liberation about them, those are the people who need to be kept outside your circle while you're doing this work.

You'll know who belongs in your support network by how they respond when things get hard. When the healing paradox hits and you're falling apart while getting better, who stays? Who can handle your mess? Who doesn't try to rush you through the process or convince you to go back to how you were?

Those are your people. Hold onto them. Let them help you. Don't try to do this alone just because you think you should be strong enough to break your own chains.

Strength isn't refusing help. Strength is knowing when you need it and being humble enough to ask for it.

The chains you're breaking were built in isolation, in moments when you felt alone, when you thought no one would understand, when you had to survive without support. Breaking them requires the opposite. It requires connection.

It requires authentic vulnerability. It requires letting people in.

So before you go any deeper into this work, before you start breaking the chains that have held you longest, I want you to ask yourself: who's in my corner? Who can I call when it gets hard? Who will remind me why this matters when I want to quit?

And if you can't answer those questions, if you realize you've been trying to do this alone, then your first step isn't breaking chains. It's building a team.

Find a therapist. Identify your accountability partners. Reach out to safe people and tell them what you're working through. Create the support network that will hold you when the healing paradox hits and breaking free feels worse than staying bound.

Because the paradox is real. It does get worse before it gets better. The re-breaking hurts more than the original break sometimes.

But here's what makes it worth it: when a bone heals correctly, it's stronger than it was before it broke. When chains break completely, you're freer than if they'd never been there at all. When healing happens properly, you don't just go back to who you were. You become who you were always meant to be.

And you don't have to do it alone.

When Chains Fight Back & Freedom Feels Strange

You'd think that once you start breaking chains, once you've committed to the work and built your support network and started doing the hard things, the rest would be easier.

You'd think liberation would feel like relief from the first moment. That freedom would be instantly recognizable as better than bondage. That once you've cut one link, the rest would fall away naturally.

But that's not how it works.

Chains fight back. And freedom, at least at first, feels really strange.

Let me explain what I mean by chains fighting back, because this is where a lot of people give up. They start doing the work. They begin to see progress. They feel lighter, freer, more hopeful than they've felt in years. And then something happens that makes them question everything.

An old trigger resurfaces stronger than before. A pattern they thought they'd broken shows up again. A person they've forgiven does something that reignites all the old anger. A fantasy they thought they'd released pulls at them with surprising force.

And they think, "I must be doing it wrong. The work isn't working. I'm never going to be free. I should just give up and go back to how things were."

This is the chain fighting back.

Chains don't just let go because you've decided you're done with them. They've been part of your identity, your coping mechanisms, your way of understanding the world for so long that your entire system resists their removal. Your mind, your body, your emotions, they all know how to function with the chains. But they don't know how to function without them.

So when you start removing them, everything in you that's been built around bondage starts sending alarm signals. Danger. Unfamiliar territory. Return to what you know. Put the chains back on. At least with them you knew what to expect.

This resistance will not show up in the same way for everyone.

For some, it's physical. Your body has been carrying stress and trauma for so long that when you start releasing it, you feel exhausted. You get sick more easily. You sleep more or can't sleep at all. Your body is detoxing, learning to exist without the adrenaline and cortisol that's been flooding your system for years.

For others, it's emotional. You start feeling things you haven't felt in years because you've finally stopped numbing yourself. And those feelings are overwhelming. The grief you've been avoiding suddenly hits you like a tsunami. Anger you've been suppressing demands attention. Fear you've been outrunning finally catches up with you.

For some, it's relational. The people in your life are used to the chained version of you. They know how to interact with you when you're bound. They have roles that depend on your dysfunction. And when you start changing, when you start setting boundaries and refusing to carry what isn't yours, they don't know what to do with the new you.

Some of them will try to pull you back. Not because they're evil, but because your chains made them feel better about their own. Not because they don't love you, but because they loved the version of you that needed them in specific ways. Not because they want you to suffer, but because your suffering was somehow serving their purposes.

They'll say things like, "You've changed," like it's an accusation. "You're not yourself anymore," as if the self you were was the one you were meant to be. "I miss the old you," not realizing the old you was drowning.

And if you're not prepared for this resistance, if you don't understand that chains fight back through the people who benefited from your bondage, you'll start to believe them. You'll wonder if maybe you have changed too much. If maybe you should go back to being who you were. If maybe freedom isn't worth losing the people who can't handle it.

But here's what I need you to understand: the people who truly love you will adjust. They'll mourn the loss of the dynamic they knew, yes. They'll be uncomfortable with your growth, maybe. But they'll ultimately celebrate your freedom because they want you to be whole more than they want you to be familiar.

The people who fight your liberation, who make you feel guilty for growing, who try to shame you back into chains, those people were never really for you. They were for the version of you that served their needs. And you cannot sacrifice your freedom for their comfort.

The chains will also fight back through your own mind. You'll have moments, maybe even days or weeks, when you're convinced this was all a mistake. When the old patterns will seem easier than the new ones. When going back to what you knew feels safer than moving forward into what you don't.

Can I tell you something? This is normal. This is part of the process. This doesn't mean you're failing.

What it means is that you're in the hard middle, the space between bondage and freedom where you're not fully in either place. You've broken some chains but you're still carrying others. You've made progress but you haven't arrived. You're better than you were but not yet who you're becoming.

And in that space, the temptation to quit is strongest.

I remember hitting this point in my own journey. I had done the work. I had forgiven people who didn't deserve it. I had let go of fantasies that had comforted me for years. I had built my support network and showed up for therapy and did all the things I was supposed to do.

And then one day, someone did something that triggered every old wound. And I felt all the old anger, all the old hurt, all the old patterns trying to reassert themselves. And I thought, "What was the point? I did all this work and I'm right back where I started."

But I wasn't back where I started. I was in a moment that felt like where I started. There's a difference.

The difference was that this time, I had tools. I had people I could call. I had awareness of what was happening instead of just being swept away by it. I had a choice about how to respond instead of just reacting from old patterns.

Now I will admit, I didn't exactly handle it the way that I should. I got angry. I felt hurt. I wanted to retreat into old ways of protecting myself.

But I did something different. I called my therapist. I reached out to my accountability partners. I acknowledged what I was feeling without letting it define what I would do. I chose forgiveness again, even though it was the hundredth time I'd had to choose it.

And slowly, the intensity passed. The chain that had been fighting back loosened its grip. The pattern that had tried to reassert itself lost its power.

That's when I learned something crucial: chains fighting back doesn't mean you're losing. It means they're losing their grip and they're desperate to hold on.

When you feel the resistance, when old patterns resurface, when people try to pull you back, when your own mind tells you to quit, that's not evidence that freedom isn't working. That's evidence that bondage is losing its hold and it's fighting for survival.

Don't give up in that moment. That's when you're closest to breakthrough.

But here's the other thing nobody prepares you for: even when the chains break, even when you're finally free, freedom itself feels strange.

You've been carrying weight for so long that when it's gone, you feel unbalanced. You've been limited for so long that when the limitations are removed, you don't know what to do with the space. You've been defined by your chains for so long that when they're broken, you're not sure who you are without them.

I watched this happen with someone I know who finally broke free from an abusive relationship. She had been chained to that person for years, defined by that dynamic, shaped by that pain. And when she finally left, when she was finally safe, when she was finally free, she didn't know what to do with herself.

She kept expecting him to show up. She kept waiting for the other shoe to drop. She kept looking over her shoulder for threats that weren't there anymore. Her body was free but her mind was still in prison, still operating as if the chains were there even though they'd been broken.

It took months for her to adjust to freedom. Months of reminding herself she was safe. Months of learning to make decisions without fear. Months of discovering who she was when she wasn't just surviving.

It may not seem like it but this is normal. This is what liberation looks like. It's not an instant transformation from bound to free. It's a slow adjustment to a reality you're not used to, learning to move without weight you've carried so long you forgot it was there.

You'll catch yourself still operating from old patterns even though they don't serve you anymore. You'll find yourself apologizing when you don't need to, shrinking when you don't have to, performing when no one's demanding it.

You'll have moments when you almost miss the chains because at least with them you knew what to expect. At least with them you had an excuse for why you couldn't move forward. At least with them you didn't have to face the responsibility of freedom.

Because that's the thing about freedom that nobody tells you: it's terrifying. When you're chained, you can blame the chains for everything you're not doing, everything you're not becoming, everywhere you're not going. But when the chains are broken, you have to face the fact that you're the only thing standing between who you are and who you could be.

That's a heavy realization. And it's why some people, even after they've done the work to break free, will slowly, unconsciously, start picking the chains back up.

They'll find new people to stay bound to. New fantasies to hide in. New unforgiveness to carry. New patterns to repeat. Not because they want to be in bondage, but because bondage is familiar and freedom is foreign, and the human mind gravitates toward what it knows, even when what it knows is painful.

Don't do that. Don't break chains just to pick up new ones. Don't do all this work just to trade one form of captivity for another.

When freedom feels strange, when you're tempted to go back to what you know, when you catch yourself reaching for chains you've already broken, stop. Breathe. Remember why you did this work in the first place.

Remember how heavy the chains were. Remember how exhausting it was to carry them. Remember what it cost you to stay bound. Remember that the strangeness of freedom is temporary but the chains were permanent until you broke them.

And then practice living free. Consciously, deliberately, intentionally practice making choices as a free person. Practice setting boundaries without guilt. Practice forgiving without keeping score. Practice letting go without picking back up. Practice being present in your actual life instead of imprisoned in imaginary ones.

It will feel awkward at first. Like learning to walk after years in a wheelchair. Your muscles aren't used to carrying you this way. Your balance is off. You'll stumble and fall and wonder if you should just go back to wheels.

But keep practicing. Keep choosing freedom even when it feels foreign. Keep breaking chains even when they fight back. Keep building the life that's possible now that you're not carrying the weight.

Because eventually, freedom won't feel strange anymore. It will feel normal. Natural. Right.

Eventually, you won't be able to imagine going back to bondage because you'll have adjusted to liberation. You'll have learned to move without chains. You'll have discovered who you are when you're not defined by what's held you.

Eventually, you'll look back at who you were when you started this journey and barely recognize that person. You'll see how much you were carrying, how small you had made yourself, how much of your life you were missing while you were bound.

And you'll be grateful you didn't quit when the chains fought back. Grateful you pushed through when freedom felt strange. Grateful you did the hard work that brought you here.

So when the resistance comes, and it will come, remember this: chains fight back because they're losing. Freedom feels strange because you're not used to it yet.

Neither of those things means you should stop.

They mean you should keep going.

The Story You Tell Yourself

You've done the work. You've named the demons. You've understood how they operate across your past, your present, and your future. You've learned about the architecture of bondage, picked up the bolt cutters of forgiveness, grieved what never was, built your support network, and prepared yourself for the resistance that comes with liberation.

The chains are breaking. Some are already gone. Others are loosening with each choice you make toward freedom.

But here's what happens next, the part that determines whether this liberation actually lasts or whether you end up right back where you started: you have to decide what story you're going to tell about all of this.

Because the demons didn't just chain you with circumstances and trauma and pain. They chained you with narratives. Stories about who you are, what you deserve, what's possible for someone like you. Stories that have been playing on repeat in your mind for so long you've forgotten they're just stories, not truth.

Guilt told you a story about permanent damage. Envy whispered a narrative about stolen destiny. Greed convinced you of perpetual insufficiency. Selfishness spun a tale of necessary isolation. Rejection wrote a script where you're fundamentally unlovable.

And you believed them. Not because you're weak or foolish, but because those stories were all you had to make sense of your pain.

But now? Now you're free enough to write a different story. Now you have the space to question the narrative. Now you can look at everything that's happened to you and decide what it means, what you're going to do with it, how you're going to let it shape who you're becoming.

The question isn't whether your past happened. It did. The question is what story you're going to tell about it going forward.

Are you the victim who never recovered? Or the survivor who refused to stay down? Are you defined by what was done to you? Or by what you did in response to it? Is your life a tragedy? Or a testimony?

You get to decide. Not the demons. Not the people who hurt you. Not the circumstances that shaped you.

You.

Because breaking chains is only half the battle. The other half is rewriting the narrative that kept you bound in the first place.

CHAPTER NINE
REWRITE THE NARRATIVE

The Stories We Inherit

Long before you knew what a narrative was, you were living inside one.

It started in the way your family talked about money. The way they spoke about relationships. The casual comments made at dinner tables and family reunions that sounded like observations but were actually prophecies being spoken over your life. The scripts handed down like sentimental items, passed from generation to generation with the same certainty as your grandmother's china or your grandfather's pocket watch.

"We've always struggled with money."
"The women in our family are strong, but the men always leave."
"Nobody in this family has ever gone to college."
"We're just not the kind of people who catch breaks."

These weren't just statements. They were stories. And stories, when repeated enough times, become reality. Not because they're true, but because we start living as if they are. We inherit narratives the same way we inherit eye color or the shape of our hands, the difference is these inheritances shape our choices, our expectations, our sense of what's possible.

I grew up hearing certain stories on repeat. Some of them were beautiful, like Mama's "come what may" and Lil'Momma's embodiment of grace. Those were narratives worth inheriting, wisdom uploaded into my spirit that would carry me through losses I couldn't yet imagine.

But there were other stories too. Ones about limitation. About what people like us could expect from life. About which doors were meant for us and which ones weren't. Stories that sounded like protection but functioned like prisons, keeping us safe from disappointment by keeping us from even trying.

The tricky thing about inherited narratives is that they don't announce themselves as stories. They present themselves as facts. As "just the way things are." As reality so obvious it doesn't need questioning. Your family doesn't sit you down and say, "Now let me tell you the limiting beliefs we're going to program into you." They just live them. They speak them. They reinforce them with every cautionary tale and every nervous warning when you start dreaming too big.

And you absorb them. Not because you're weak or gullible, but because you're human. Because the people who raised you are the first people who teach you about the world, and their understanding of the world becomes your understanding. Their limitations become your ceiling. Their fears become your boundaries.

Until you decide they don't have to be.

Here's what I need you to understand: recognizing scripts is not the same as disrespecting your family. Questioning inherited narratives doesn't mean you're ungrateful for everything your people gave you or the struggles they endured to give you. You can honor the strength it took for them to survive their circumstances while also recognizing that survival mode shouldn't be your final destination.

Your grandmother might have had to accept certain limitations because of the world she lived in, the opportunities she was denied, the doors that were closed to her because of her gender or her race or her economic reality. That was her story. That was her fight. And she fought it with everything she had.

But her story doesn't have to be your story. Her ceiling doesn't have to be your ceiling.

This is the difference between scripts and destiny. Scripts are written by circumstances, by fear, by the limitations imposed on previous generations. Destiny is written by purpose, by calling, by the specific assignment God has for your life. Scripts tell you what's realistic based on where you came from. Destiny tells you what's possible based on where you're going.

And sometimes, the most loving thing you can do for the people who came before you is to go further than they could. To dream bigger than they were allowed to dream. To break the cycle not as a rejection of them, but as a fulfillment of what they would have wanted for you if they'd had the freedom to want it.

Because when you really think about it, what did they sacrifice for? What did they endure for? They didn't struggle so you could stay exactly where they were. They struggled so you could have more options than they had. More freedom. More possibilities.

Isaac Newton once said, "If I have seen further, it is by standing on the shoulders of giants." Those giants in your life had to create the platform upon which you could see further, beyond the script, and into possibility. They built the foundation so you could build higher.

My family wanted me to do something they only dreamed of: going to college, getting a good education, securing a good job, and leaving a profound mark on this world. So I lived that dream as the first in my family to go all the way to a doctorate. I became a department leader within my university. I published books and presented at conferences they'd never heard of and couldn't have conceived. I'm here in this moment, writing these words, encouraging you to rewrite your narrative because someone stood on their shoulders so I could see far enough to know it's possible.

And now you're standing on theirs. And mine. And everyone else's who dared to push past the script.

The narrative you inherited might have been exactly what your family needed to survive their circumstances. But surviving and thriving are two different things. And if you're going to step into the fullness of who you were created to be, you're going to have to examine which stories you're carrying and decide which ones still serve you.

Some of them will be worth keeping. Mama's "come what may" earned its place in my spirit because it wasn't a narrative of limitation. It was a declaration of endurance, a reminder that I could face whatever came because I was standing on something solid.

But other stories? The ones that told me what I couldn't do, who I couldn't become, what I shouldn't even try? Those had to be questioned. Examined. And ultimately, rejected.

Not with anger. Not with bitterness. But with clarity.

Because you can't chase your destiny while dragging someone else's limitations behind you.

The Stories Demons Tell

Family narratives are powerful, but they're not the only stories shaping your life. The demons we've been chasing throughout this book don't just attack you with circumstances and feelings. They attack you with narratives. Carefully crafted stories designed to keep you exactly where they want you: stuck, afraid, and convinced that freedom isn't for someone like you.

Remember, these demons have names: Guilt, Envy, Greed, Selfishness, and Rejection. And each one comes with its own script, its own lie masquerading as truth, its own story that sounds so convincing you forget it's fiction.

Let me show you the stories they tell.

Guilt's Story: "You're Permanently Damaged"

Guilt doesn't just remind you of what you've done wrong. It tells you a story about who you are because of what you've done. It takes your mistakes and transforms them into your identity. It takes your past and makes it your permanent address.

Guilt's narrative goes something like this: "You had your chance and you blew it. You hurt people who trusted you. You made choices that can't be unmade. And because of that, you don't get to move forward. You don't get to be free. You don't get to be happy. You're permanently damaged goods, and the best you can hope for is to serve your sentence quietly and try not to hurt anyone else."

This is the story that keeps victims of abuse silent. The story that convinces people they deserved what happened to them. The story that says redemption is for other people, not for you. Guilt's story doesn't just acknowledge that you made a mistake—it insists that you are the mistake.

And here's the insidious part: Guilt backs up its story with evidence. It replays your failures on repeat. It shows you the faces of people you hurt. It points to the consequences of your choices as proof that you're beyond repair. It sounds so reasonable, so justified, so obviously true that you stop questioning whether it actually is.

But Guilt's story leaves out something crucial: Grace. Transformation. The possibility that who you were doesn't have to define who you're becoming. Guilt's story has no room for growth because growth would mean Guilt loses its power over you.

Envy's Story: "Everyone Else Got What Should Have Been Yours"

Envy tells a different story, but it's just as poisonous. Envy's narrative is about stolen destiny, about a cosmic injustice that gave everyone else what rightfully belonged to you. Envy whispers that you were supposed to have that career, that relationship, that opportunity, that blessing. But somehow, through no fault of your own, it went to someone less deserving.

Envy's story sounds like this: "You worked just as hard. You sacrificed just as much. You deserved it more. But they got lucky. They knew the right people. They were in the right place at the right time. They got what should have been yours, and now you're stuck watching them live the life that was meant for you."

This story is particularly dangerous because it contains a kernel of truth. The harsh reality that we skate by is that life isn't fair. Sometimes people do get opportunities they didn't earn. Sometimes you do work harder than the person who got promoted. Sometimes the less talented person does get the break you've been praying for.

But Envy takes that kernel of truth and builds an entire narrative around it, one that poisons every good thing in your life. Envy makes you resent your friend's marriage because yours ended in divorce. Envy makes you bitter about your coworker's promotion because you've been there longer and worked harder. Envy makes you unable to celebrate anyone else's success because you're too busy mourning what you think you lost.

Envy's story keeps you stuck in comparison mode, always measuring your life against someone else's highlight reel. And as long as you're focused on what everyone else has, you can't see what you have. You can't appreciate your own blessings. You can't pursue your own purpose because you're too busy chasing someone else's.

Greed's Story: "You're Always One Acquisition Away"

Greed's narrative is about perpetual insufficiency. No matter how much you have, Greed tells you it's not enough. No matter what you achieve, Greed insists there's one more thing you need before you can finally be satisfied, finally be secure, finally be enough.

Greed's story goes like this: "You're almost there. Just one more promotion and you'll feel successful. Just a little more money in savings and you'll feel secure. Just one more relationship and you'll feel complete. Just one more achievement and you'll finally be worthy. You're so close. Don't stop now. Keep chasing. Keep acquiring. Keep consuming. The thing that will finally satisfy you is just around the corner."

Except it never is. Because Greed's story has no ending. There is no "enough" in Greed's narrative. Every finish line is revealed to be just another starting line. Every summit reached shows you there's another mountain to climb. Greed promised you that satisfaction was just one acquisition away, but once you get it, Greed moves the goalpost and tells you there's something else you need.

This isn't just about money, though it certainly includes that. Greed's story applies to relationships, achievements, experiences, validation. It's the insatiable appetite that can never be filled because the hunger isn't really about what you're consuming. It's about the hole you're trying to fill.

And as long as you believe Greed's story, you'll spend your entire life chasing what you already have: enough.

Selfishness's Story: "You Can Only Trust Yourself"

Selfishness tells a story about necessary isolation. It insists that vulnerability is weakness, that needing others is failure, that the only person you can truly count on is yourself. Selfishness takes the pain of past betrayals and builds a fortress around your heart, convincing you that safety lies in self-sufficiency.

Selfishness's narrative sounds like protection: "People will let you down. They'll use you. They'll leave when things get hard. The only way to avoid getting hurt again is to never need anyone. Keep your guard up. Stay in control. Don't let anyone close enough to hurt you. You're the only one who will never abandon you."

This story seems wise until you realize it's a prison. Selfishness convinces you that isolation equals safety, but what it actually delivers is loneliness dressed up as strength. It tells you that asking for help means you're weak, that depending on others means you're inadequate, that trusting anyone is foolish.

Selfishness's story keeps you from the very connections that could heal you. It makes every relationship transactional because vulnerability feels too dangerous. It turns love into leverage and friendship into potential betrayal waiting to happen. It robs you of community, of support, of the reminder that you were never meant to carry everything alone.

Rejection's Story: "You're Fundamentally Unlovable"

And then there's Rejection, perhaps the most devastating storyteller of all. Rejection doesn't just tell you that someone didn't choose you. It tells you that no one ever will. That there's something fundamentally wrong with you that makes you unworthy of love, belonging, and acceptance.

Rejection's story goes like this: "They saw the real you and they left. They got close enough to know who you actually are and they decided you weren't worth staying for. And they're right. Because you're too much or not enough, too broken or too difficult, too needy or too distant. You're fundamentally unlovable, and every relationship is just a countdown to when they figure that out and leave like everyone else."

This is the story that makes you sabotage relationships before they can fail. The story that keeps you from being your authentic self because you're convinced that the real you is unacceptable. The story that interprets every conflict as confirmation that you're too much trouble, every moment of distance as proof that abandonment is coming.

Rejection's story is so convincing because it's built on real pain. Real abandonment. Real moments when people chose not to choose you. But Rejection takes those moments and builds them into an identity, a permanent state of being rather than a painful experience you survived.

Here's the truth that Rejection's story leaves out: the person who rejected you didn't have the authority to define your worth. Their choice to leave says more about them, their capacity, their readiness, their own wounds than it does about your value. You were rejected. That's a fact. But you are not rejection. You are not defined by who didn't choose you.

The Common Thread

Do you see the pattern yet? Each demon's story starts with something real—a genuine mistake, an actual disappointment, a legitimate hurt—and then builds an entire identity around it. Each one takes a moment in time and turns it into a permanent state of being. Each one whispers that this is just how things are, how you are, how life is, and there's nothing you can do about it.

These stories are so convincing because they're not entirely lies. You did make mistakes. Life isn't always fair. People did hurt you. But the demons take those truths and twist them into chains, narratives designed to keep you from the very freedom that's available to you.

The question is: are you going to keep believing their stories? Or are you ready to write a different one?

The Difference Between Victim And Survivor

There's a moment in every person's story where they stand at a crossroads. Behind them is everything that's happened—the trauma, the betrayal, the loss, the disappointment, all of it real and painful and undeniable. In front of them are two paths, and both paths start from the exact same place.

One path leads to victim. The other leads to survivor.

Let me be clear about something: both identities are earned through suffering. Both start with legitimate pain. Both begin with something that was done to you, something you didn't ask for and didn't deserve. The difference isn't in what happened. The difference is in what you do with what happened.

A victim is someone who stays in the story as it was written by their circumstances. A survivor is someone who takes that story and writes a different ending.

I want to make this absolutely clear: acknowledging that something terrible happened to you is not playing the victim. Calling out abuse for what it is, is not playing the victim. Grieving your losses is not playing the victim. Seeking justice is not playing the victim. Working through trauma is not playing the victim.

Playing the victim is when you let what happened to you become your permanent identity. When you use your past as a reason to stay stuck. When you make your pain your personality. When you refuse every lifeline thrown to you because staying in the victim role has become more familiar than the work of becoming a survivor.

I've seen it happen. I've watched people build entire lives around their wounds, careers around their trauma, identities around their pain. They introduce themselves by their scars. They lead every conversation back to what was done to them. They measure every new relationship by how much sympathy they can extract from it.

And I'm not saying this to judge them. I'm saying it because I understand the temptation. Because there's something oddly comfortable about staying in victim mode. You know the terrain. You know what to expect. And most importantly, you're not responsible for changing anything because you've already been hurt enough, right? The world owes you something, and until you get it, you're justified in staying exactly where you are.

Except that's not true. And deep down, you know it's not true.

The world doesn't owe you healing. The people who hurt you aren't going to show up and make it right. The circumstances that broke you aren't going to magically reassemble themselves into something better. And waiting for any of those things to happen before you start living again is just another way of staying chained.

A survivor understands something profound: what happened to you is not your fault, but healing from it is your responsibility.

Not because that's fair. Not because you deserve to carry that burden. But because no one else can do it for you. Your healing is not going to come from the person who hurt you finally apologizing. It's not going to come from getting back what was taken from you. It's not going to come from justice being served or the world acknowledging your pain.

Your healing comes from the decision to stop waiting for external validation and start doing the internal work.

This is the choice that separates victims from survivors. Victims wait for someone to rescue them. Survivors realize they have to rescue themselves. Victims rehearse their pain. Survivors process it. Victims use their past as an excuse. Survivors use it as fuel.

Both started from the same place. Only one stayed there.

I know this is hard to hear. I know it sounds like I'm placing an unfair burden on people who have already carried too much. But here's what I've learned from my own journey and from watching others navigate theirs: staying in victim mode doesn't actually protect you from more pain. It just guarantees that the pain you've already experienced continues to define you.

Survivor mode doesn't mean you forget what happened. It doesn't mean you pretend it didn't hurt. It doesn't mean you're suddenly okay with what was done to you. Survivor mode means you refuse to let the worst thing that ever happened to you become the only thing that defines you.

It means you look at your scars and say, "Yes, that happened to me. And here's what I did with it."

Let me tell you about someone I knew who made that shift. She'd been through hell—abuse that started in childhood and followed her into adult relationships. For years, she introduced herself through her trauma. "I'm a survivor of domestic violence." "I'm dealing with PTSD from childhood abuse." Every conversation, every relationship, every opportunity was filtered through that lens.

And I'm not saying she was wrong to name what happened to her. Naming it was necessary. Acknowledging it was essential. But at some point, she realized that her entire identity had become wrapped up in what had been done to her. She wasn't a person who had survived trauma. She was trauma in the flesh.

The shift happened when she started saying, "Yes, that happened to me, and I'm also a mother. And an artist. And someone who makes people laugh. And someone who's learning to trust again. And someone who's discovering what she's capable of when she's not just surviving but actually living."

Same past. Same pain. Same scars. Different story.

That's the difference between victim and survivor. A victim's story ends with the trauma. A survivor's story begins there.

And here's what nobody tells you: making that shift feels terrifying. Because victim mode, for all its limitations, comes with certain benefits. People feel sorry for you. They cut you slack. They don't expect too much from you. They treat you with kid gloves. And if you've been hurt badly enough, there's something appealing about living in a world where everyone knows you've been through hell and adjusts their expectations accordingly.

But survivor mode? That's different. Survivors don't get the same kind of sympathy. People expect things from survivors. They expect you to keep moving forward. They expect you to handle challenges. They expect you to show up even when it's hard. The world stops making allowances for your pain because it sees that you're no longer imprisoned by it.

And that can feel like loss. Like giving up the one thing that made people care about you or cut you some slack. Like stepping out of protective custody and back into a world that might hurt you again.

But here's the reality: survivor mode is freedom. It's the difference between being defined by what happened to you and being defined by how you responded to it. It's the difference between letting your story be written by your circumstances and taking the pen back.

You get to choose. Right now, in this moment, you get to choose.

So I ask you, are you going to stay in the story as it was written? Or are you going to write a different ending?

Because both paths start from the same place. Only one actually leads to freedom.

Reclaiming Your Story Through Truth-Telling

There's a particular kind of power that comes from telling the truth about your life. Not the sanitized version. Not the version that makes everyone comfortable. Not the version that minimizes your pain or exaggerates your strength. The real version. The one that says, "Yes, that happened to me, AND here's what I did with it."

That "AND" is everything.

Most people get stuck in one of two places when it comes to their story. They either stay in the "Yes, that happened to me" part—rehearsing their trauma, reliving their pain, making their past the entire narrative. Or they skip straight to some forced positivity that pretends the hard parts never happened, that tries to jump from wound to wisdom without acknowledging the work it took to get there.

But truth-telling requires both. It requires you to own what happened without being owned by it. To acknowledge the pain without being imprisoned by it. To honor the wound while also honoring the healing.

This is what it means to reclaim your story.

When you say, "Yes, that happened to me, AND here's what I did with it," you're doing something revolutionary. You're separating the event from your identity. You're distinguishing between what was done to you and who you are. You're taking the pen back from the demons who've been writing your narrative and declaring that from now on, you're the author.

Let me show you what this looks like in practice.

"Yes, I was abused as a child, AND I chose to break the cycle instead of continuing it."

"Yes, my marriage ended in betrayal, AND I learned that my worth isn't determined by who chose to stay or leave."

"Yes, I failed publicly and spectacularly, AND I discovered that failure isn't fatal."

"Yes, I grew up in poverty, AND I refused to let scarcity define my sense of possibility."

"Yes, I was rejected by people I loved, AND I learned that being chosen by the wrong people would have been worse than being rejected by them."

Do you see what's happening in each of those statements? The first part acknowledges the reality. It doesn't minimize it or pretend it didn't hurt. It says, "This is what happened, and it was real, and it mattered."

But then comes the "AND." Not "but," which would dismiss or negate the first part. "AND," which holds both truths simultaneously. Yes, something terrible happened. AND, you did something with it. Yes, you were wounded. AND, you chose to heal. Yes, you experienced loss. AND, you found something in the midst of it.

This is the difference between staying in your story and reclaiming it.

When you stay in your story, every time you tell it, you're reinforcing the narrative that the demons wrote. You're rehearsing your helplessness. You're reminding yourself and everyone else that you are fundamentally defined by what was done to you.

But when you reclaim your story, every time you tell it, you're reinforcing something different. You're declaring agency. You're demonstrating growth. You're showing that you're not just a person things happened to—you're a person who responded, who chose, who transformed.

Now here's where this gets tricky: reclaiming your story doesn't mean rushing to the positive. It doesn't mean slapping a happy ending on something that's still unresolved. It doesn't mean forcing yourself to be grateful for trauma or pretending that suffering was a gift.

Some of you aren't ready for the "AND" yet. And that's okay. Some of you are still in the "Yes, this happened to me" stage, and you need to stay there for a while. You need to name it. Grieve it. Feel it. Process it. And anyone who tries to rush you to the "AND" before you're ready is doing you a disservice.

But here's what I need you to understand: the goal is to get to the "AND." Not to stay indefinitely in the wound. The "Yes, this happened to me" is necessary, but it's not sufficient. At some point, if you're going to move from victim to survivor, from surviving to thriving, you have to ask yourself: "What am I going to do with this?"

Not "Why did this happen?" That question keeps you stuck because you're waiting for an answer that probably isn't coming. "Why" is a backward-looking question that searches for meaning in the event itself.

But "What am I going to do because this happened?" is a forward-looking question. It doesn't require you to understand why something happened in order to decide what you're going to do with it. It shifts you from passive to active. From victim to author.

This is the question that changes everything.

When my mother died and then Mama died just months later, I spent a long time in the "Yes, this happened" stage. I was numb. Broken. Unable to see anything beyond the loss. And if someone had told me in that season to find the silver lining or be grateful for the lesson, I would have had some choice words for them.

Slowly but surely, I started asking different questions. Not "Why did God let this happen?" but "What am I going to do now that it has?" Not "How do I make sense of this loss?" but "How do I honor what they gave me by the way I live going forward?"

Those questions didn't erase the pain. They didn't make the loss okay. But they gave me a way to move forward without pretending the loss didn't matter.

And that's when the "AND" became possible.

Yes, I lost two of the women who shaped me most. AND, their wisdom lives on in how I stand firm when life throws its punches. Yes, 2020 broke me in ways I'm still discovering. AND, I learned that I'm strong enough to survive being broken and still choose to keep living.

That's reclaiming your story through truth-telling. It's not about toxic positivity or spiritual bypassing. It's about refusing to let the demons who attacked you also get to write the ending.

Because here's what I figured out that Guilt wants: Guilt wants your story to end with condemnation. "I did something terrible, and therefore I am terrible, and nothing can change that." But truth-telling says, "Yes, I made a mistake, AND I learned from it and chose differently going forward."

Envy wants your story to be about what everyone else got that you didn't. "They have what should have been mine, and my life will always be less than theirs." But truth-telling says, "Yes, they got opportunities I didn't, AND I'm going to build something meaningful with what I do have."

Greed wants your story to be about perpetual insufficiency. "No matter what I achieve, it will never be enough." But truth-telling says, "Yes, I have ambitions and goals, AND I'm learning to recognize and celebrate enough."

Selfishness wants your story to be about necessary isolation. "People hurt me so I can never trust again." But truth-telling says, "Yes, I was betrayed, AND I'm choosing to risk vulnerability again because connection is worth the risk."

Rejection wants your story to be about fundamental unworthiness. "They left because something is wrong with me." But truth-telling says, "Yes, they left, AND their leaving doesn't define my worth."

Every time you tell your story with the "AND," you're rewriting the narrative the demons tried to impose on you. You're taking back the authority they stole. You're declaring that what happened to you is part of your story, but it's not the whole story.

And the more you practice truth-telling, the more natural it becomes. The "AND" gets stronger. The demons' version gets quieter. Your voice gets clearer.

Until one day you realize: you're no longer telling the story the demons wrote. You're telling the story you're writing.

And that's when everything changes.

Writing New Chapters While Honoring Old Ones

Here's something I wish someone had told me earlier: rewriting your narrative doesn't mean erasing your history.

There's this temptation, once you start doing the work of breaking free from demon narratives and reclaiming your story, to want to wipe the slate clean. To pretend the hard chapters never happened. To skip over the painful parts and start fresh as if you're a completely different person with no connection to who you were before.

But that's not how healing works. That's not how wholeness works. And honestly, that's not even how good stories work.

The most powerful stories aren't the ones where the hero emerges unscathed. They're the ones where the hero carries their scars into their victory. Where the wounds become wisdom. Where the past informs the future without imprisoning it.

You can't erase the past, but you can change its meaning.

Think about it this way: every chapter you've already lived is part of the larger story. Some of those chapters were beautiful. Some were brutal. Some were mundane. Some were transformative. But they all brought you here, to this moment, to this choice about what comes next.

When you rewrite the narrative, you're not deleting those chapters. You're changing how they connect to what comes after. You're deciding what they mean in the context of the whole story rather than letting them define the entire plot.

Let me show you what this looks like.

If your early chapters included abuse, you don't have to pretend that didn't happen in order to write new chapters about healing. The abuse is part of your story. It shaped you, scarred you, taught you things you wish you'd never had to learn. But it doesn't get to write the rest of the book. You can honor the reality of those chapters while also writing new ones where you're no longer defined by what was done to you.

If your middle chapters included failure, betrayal, or loss, you don't have to minimize those experiences to move forward. They happened. They hurt. They matter. But they're chapters, not the conclusion. You can acknowledge the weight of what you went through while also recognizing that the story isn't over yet.

This is what integration looks like. Not erasure. Integration.

Erasure says, "That never happened," or "That doesn't matter," or "I'm completely over it." Erasure is dishonest, and deep down, you know it. You can't convince yourself that something that fundamentally shaped you is irrelevant. And pretending otherwise just means you're still giving it power by working so hard to deny it.

Integration says, "Yes, that happened. It was real. It shaped me. And now I'm taking what I learned from it and using it to write what comes next."

Integration means you can talk about the hard chapters without living in them. You can acknowledge your scars without making them your identity. You can honor what you survived without being defined by survival mode.

I think about my grandmothers often when I'm writing new chapters in my own life. Mama and Lil'Momma gave me so much, uploaded so much wisdom into my spirit, prepared me for battles they knew were coming even if I didn't. Their influence is woven into every choice I make, every challenge I face, every moment I choose to stand firm instead of falling apart.

But here's the thing: honoring them doesn't mean living exactly the life they lived. It doesn't mean accepting the same limitations they had to accept. It doesn't mean staying in survival mode because that's all they knew how to teach me.

Honoring them means taking what they gave me and building something new with it. Taking their "come what may" and applying it to situations they never faced. Taking Lil'Momma's grace and extending it in ways she might never have had the opportunity to. Taking their strength and using it to break cycles they couldn't break, to reach heights they couldn't reach, to dream dreams they weren't allowed to dream.

That's not betrayal. That's completion. That's taking their story and extending it into mine. That's writing new chapters that honor old ones by building on the foundation they laid rather than staying trapped in the structure they were forced to inhabit.

The same is true for you and your story.

Whatever happened in your early chapters, whatever shaped you, wounded you, formed you—it doesn't have to determine what you write next. But it will inform it. And that's actually a good thing, as long as you're choosing what lessons you take forward.

Maybe your early chapters taught you that love is conditional and people leave. That's what you learned. That's the narrative that got written. But in your new chapters, you get to decide: am I going to let that lesson keep me isolated? Or am I going to use that painful education to recognize genuine love when I see it, to appreciate loyalty when I find it, to value people who stay?

Maybe your middle chapters taught you that failure is fatal and mistakes are unforgivable. That's the story Guilt told you. That's the narrative that kept you stuck. But in your new chapters, you get to decide: am I going to let that fear keep me from trying anything risky? Or am I going to use those failures as proof that I can survive falling and still get back up?

Maybe your recent chapters taught you that you're always one step behind everyone else, that you're watching from the sidelines while everyone else lives the life you wanted. That's Envy's story. But in your new chapters, you get to decide: am I going to spend the rest of my life comparing? Or am I going to use that painful awareness of what I don't have to clarify what I actually want and go after it?

This is how you honor old chapters while writing new ones. You don't pretend the old chapters didn't happen. You don't minimize what they cost you. But you also don't let them dictate the plot going forward.

You take the lessons. You leave the chains.

And here's something else: writing new chapters doesn't mean you'll never reference the old ones. It doesn't mean you can never talk about what happened, never grieve what was lost, never feel the weight of what you carried. It just means that when you reference those chapters, you're doing it from a different place.

You're not stuck in them. You're standing in your present, looking back with perspective, recognizing how far you've come. You're not rehearsing trauma. You're bearing witness to transformation.

There's a difference between saying, "This terrible thing happened and I'll never recover" and saying, "This terrible thing happened and here's how I survived it and what I learned from it and how I'm different now because of it."

One keeps you trapped in the old chapter. The other shows you've moved on to new ones while carrying the wisdom forward.

Your history becomes your testimony. Your pain becomes your platform. Your scars become your credentials for helping others who are still fighting battles you've already won.

That's what it means to write new chapters while honoring old ones. You're not erasing your story. You're continuing it. You're not pretending you're someone else. You're becoming more fully yourself by integrating everything you've been through into who you're becoming.

And the beautiful thing about this? Once you realize you're the author now, once you take the pen back from the demons who were writing your story, you start to see that every chapter going forward is yours to write.

You don't have to ask permission. You don't have to wait for perfect conditions. You don't have to know exactly how it's going to turn out before you start writing.

You just have to decide: what do I want this next chapter to say about who I'm becoming?

Because the story isn't over. Not even close. You've survived chapters that should have destroyed you. You've endured plot twists that would have ended lesser stories. You've been the protagonist in a narrative that demons tried to control, and you're still here. Still standing. Still writing.

So what comes next is up to you. The old chapters happened. They shaped you. They matter. But they don't get to write what comes next.

You do.

CHAPTER TEN
FROM VICTIM TO AUTHOR

There's a manuscript sitting in a drawer somewhere in my house. Well, not a physical drawer anymore—it's digital now —but you know what I mean. It's a half-finished book that I couldn't touch for months after my mother died. She was the only person who had read those pages. The only one who knew what I was trying to say, what I was working toward, what those words meant to me.

And when she died, I couldn't look at it. Couldn't open the file. Couldn't even think about writing without feeling like the ground was collapsing underneath me.

Because here's what nobody tells you about losing someone who believed in your story: it feels like losing permission to keep telling it. Like their death erased not just their presence but also their validation. Like the story you were writing was only worth writing because they were there to read it.

I sat with that manuscript closed for what felt like forever. Numb. Shut down. Convinced that whatever I had to say died with her.

But here's what I didn't understand then, what I'm still learning now: that paralysis? That inability to pick up the pen? That wasn't grief alone. That was the demons whispering that my story ended when hers did. That I was a character in someone else's narrative rather than the author of my own. That my voice only mattered if she was there to hear it.

And as long as I believed that lie, I stayed stuck. A victim of loss rather than a survivor building something new from the rubble.

The Role Of Testimony

Let me tell you what changed.

It wasn't a lightning bolt moment. It wasn't some profound revelation that made everything make sense. It was a slow, painful realization that my survival—from COVID, from loss, from all of it—wasn't just for me. That the story I was living, the one I almost didn't get to finish, had a purpose beyond my own understanding.

I survived COVID when I wasn't supposed to. The doctors told my family to prepare for the worst. I remember lying in that hospital bed, unable to move my arms, unable to speak, feeling like death was in the room with me, waiting. The room smelled of pain, despair, and antiseptic—a scent I'll never forget. It felt like a basement with no windows, no sense of time, just darkness and the constant beeping of monitors. Bodies around me were being removed. One day someone would be next to me, and the next, they were gone. I could hear people coding across from me, nurses cautioning families about ventilators. Death wasn't an abstract concept—it was in the room, patient, methodical, working its way through the unit bed by bed. And I was convinced I was next.

The nurse said I might need a ventilator, and I knew what that meant. I knew the odds going into it. What I didn't know in that moment was that my mother got put on one.

But somehow, I'm still here.

And for the longest time, I couldn't reconcile that. Why did I survive when my mother didn't? Why did I get to keep breathing when so many others—eleven people known personally to me in 2020 alone—didn't? What was I supposed to do with this undeserved continuation of my story?

Then it hit me: testimony.

My survival wasn't random. My mother's death wasn't meaningless. The fact that I'm still here, still writing, still speaking, still showing up—that's not just luck or chance or medical intervention. That's favor with a purpose. As hard as it is for me to accept, that's a test that became a testimony.

And if I keep my story to myself, if I let the demons convince me that my voice doesn't matter or that my pain is too personal to share or that nobody needs to hear what I've been through, then I'm wasting the very thing I was kept alive to give.

Your story is not just for you. Your survival is not just about you. Your healing is not just about you.

When you share your testimony—not to perform, not to impress, not to gain sympathy, but to genuinely say "I went through this and here's what I learned and here's how I'm different now"—you do something powerful. You give permission to people who are still in their crisis. You show them that survival is possible. You demonstrate to the world that the demons don't get the last word.

But there is something else I had to learn: testimony isn't just about helping others. It's also about reinforcing your own freedom.

Reinforcing Your Own Freedom Through Testimony

I didn't realize it at first but there's something that happens when you say your truth out loud. When you stop hiding what you've been through. When you name what tried to destroy you and declare that it didn't succeed.

You break the power of silence.

For years, I lived in strategic silence about parts of my identity. I was gay, and I knew it, but I also knew that being open about it could close doors. Could limit opportunities. Could cost me positions, relationships, credibility. So I navigated carefully. Revealed selectively. Managed perceptions. Calculated risk.

And I was simply exhausted from the performance.

At the time, there was something I just didn't understand: every time you hide your truth to protect your future, you reinforce the lie that your authentic self is your biggest obstacle. Every time you code-switch or perform or present a palatable version of yourself, you teach yourself that who you really are isn't enough. Every time you choose silence over honesty, you give the demons more authority over your narrative.

But when you speak your truth—when you say "I'm gay" or "I almost died" or "I lost my mother and I'm still figuring out how to live without her" or whatever your truth is—you take back authority. You declare that the demons don't get to write your story anymore. You reinforce your own freedom by refusing to live in captivity to fear.

And the beautiful thing? Every time you tell your story with honesty, it gets a little easier. The demons' version gets a little quieter. Your voice gets a little clearer.

I remember the first time I was fully open about being gay in a professional setting. My heart was pounding. I was calculating all the ways this could go wrong. All the opportunities I might lose. All the people who might reject me.

But you know what happened? I exhaled. For the first time in years, I felt like I could breathe deeply. Like I wasn't performing anymore. Like I could finally show up as myself instead of as a carefully curated version designed to minimize risk.

And that peace—that freedom—was worth more than any door that might close because of it.

Where the Spirit of the Lord is, there is liberty. Remember that from Chapter 2? If your identity feels like captivity, that's not God. If your dream requires you to hide your truth, that's not your destiny. If the future you're chasing demands that you live in fear of being fully seen, then you're not chasing freedom—you're chasing another chain.

Your testimony—spoken out loud, lived authentically—reinforces the truth that you are free. And every time you tell it, you're not just helping someone else. You're reminding yourself that the demons don't own you anymore.

From Passive Character To Active Author

Here's where everything shifts.

For most of my life, I felt like a character in someone else's story. Like I was reacting to circumstances rather than creating them. Like my job was to survive the plot rather than write it.

COVID happened to me. Loss happened to me. Rejection happened to me. Discrimination happened to me. Trauma happened to me.

And all of that is true. Those things did happen to me. I didn't choose them. I didn't ask for them. I didn't deserve them.

But at some point, I had to decide: am I going to let what happened to me define what happens next? Am I going to let the demons who attacked me also get to write my ending? Am I going to spend the rest of my life being a victim of my circumstances, or am I going to become the author of my future?

That's the shift from victim to author. And it's not about denying what happened. It's not about pretending the pain wasn't real or that the loss doesn't matter. It's about recognizing that you have authority over what comes next.

I remember the exact moment I decided to become the author again.

It was a dream. My mother appeared to me, and in the dream, we were having a conversation we'd actually had years earlier, back around Christmas 2014. I had finished my dissertation the previous December—December 2013—and almost a year later, I was still exhausted. Completely drained. I'd promised myself that I didn't want to read anything—not even a stop sign—because I had consumed so many books during my doctoral program. And I definitely didn't want to write anything else. I just wanted to exist. Nothing more. No pressure. No expectations. No performance.

She looked at me in that dream the same way she'd looked at me all those years ago and said, "You have too much talent to let it go to waste."

Then she said something that broke me: "I wish I had the opportunity and potential you had when I was your age."

And I woke up.

In that moment, I realized she was seeing something in me that I didn't want to see in myself. I didn't want to be anything special. I didn't want to have potential or talent or opportunity. I just wanted to exist without the weight of expectation, without the pressure of purpose, without the responsibility of my own gifts.

But she saw it. And even in death, even in a dream, she was still uploading wisdom into my spirit. Still reminding me that my voice mattered. Still refusing to let me waste what I'd been given.

That's when I opened the file. That's when I started writing again. Not because the grief was gone—it wasn't. Not because I suddenly had all the answers—I didn't. But because I realized that staying silent, staying stuck, staying in victim mode was wasting the very thing she'd seen in me all along.

You're not just surviving the plot anymore. You're writing it.

When I finally opened that manuscript again—the one I couldn't touch after my mother died—I realized something. She wasn't the reason the story mattered. She was one of the first people to see its value, yes. But the story mattered because it was true. Because it was mine. Because it had something to say that people needed to hear.

And when I completed "The What If Factor" in 2021, nearly a year after her death, it wasn't just about honoring her memory. It was about reclaiming my voice. About declaring that my story didn't end when hers did. About taking the pen back from grief and loss and fear and writing something new.

That's what it means to move from passive character to active author. You stop waiting for life to happen to you and start deciding what you're going to do with what's already happened. You stop asking "Why did this happen?" and start asking "What am I going to do because this happened?"

You take authority over the narrative going forward.

I want to be absolutely clear: this doesn't mean you have control over everything. You don't get to decide whether you get sick. You don't get to decide whether people accept you. You don't get to decide whether loss comes knocking. Those things are going to happen whether you author them or not.

But you do get to decide what those things mean. You get to decide how you respond. You get to decide whether they become your ending or just a difficult chapter in a much longer story.

You're no longer just surviving the plot—you're writing it.

And when I learned this, here's what I discovered: once you realize you're the author, everything changes. You start making different choices. You start showing up differently.

You start seeing yourself not as a victim of circumstances but as someone with agency, purpose, power.

Before, I was constantly battling for acceptance. For validation. Every room I walked into, I was performing—calculating what version of myself would be most palatable, most acceptable, most likely to keep me safe. I was exhausting myself trying to prove I was worthy of being there, worthy of the opportunity, worthy of taking up space.

After? I walk into rooms knowing I belong there. Not because I'm perfect or because I've figured everything out, but because I'm done performing. I'm done trying to earn approval from people who were never going to give it anyway. I'm done shrinking myself to fit into spaces that were too small for who I actually am.

Before, my identity felt like a liability I had to manage. After? It's just who I am. Before, I was reacting to everyone else's story about me. After? I'm writing my own.

You start living like your story matters. Because it does.

The Story God Tells About You

But here's where it gets really interesting—and this is something I'm still wrestling with, still learning, still trying to reconcile.

There's the story I tell about myself. And then there's the story God tells about me. And sometimes they don't match up.

I look at my life and I see survival by the skin of my teeth. I see loss and grief and struggle. I see doors that closed and opportunities that didn't work out and pain that I'm still carrying. I see all the ways I almost didn't make it, all the times I wanted to give up, all the moments when I felt completely alone.

That's my version.

But God's version? His version is different. His version sees favor where I see near-misses. His version sees purpose where I see randomness. His version sees a calling where I see chaos.

His version says I survived COVID not in spite of the odds but because of a specific assignment. That my mother's death, as devastating as it was, doesn't get to write my ending. That my identity as a gay man is not a disqualification from my destiny but part of how He wired me for purpose. That every closed door and every rejection and every moment of pain was preparing me for something I couldn't see yet.

His version is bigger than mine. It just took me some time to realize it.

Let me give you an example.

For years, I missed out on what looked like lucrative job opportunities. And my story about that was simple: people could see what I felt about myself. That I wasn't good enough. That I wasn't worthy. Even though I looked like a diamond on paper—the degrees, the experience, the credentials—there was something in some deep, dark corner of my presentation that screamed "not enough." And I believed that's why doors kept closing.

But then something shifted. My territory began to enlarge. I started getting tapped to fix programs and policies that were broken. My ability to tell a story through data became the cornerstone of operations I was brought into. People started seeking me out not despite who I was, but because of the unique perspective and skill set I brought.

And I realized: God's story was never about me being "not enough." His story was about preparation. About waiting until I was ready. About positioning me in places where my gifts wouldn't just be tolerated but actually needed.

As bad as I wanted those opportunities I had to realize that when He said in Psalm 121:3, "He will not suffer thy foot to be moved," He meant it. He wasn't letting me stumble into opportunities where I'd have to shrink myself or perform or code-switch to survive. He was making sure that when the doors opened, they were doors I could walk through as myself.

I stopped looking at what I thought was the measure of my worth—external validation, titles, salaries, other people's approval. And I started accepting that through the power of God Almighty, I was able to do great things. Not because I finally became worthy, but because I'd always been worthy and was finally starting to believe it.

The greatest thing I learned through it all: sometimes the story God is telling about you is so much larger than what you can see in your present moment that you have to trust His narrative even when yours feels small.

When I was in that hospital bed, unable to breathe, watching my oxygen levels drop, my story was "I'm dying." But God's story was "Not yet. There's more for you to do."

When I lost my mother and couldn't write for months, my story was "This is too much. I can't do this." But God's story was "Grieve. Rest. And then pick up the pen again because your voice matters."

When I was afraid to be open about being gay because of what it might cost me, my story was "Hide to survive." But God's story was "Where my Spirit is, there is liberty. You don't have to perform. You don't have to hide. I made you exactly as you are, and there's purpose in that."

Reconciling these two narratives—mine and His—is still an ongoing process. Some days His version makes sense to me. Some days I can see how everything connects, how the pain had purpose, how the struggle produced strength.

Other days, I'm still asking questions. Still wrestling. Still trying to make sense of why some things happened the way they did.

And I think that's okay. I think faith doesn't require me to have it all figured out. It just requires me to trust that His version is true even when mine feels incomplete.

Sometimes His story about you aligns perfectly with what you see. And sometimes His story is so much bigger than you imagined that you just have to trust Him with the ending.

Because here's the truth: you're the author of your response, your choices, your attitude, your next steps. But you're not the Author of the whole story. There's a larger narrative at play. A divine plot that's been unfolding since before you were born. A purpose that's bigger than your individual circumstances.

And your job isn't to write God's part of the story. Your job is to write yours—with honesty, with courage, with authenticity—and trust that He's weaving it into something beautiful even when you can't see the full picture yet.

The Cost Of Authorship

Now, let me be honest about something that nobody warned me about: becoming the author of your story will cost you something.

Some people won't understand. Some will say you've changed. And they're right—you have. But they'll say it like it's a bad thing, like you were better when you were smaller, quieter, more manageable. They liked you better when you were a character they could predict, not an author writing plot twists they didn't see coming.

I am sorry to tell you this but some relationships won't survive your authenticity. I learned this the hard way. You'll try to hang onto people you should have long let go of because they simply don't fit the story you're trying to write anymore. They were cast members in the victim narrative, and they don't know what to do with you now that you're writing something different.

Some opportunities will disappear when you stop performing. Some doors will close specifically because you're being authentic. Some spaces won't have room for the real you because they only had space for the version you were pretending to be.

And you know what? That's okay.

Because what you gain—true peace, genuine connection, actual purpose, the freedom to breathe deeply for the first time in years—is worth infinitely more than what you lose.

I learned something valuable: if it's worth having, it will cost you something. But the value you gain in obtaining whatever that is—your voice, your freedom, your authentic self—is far more than what you lost.

The people who leave when you stop performing weren't meant for the real story anyway. They were attached to the character you were playing, not the author you're becoming. The doors that close when you show up as yourself weren't your doors to begin with. The opportunities you lose when you stop hiding your truth weren't opportunities—they were prisons with better titles.

So yes, there's a cost. But staying a victim costs more. Staying silent costs more. Staying in captivity while calling it safety costs more.

And once you experience the freedom of being the author, once you taste the peace of showing up as yourself, once you realize that your story matters and your voice has power—you'll never want to go back to being a character in someone else's narrative.

The cost is real. But it's worth it.

What Story Are You Telling?

So I am curious about something: what story are you telling?

Are you still letting the demons write your narrative? Still letting past trauma define your identity? Still letting fear dictate your future? Still performing a version of yourself that you think will keep you safe? Still battling for acceptance and validation from people who were never going to give it?

Or are you ready to take the pen back?

Because here's what I know: your test is meant to become your testimony. Your survival has a purpose. Your voice matters. Your story—messy and painful and imperfect as it is—can be the very thing that helps someone else break free.

You're not just a character in someone else's story. You're the author of what comes next.

So write it. Write it honestly. Write it courageously. Write it authentically.

Here's your first step: Write it down. Literally. Take out a piece of paper or open a document and write this sentence: "I am the author of what comes next."

Then write one thing—just one—that you're ready to do differently because you're done being a victim and ready to be an author. Maybe it's speaking a truth you've been hiding. Maybe it's setting a boundary you've been afraid to set. Maybe it's letting go of a relationship that's keeping you stuck. Maybe it's pursuing something you've been too scared to try.

Write it. Say it out loud. Then do it.

That's how you take the pen back. One word at a time. One choice at a time. One honest, courageous, authentic act at a time.

And trust that the God who kept you alive through your darkest chapter has a purpose for every word that comes after. Trust that the story He's telling about you is bigger than you can imagine. Trust that you were made for this—not to be a passive character surviving someone else's plot, but an active author writing something beautiful from the rubble.

Your story isn't over. It's just getting started.

CHAPTER ELEVEN
CREATING LASTING CHANGE

So, you've done the work. You've named the demons. You've broken the chains. You've rewritten the narrative. You've moved from victim to author. You've even shared your testimony and stepped into your power.

And now you're wondering: how do I make this last?

There is something that people forget to tell you about transformation: the breakthrough is just the beginning. The moment you break free, the moment the chains snap, the moment you declare your liberation—that's exhilarating. That's powerful. It even starts to feel like the finish line.

But it's not the finish line. It's really the starting line.

The real work begins when the adrenaline wears off. When the moment of clarity fades and Monday morning arrives with all its ordinary demands. When nobody's applauding your breakthrough anymore because they expect you to just be this new person now. When the demons you defeated start whispering again, quieter this time, testing to see if the door's still locked.

That's when you discover the gap between liberation and transformation. Between knowing you're free and actually living free. Between declaring you're different and truly becoming different.

And that gap? That's where most people lose what they fought so hard to obtain.

Why Change Doesn't Stick

I want to tell you about the fitness center phenomenon.

Every January, gyms explode with new members. People show up motivated, determined, armed with resolutions and intentions and brand-new workout clothes. They're going to transform their bodies. Change their lives. Finally become the person they know they're supposed to be.

And for a week, maybe two, they show up. They push through the discomfort. They feel the burn and tell themselves it's working.

Then February arrives. And the gym is empty again. I know that all to well because I was in that number, except unlike most, I at least made it to March.

I don't believe it's because those people didn't want to change. It's not even because they were lying to themselves or didn't try hard enough. It's because they confused motivation with transformation. They mistook the emotional high of a new beginning for the actual work of rewiring their entire system.

I had to learn something very important: motivation gets you started, but it won't keep you going. Motivation is an emotion, and emotions are temporary. They rise and fall based on circumstances, moods, how much sleep you got, whether someone encouraged you or discouraged you, whether you feel like it or not.

If your transformation depends on feeling motivated, you're going to end up right back where you started the moment life gets hard and motivation evaporates.

The demons know this and they are counting on it happening. Guilt knows that if it just waits long enough, your determination will fade. Envy knows that if it stays quiet for a few weeks, you'll forget why you were fighting so hard to stop comparing yourself to others. Greed knows that once the thrill of "enough" wears off, the appetite for "more" will resurface. Selfishness knows that isolation feels safer when you're tired of the vulnerability that connection requires.

Rejection knows that the fear of being hurt again will eventually outweigh the risk of being authentic.

They're patient. They have been at this longer than you have been alive. They know how to wait you out. They know that if they can just outlast your motivation, they can reclaim the territory you took back.

Just like I was on this journey you are probably saying to yourself, so if motivation isn't the answer, what is?

The Architecture Of Sustainable Transformation

Let me tell you something I learned the hard way: you don't need more motivation. You need better systems.

Transformation that lasts isn't built on dramatic gestures and intense emotions. It's built on small, consistent actions that become so automatic you don't have to think about them anymore. It's built on infrastructure that supports who you're becoming even when you don't feel like being that person.

Think about it like this: when you break a chain, you don't just walk away and hope it stays broken. You have to build something new in the space where the chain used to be. You have to create patterns that reinforce your freedom instead of patterns that invite bondage back in.

I used to think discipline was about forcing myself to do hard things through sheer willpower. And don't get me wrong, sometimes it is. But sustainable discipline is actually about removing the need for willpower by making the right choices automatic.

Let me give you an example. When I was working to break free from the demon of Rejection, one of my patterns was people-pleasing. I would say yes to things I didn't want to do, commit to things that drained me, perform in ways that exhausted me, all because I was terrified of disappointing people and giving them a reason to reject me.

Breaking free meant learning to say no. In doing so, here is what I discovered: if I relied on willpower alone, if I had to fight that battle every single time someone asked something of me, I would lose every time. Because eventually I'd be too tired to fight. Eventually I'd give in just to stop feeling the internal conflict.

So instead of relying on willpower, I built a system. I created boundaries before the requests came. I established clear criteria for what I would and wouldn't commit to. I practiced specific phrases I could use to decline gracefully. I identified trusted people who could help me reality-check whether something was actually mine to do or just my people-pleasing trying to take over.

Then when the requests came—and trust me, they always do—I didn't have to reinvent the wheel every time. I didn't have to rely on motivation or muster up courage in the moment. I had a system. A structure. A pre-made decision that my old pattern couldn't argue with because it wasn't negotiable anymore.

That's what sustainable transformation looks like. Not heroic moments of willpower, but ordinary moments of following the system you built to protect your freedom. And you cannot be worried about what people think about protecting your freedom.

Small, Consistent Actions Over Dramatic Gestures

In this journey, there was something else I had to learn: transformation happens in the unsexy middle, not in the dramatic beginning.

We love dramatic beginnings. The moment you stand up and declare you're done being a victim. The day you finally cut off the toxic relationship. The night you decide you're going to stop living in fear. Those moments matter. They're necessary. They're the line in the sand that says "no more."

But transformation doesn't happen in that moment. Transformation happens in the ten thousand moments after that moment, when nobody's watching and nobody's cheering and you have to make the same choice again even though it's not exciting anymore.

It happens when you choose forgiveness for the hundredth time even though you're exhausted from forgiving. When you set the same boundary for the thirteenth time with the same person who still doesn't respect it. When you show up to therapy even when you don't feel like processing anything else. When you call your accountability partner even though you just want to handle it alone like you always have.

Those small, unglamorous, repetitive choices—that's where transformation becomes permanent.

I think about my grandmothers again here. Mama and Lil'Momma didn't become the women they were through one dramatic moment of spiritual awakening. They became who they were through decades of small, faithful choices. Getting up every morning and choosing to trust God even when circumstances screamed that He'd abandoned them. Showing grace to people who didn't deserve it, again and again and again, until grace became who they were instead of just something they did.

That's the architecture of lasting change. Not one big decision, but thousands of small ones. Not dramatic transformation, but incremental transformation that compounds over time until one day you look back and realize you're not the same person you used to be.

The demons really hate this kind of change because they can't fight it the way they fight dramatic gestures. They can't convince you to give up when there's no single moment to give up on. They can't undermine your motivation when you're not relying on motivation. They can't break your will when you're not using willpower.

All they can do is watch while you slowly, consistently, faithfully build a life they can't control anymore.

The Relapse Reality

Now let me tell you something you need to hear, something that most self-help books won't tell you because it doesn't sound inspirational: you're going to slip. You're going to have moments when the old patterns resurface. You're going to find yourself responding the way you used to respond, thinking the way you used to think, falling back into behaviors you swore you'd left behind.

And when that happens, the demons are going to tell you that you failed. That the transformation wasn't real. That you're still the same person you've always been and you might as well stop pretending otherwise.

But here's what I need you to understand: setbacks aren't failures. They're information.

When you slip back into an old pattern, you're not erasing all the progress you made. You're identifying which areas still need more work. You're discovering which triggers still have power. You're learning which support structures need to be strengthened.

I remember a moment, months after I thought I'd dealt with the demon of Rejection, when someone I respected deeply criticized something I'd created. And immediately, without even thinking about it, I felt that familiar spiral start. That voice telling me I was never good enough, that I should've known better than to put myself out there, that rejection was inevitable and I'd just been fooling myself thinking I could be free from it.

For about thirty minutes, I believed those lies. I sat with that shame. I felt that old pattern trying to reassert itself.

But then something different happened. I recognized it. I named it. I said out loud, "This is Rejection trying to reclaim territory, and it's not for sale."

And the power of that moment wasn't that I didn't slip. The power was that I caught myself slipping and made a different choice. I called someone I trusted. I processed it out loud instead of hiding in shame. I separated the legitimate feedback from the demon's narrative about my worth.

That's what transformation looks like in real time. Not perfection. Not never struggling. But struggling with awareness and tools and support instead of struggling alone in the dark.

Neuroscience backs this up. Your brain has pathways—literal neural pathways—that were built over years of thinking certain ways, responding certain ways, believing certain things about yourself. Those pathways don't disappear just because you decided you're done with them.

But here's the beautiful part: your brain is plastic. Neuroplasticity means you can build new pathways. You can rewire your responses. You can literally change the way your brain works through repetition and consistency.

Rewiring Your Default Settings

There's this concept I learned called the 10,000-rep rule, or as K. Anders Ericsson called it, the 10,000-hour rule. It takes roughly ten thousand repetitions of a new behavior before it becomes automatic. Before it becomes your default instead of something you have to consciously choose.

Ten thousand times.

Let that sink in. Not ten times. Not a hundred times. Ten thousand times of choosing differently before your brain stops fighting you and just does the new thing without you having to force it.

That's why transformation is a long game. That's why you can't give up after the first hundred reps when it still feels hard. That's why the demons are so confident they'll win you back—because they know most people quit long before they hit ten thousand.

But here's what I want you to know: every single rep counts. Every time you choose forgiveness instead of holding a grudge, that's one rep. Every time you set a boundary instead of people-pleasing, that's one rep. Every time you practice gratitude instead of giving in to Envy, that's one rep. Every time you choose enough instead of chasing more, that's one rep. Every time you reach out for connection instead of isolating, that's one rep.

They add up. Slowly, gradually, almost imperceptibly, they add up. Until one day you realize you didn't even think about it. You just responded the new way automatically. The demon showed up and your brain didn't even register it as a threat anymore because the new pathway was so well-established that the old one couldn't compete.

That's when you know the transformation is sticking. Not when it feels easy in the moment of decision, but when it stops feeling like a decision at all. When who you're becoming is just who you are.

The People Factor

There is another key that determines whether change sticks: who you're doing it with.

You cannot transform in isolation. I don't care how strong you are, how disciplined, how committed—if you're trying to do this alone, you're going to fail. Not because you're weak, but because transformation was never meant to be a solo project.

The people around you will either reinforce your transformation or undermine it. There's no neutral ground.

They're either helping you become who you're meant to be, or they're pulling you back toward who you used to be.

And sometimes, the people pulling you back aren't doing it maliciously. They're not trying to hurt you. They're just comfortable with the old version of you. They know how to relate to that person. They have roles that make sense when you're operating in your old patterns. And your transformation makes them uncomfortable because it disrupts their comfort.

Remember what I said in Chapter 8 about how chains fight back through the people who benefited from your bondage? That applies here too. The people who got something out of your people-pleasing will resist your boundaries. The people who felt better about themselves when you were struggling will feel threatened by your success. The people who bonded with you over shared dysfunction will feel abandoned when you start healing.

And you have to be willing to let them go. Or at least, you have to be willing to renegotiate those relationships with very clear boundaries about what you will and won't tolerate.

But you also need to be intentional about surrounding yourself with people who are going where you're going. People who celebrate your growth instead of resenting it. People who call you forward instead of calling you back. People who remind you of who you're becoming on the days you forget.

I call these people my "freedom reinforcers." They're the ones who don't let me get away with old patterns. The ones who lovingly call me out when I'm slipping. The ones who believe in my transformation even when I'm doubting it. The ones who have their own chains breaking so they understand the battle I'm fighting.

Find your freedom reinforcers. Invest in those relationships. Show up for them the way they show up for you. Because lasting change doesn't happen in a vacuum—it happens in community.

Maintaining Vigilance Without Living In Fear

Now here's the tension you have to manage: you need to stay alert to the demons' tactics, but you can't live in constant fear that they're going to destroy everything you've built.

Vigilance is not the same as paranoia. Vigilance means you're aware of your triggers. You know which situations are most likely to resurrect old patterns. You recognize the early warning signs when a demon is trying to slip back in. You have people who can help you spot blind spots.

But paranoia means you never rest. You never trust your own transformation. You're so afraid of slipping that you live in constant hypervigilance, which is just another form of bondage.

I had to learn this balance. For a long time after I started breaking free, I was exhausting myself trying to anticipate every possible way the demons might return. I was overanalyzing every thought, every feeling, every interaction, terrified that if I let my guard down for even a moment, everything would fall apart.

But that's not freedom. That's captivity with a different face.

Real freedom means you're aware without being controlled by the awareness. You're alert without being anxious. You know the demons are still out there, still looking for opportunities, but you trust that the work you've done has built something strong enough to withstand their attacks.

You trust your systems. You trust your community. You trust that even if you slip, you have what you need to recover. You trust the process of transformation instead of trying to control every single variable.

That's the vigilance that sustains freedom without stealing your peace.

The Long Game: What Success Really Looks Like

So now, let me tell you what success doesn't look like: it doesn't look like arrival. It doesn't look like a moment where you finally get to declare "I made it" and stop growing.

Because there is an unsettling truth that nobody wants to hear: transformation doesn't have a finish line. You don't reach a point where you're done, where you've conquered all the demons, where you never have to be intentional about your choices again.

I know that's not the inspirational message you wanted. You wanted me to tell you that if you just do these steps, follow this formula, put in the work, eventually you'll arrive at a place where it's easy. Where you're free and you never have to fight again.

But that would be a lie. And I truthfully care too much about you to lie.

The unadulterated truth is this: transformation is a marathon with no finish line. It's a lifelong process of becoming. The demons may lose power, but they don't lose presence. The old patterns may get weaker, but they don't get erased. The healing may go deep, but there will always be layers you haven't discovered yet.

And that's not discouraging. That's actually liberating. Because it means you can stop putting pressure on yourself to be perfect. You can stop waiting to arrive before you start living. You can embrace the process, the journey, the ongoing work of becoming, instead of constantly measuring yourself against some imaginary standard of "healed" or "free" or "transformed."

Hear me when I say this: success isn't about reaching a destination. Success is about who you're becoming along the way.

It's about looking back and realizing that the person you were a year ago would be amazed at the person you are today. It's about recognizing that the situations that used to destroy you now just challenge you. It's about watching yourself choose differently, respond differently, think differently, and knowing that the work is paying off even if it's not finished.

Success is waking up one morning and realizing you haven't thought about that demon in weeks because you've been too busy living your life to let it rent space in your head. It's the moment someone tries to trigger you and you don't react the way you used to. It's the day you realize you're actually enjoying your life instead of just surviving it.

That's what success looks like. Not perfection. Progress. Not arrival. Direction. Not never struggling. But struggling with more tools, more support, more awareness than you had before.

And you know what? That's enough. That's more than enough. That's everything.

The Choice You Make Every Day

So here's where we land: creating lasting change isn't about one big decision. It's about the choice you make every single day to keep showing up to your own transformation.

It's the choice to follow your system even when you don't feel like it. The choice to do the rep even when you're tired of reps. The choice to reach out for support even when you want to handle it alone. The choice to stay alert without living in fear. The choice to celebrate progress instead of obsessing over perfection. The choice to believe that who you're becoming is worth the work it takes to get there.

That's what makes change last. Not intensity. Consistency. Not motivation. Systems. Not dramatic moments. Ordinary faithfulness. Not arrival. Direction.

You've broken the chains. You've rewritten the narrative. You've become the author.

Now it's time to write a story that doesn't just start with freedom—it sustains it.

Every day, you get to make that choice again. Every day, you get to be faithful to who you're becoming. Every day, you get to add another rep to the ten thousand that will rewire your brain.

And every day, you get closer to the version of yourself who doesn't just know they're free—they live like it.

That's the long game. That's the architecture of sustainable transformation. That's what it means to create lasting change.

So the question becomes, are you ready to build something that lasts?

CHAPTER TWELVE
EMBRACE A NEW FUTURE

Possibility Thinking

There's a moment that comes after you've done all the work we've talked about in this book. After you've named the demons, broken the chains, rewritten the narrative, and built systems to make change last. It's a quiet moment, but it's one of the most disorienting experiences you'll ever have.

It's the moment when you realize you're actually free.

And then you ask yourself: now what?

Because there is something nobody tells you about freedom—it's terrifying. Not the kind of terror that comes from being chased, but the kind that comes from standing in an open field with no walls, no chains, no limits, and realizing you have to decide where to go next. You've spent so much energy escaping captivity that you never actually thought about what you'd do once you got out.

The demons kept you so busy surviving that you forgot how to imagine thriving. They trained you to think in terms of "how do I make it through today" instead of "what could tomorrow look like?" They convinced you that your only goal was damage control, that the best you could hope for was to minimize the harm and keep your head down.

But now? Now you're standing at the edge of possibility, and you don't even know what's possible anymore.

Let me tell you what I discovered when I got to this place: your imagination has atrophied. The demons didn't just steal your present and chain you to your past. They robbed you of your ability to dream about your future. And now that you're free, you have to relearn how to think in possibilities instead of limitations.

This is what I call possibility thinking. It's not toxic positivity or wishful thinking or pretending problems don't exist. It's the discipline of opening your mind to futures you couldn't even imagine while you were chained. It's asking yourself questions that feel dangerous because they require you to believe that better is actually available to you.

What becomes possible when Guilt no longer defines you?

Think about it. What doors open when you stop carrying shame everywhere you go? What relationships could you build if you weren't constantly apologizing for existing? What risks could you take if you believed that one mistake doesn't make you a mistake? What could you create if you stopped punishing yourself for not being perfect?

Guilt has kept you small. It's convinced you that you need to stay in the shadows, that you don't deserve to take up space, that your voice doesn't matter because your past disqualifies you. But what if that's a lie? What if the very experiences Guilt used to shame you are actually the foundation for the work you're meant to do?

What if your story—the messy, painful, imperfect story that Guilt told you to hide—is exactly what someone else needs to hear to know they're not alone?

Who could you become if Envy stopped poisoning your perception?

I want you to really sit with that question. Who could you become if you stopped measuring your life against everyone else's insta-reel? If you stopped believing that their blessing is your curse? If you could celebrate someone else's success without it making you feel like a failure?

Envy has kept you trapped in comparison prison. It's stolen your joy by convincing you that what you have isn't enough because someone else has more. It's made you resent people who aren't your enemies and covet lives that weren't meant for you.

But what if you could look at your own life with fresh eyes? What if you could see your unique path as exactly that —unique—instead of inferior? What if you stopped trying to duplicate someone else's journey and started getting curious about where your own road leads?

What becomes possible when you stop letting other people's seasons define yours? When you stop treating their harvest like evidence of your failure? When you can genuinely say "I'm happy for you" and mean it, not because you're performing spirituality but because you've learned that there's enough blessing to go around?

That's when you discover your own gifts. That's the moment you find your own voice. It's also the moment when you stop being a cheap copy of someone else and start being the original you were created to be.

What could you build if Greed stopped running your life?

Imagine waking up one morning and realizing you're satisfied. Not because you finally got everything you wanted, but because you decided that what you have is enough. Not settling. Not giving up. Just recognizing that the hamster wheel you've been running on doesn't actually go anywhere.

Greed has convinced you that happiness is always one more thing away. One more promotion, one more purchase, one more achievement, and then you'll finally feel whole. But you know the truth by now, don't you? You've chased "more" long enough to realize it's a mirage. Every time you get there, "there" moves further away.

What if you could step off the wheel? What if you could invest in relationships instead of returns? What if you could be present for your kids' childhood instead of working overtime to buy them things they don't need? What if you could build a life instead of building a resume?

That's what becomes available when Greed loses its grip. You get your time back. You get your energy back. You get to enjoy what you already have instead of constantly chasing what you don't. You discover that contentment isn't about having everything—it's about wanting what you have.

What relationships could you actually experience if Selfishness stopped isolating you?

Because that's what Selfishness does, isn't it? It tells you that self-protection is survival. That trusting people is dangerous. That vulnerability is weakness. That you have to do everything yourself because no one else will do it right. And before you know it, you're an island. Successful maybe. Independent definitely. But alone.

Selfishness has robbed you of community. It's convinced you that needing people means you're failing, that asking for help means you're weak, that letting someone see your struggle means you're a burden. So you carry everything by yourself until you collapse under the weight of it.

But what if you could let people in? What if you could ask for help without shame? What if you could show up imperfect and messy and still be loved? What if you could collaborate instead of controlling everything? What if you could trust that other people's gifts complement yours instead of competing with them?

That's when you discover what you were actually created for—connection. Real connection, not the performative kind where everyone pretends they have it together. The kind where you can say "I'm struggling" and someone says "me too" and you realize you've been fighting the same battles alone when you could have been fighting them together.

Who could you love if Rejection stopped convincing you that you're unlovable?

This is the big one, isn't it? The demon that has whispered in your ear since childhood that there's something fundamentally wrong with you. That people leave because of who you are. That love is conditional and you'll never meet the conditions. That it's safer to reject yourself first than to risk someone else doing it.

Rejection has built walls so high that even people who want to love you can't get in. It's made you sabotage good relationships because you're so convinced they'll end badly that you'd rather control when and how they end. It's turned intimacy into a threat and vulnerability into a death sentence.

But what if you could let those walls come down? What if you could believe that you're worthy of love not because you've earned it but because you exist? What if you could receive affection without waiting for the other shoe to drop? What if you could trust that people who choose you actually mean it?

What becomes possible when you stop punishing new people for old wounds? When you can show up as your full self and trust that your full self is enough? When you can say "I love you" without immediately adding "but I understand if you don't feel the same way"?

That's when you discover what you've been afraid of your whole life: you are actually lovable. Not a perfect version of you. Not a performance. Not who you think you should be. The real you. Messy, imperfect, still-figuring-it-out you. That person is worthy of love. The truth is you always has been.

The Future You Couldn't Imagine While Chained

So here's what I'm asking you to do right now, in this moment: give yourself permission to imagine.

Not just small, safe, realistic dreams. Not the cautious hopes that feel achievable. I'm talking about the futures that feel too good to be true. The possibilities that make you nervous to even think about because what if you let yourself want them and they don't happen?

I want you to imagine them anyway.

Because the demons spent years training you not to dream. They taught you that hope is dangerous, that wanting more is greedy, that believing in better is setting yourself up for disappointment. They convinced you that lowered expectations equal protection from pain.

But you know what lowered expectations actually equal? A smaller life than the one you were created for.

You've done the work. You've named the demons. You've broken the chains. You've built the systems to make change last. And now, right now, you're standing at the threshold of possibility.

The question is: are you brave enough to walk through it?

Trusting The Process You Can't See

So, here's where it gets uncomfortable.

You've opened your mind to possibility. You've imagined futures that feel almost too good to be true. You've asked yourself what becomes available when the demons lose their power. And now you're standing at the starting line of something new, and you realize something that makes your stomach drop: you have no idea how to get there.

You can see the destination. You can imagine what freedom looks like, what wholeness feels like, what purpose sounds like. But the path? The actual steps from here to there? That part is foggy at best and completely invisible at worst.

And that terrifies you. Because it terrified me.

Because you're a planner. A strategist. Someone who needs to see the whole staircase before taking the first step. You want guarantees, timelines, detailed instructions. You want to know that if you do A and B, then C will definitely happen. You want to trace the path the same way you've been trained to trace everything else.

But here's what I need you to understand: transformation doesn't work that way. Freedom doesn't come with a roadmap. Purpose doesn't reveal itself all at once on day one.

Remember what we talked about all the way back in Chapter 1? The difference between tracing and trusting?

Tracing is following someone else's blueprint. It's looking at how they did it and trying to replicate their steps. It's safe, it's predictable, it's controllable. But it's also exhausting, and more importantly, it's not your path. Their journey doesn't account for your demons, your gifts, your story, your calling.

Trusting is completely different. Trusting is taking the next right step even when you can't see the one after that. It's believing that the path will reveal itself as you walk it. It's accepting that some seasons are about preparation, not arrival. It's making peace with the fact that delay doesn't mean denial.

Abraham didn't know where he was going when God told him to leave. He just knew he had to go. He packed up his whole life, said goodbye to everything familiar, and started walking toward a promise he couldn't see. That's not foolishness. That's faith. And faith, by definition, requires trust in what you cannot see.

The wilderness you're walking through right now? It's not punishment. It's preparation.

I know it doesn't feel that way. I know it feels like you're wandering in circles, like you should be further along by now, like everyone else is arriving while you're still in the desert. But what if this season isn't about reaching the destination? What if it's about becoming the person who can handle what's waiting on the other side?

Because here's the truth: if God gave you everything you asked for right now, today, this moment, you wouldn't be ready for it. You'd take your unhealed patterns into your new season. You'd bring your demons into your destiny. You'd sabotage your breakthrough with the same behaviors that kept you bound.

The wilderness is where that gets sorted out. It's where you learn who you are when nobody's watching. It's where you discover what you're actually made of. It's where you build the character that your calling requires.

Moses spent forty years in the desert before he led anyone out of Egypt. David was anointed king as a teenager but didn't wear the crown until he was thirty. Joseph had the dream at seventeen but didn't step into it until he was thirty. Jesus himself spent thirty years in obscurity before three years of ministry.

The space between promise and fulfillment isn't wasted time. It's sacred time. It's the season where God builds in you what He's already prepared for you.

So yes, you're going to have to trust the process you can't see. You're going to have to walk by faith, not by sight. You're going to have to take the next right step without knowing where step fifty leads. You're going to have to make peace with mystery, with waiting, with not having all the answers.

And that's not weakness. That's actually the most courageous thing you can do. Because trusting requires more strength than controlling. Surrendering requires more power than grasping. Believing requires more faith than seeing.

You don't need to see the whole staircase. You just need to take the first step. And then the next one. And then the next one. The path reveals itself to those who walk it, not to those who demand to see it all before they start.

Permission To Build And Dream Again

There comes a moment after the chains break when you look around at your life and realize something unsettling: you've spent so much energy tearing down what was toxic that you forgot to think about what you want to build in its place.

You've dismantled the lies. You've walked away from relationships that kept you small. You've quit the job that was killing your soul. You've set boundaries with family members who treated you like a doormat. You've done the demolition work, and now you're standing in the rubble wondering what comes next.

And there's this voice in your head—maybe it's your own, maybe it's an echo of the demons you've been fighting—that whispers: "What if you tear everything down and discover you don't know how to build anything better?"

Let me tell you something: that fear is normal. That hesitation is understandable. Because building requires something that destruction doesn't: hope. And hope, after years of disappointment, feels dangerous.

But here's what I need you to understand: you have permission to build again.

You have permission to dream about relationships built on authenticity instead of performance. To imagine friendships where you don't have to perform or pretend or hide the parts of yourself you think are too much or not enough. To believe that there are people out there who will love the real you, not the version you've been performing.

You have permission to pursue work that actually means something to you. Not just a paycheck. Not just security. Not just what your parents wanted or what looks impressive or what society says success should look like. Work that aligns with who you actually are and what you're actually called to do. Work that energizes you instead of draining you. Work that feels like purpose instead of penance.

You have permission to make choices guided by purpose instead of fear. For how long have you been making decisions based on what might go wrong instead of what could go right? How many opportunities have you turned down because you were afraid of failure? How many risks have you avoided because you couldn't guarantee the outcome?

Fear has been your primary decision-maker for too long. Sure, it's kept you safe. But it's also kept you stuck. And now that you're free, you get to choose a different guide. You get to ask "does this move me toward my purpose?" instead of "what if this doesn't work out?"

That doesn't mean you become reckless. That doesn't mean you ignore wisdom or throw caution to the wind. It means you stop letting fear have veto power over your future.

You have permission to imagine what could be instead of just protecting yourself from what might go wrong.

Because here's what happens when you only think defensively: you build a life that's safe but small. You construct walls instead of bridges. You protect yourself so well that nothing can hurt you, but nothing can reach you either. You survive, but you don't thrive.

Building requires vulnerability. It requires you to believe that something good is possible even though you've experienced so much bad. It requires you to plant seeds even though you've watched other gardens die. It requires you to open your heart even though it's been broken before.

And yes, that's terrifying. Yes, there's risk involved. Yes, you might build something beautiful and watch it fall apart. But you might also build something that lasts. You might also create something that changes your life. You might also discover that you're capable of so much more than survival.

The old has been torn down. And that's painful, I know. You're grieving what you had to leave behind, even the toxic things, because at least they were familiar. At least you knew how to navigate them. This new territory feels uncertain and unstable.

But you know what else it is? It's yours. This blank canvas, this empty space, this fresh start—it's all yours. And you get to decide what you're going to create with it.

So what do you want to build?

Not what do your parents want. Not what would impress people. Not what seems safest. What do you actually want? What makes you come alive? What would you create if you knew you couldn't fail? What would you pursue if you weren't afraid of judgment? What would you build if you truly believed that you deserve good things?

Start there. Start with one small brick. One honest conversation. One brave choice. One authentic connection. One purposeful step.

You don't have to build Rome in a day. You just have to be willing to lay the first stone.

Becoming Comfortable With Your Own Company

Here's something nobody talks about when they talk about freedom: once you break the chains and clear out the noise and set all the boundaries, you're going to end up alone with yourself. And for many of us, that's the most terrifying part of the entire journey.

Because who are you when nobody's watching? Who are you when you're not performing for approval or managing someone else's emotions or trying to prove your worth? Who are you in the silence, in the stillness, in the space between distractions?

For years, maybe your whole life, you've avoided that question. You've stayed busy. You've filled every moment with noise, with people, with tasks, with anything that keeps you from sitting in a room with yourself and actually paying attention to what's there.

The demons loved that, by the way. They thrived in the chaos. They used your busyness against you, convincing you that constant motion equals productivity, that exhaustion equals value, that if you just never stopped moving, you'd never have to confront what you were running from.

But now? Now you're free. And freedom, as it turns out, is quiet. There's space in it. Room to breathe. Room to think. Room to feel. And in that room, you have to face yourself.

That's where the real work begins.

I took me a long time to realize that self-acceptance isn't a luxury. It's not something you get to after you fix everything else. It's the foundation for everything else. Because if you can't make peace with who you are, you'll spend the rest of your life trying to become someone else. You'll carry your freedom like a burden instead of wearing it like a crown.

Let me be clear about something: self-acceptance doesn't mean you stop growing. It doesn't mean you settle for patterns that don't serve you or refuse to acknowledge areas where you need to change. It means you stop hating yourself while you grow. It means you can look in the mirror and say "I'm a work in progress, and that's okay."

It means you can hold two truths at the same time: I am enough right now, AND I'm becoming more. I am loved as I am, AND I'm being transformed. I am whole, AND I'm still healing.

That's the "AND" framework we talked about back in Chapter 10, remember? You don't have to choose between accepting yourself and growing. You get both. You need both.

Because here's the crazy thing that happens when you can't sit with yourself: you look for other people to fill the void. You need constant validation because you can't validate yourself. You need someone to tell you you're okay because you don't believe it when you say it. You need external noise because internal silence feels like drowning.

And that's not connection. That's dependency. That's using people as distractions from yourself.

Real connection—the kind that actually nourishes you instead of draining you—can only happen when you're comfortable being alone. Because if you need someone to complete you, you'll attract people who need to be needed. If you can't handle solitude, you'll settle for any company just to avoid it. If you don't know who you are by yourself, you'll become whoever the person you're with needs you to be.

But when you're comfortable in your own skin? When you can sit in silence and not feel like you're suffocating? When you can spend a Saturday alone and actually enjoy your own company? That's when you stop settling. That's when you stop performing. That's when you start attracting people who love you for who you actually are instead of who you're pretending to be.

There's a difference between loneliness and solitude, and you need to learn it.

Loneliness is the ache of feeling disconnected even when you're surrounded by people. It's the empty feeling that comes from shallow connections and surface-level conversations. It's being at a party and feeling invisible. It's being in a relationship and feeling alone.

Solitude is different. Solitude is choosing to be alone because you value your own presence. It's the peace that comes from not having to perform or explain or justify yourself to anyone. It's the space where you hear yourself think, where you figure out what you actually believe instead of just echoing what others have told you.

To put it simply: Loneliness depletes you. Solitude restores you.

And you can't build a sustainable future if you're terrified of being alone with yourself. Because there will be seasons —probably many of them—when you're the only person you have. When friends are busy. When relationships end. When family disappoints. When the crowd moves on to the next thing.

And if you haven't learned to be your own good company, those seasons will destroy you.

But if you've done the work? If you've made peace with the person in the mirror? If you've learned that being alone doesn't mean being lonely? Then those seasons become sacred. They become opportunities for growth instead of threats to your stability.

So here's what I'm asking you to do: spend time with yourself. Not as punishment. Not because you have to. Because you want to. Get curious about who you are when nobody else is in the room. Discover what you actually like instead of what you've been told you should like. Figure out what brings you joy, what makes you laugh, what makes you feel alive.

Learn to enjoy your own company. Because you're going to be with yourself for the rest of your life. You might as well like the person you're traveling with.

The Faith To Step Forward & Releasing Control

So we've come full circle. Back to where we started in Chapter 1, back to the fundamental choice that determines everything: are you going to trace, or are you going to trust?

You know the path forward exists. You've opened your mind to possibility. You've made peace with not seeing every step. You've given yourself permission to build. You've learned to be comfortable with yourself. And now you're standing at the edge, and there's one last thing standing between you and your future: your need to control it.

Control feels like safety. It feels like wisdom. It feels like the responsible thing to do. You've been hurt before by things you didn't see coming, by people you trusted who betrayed you, by circumstances that blindsided you. So now you hold everything with a tight fist. You micromanage. You over plan. You try to anticipate every possible problem so you're never caught off guard again.

But here's what I've learned: the tighter you grip, the less you can actually hold.

Control is an illusion. The sobering truth is: it always has been. You were never actually in control of other people's choices, of circumstances beyond your influence, of outcomes you couldn't predict. What you had was the exhausting work of trying to manage the unmanageable and the anxiety that comes from believing you're responsible for things you were never meant to carry.

And now you're free from the demons that chained you, but you're in danger of becoming chained to something else: the need to orchestrate your own liberation. To manage your own transformation. To guarantee your own breakthrough.

But that's not how faith works.

Faith requires you to step forward even when you can't see where you're stepping. It requires you to release outcomes you can't control. It requires you to trust that the God who brought you out of captivity knows how to lead you into destiny.

Remember Abraham? He didn't just not know where he was going. He also didn't know how he'd get there, how long it would take, what obstacles he'd face, or what the journey would cost him. He just knew he had to go. And that was enough.

That's what I'm asking you to embrace now: the faith to move toward destiny even when the path isn't clear. Even when you can't guarantee the outcome. Even when it feels safer to stay where you are than to step into the unknown.

Because staying where you are isn't actually safe. It's just familiar. And no matter how safe it feels, familiar pain is still pain.

So, here's what releasing control actually looks like: it's making the next right decision and trusting God with the results. It's doing your part and letting go of the parts that were never yours. It's planting seeds without demanding to see the harvest on your timeline. It's showing up faithfully to your own life without needing to script everyone else's role in it.

Releasing control doesn't mean you become passive. It doesn't mean you stop taking action or making plans or working toward goals. It means you stop believing that your worth is tied to outcomes you orchestrate and start trusting that God's plans are better than your blueprints.

It means you can say "I don't know how this is going to work out" without spiraling into anxiety. You can admit "I can't see the next five steps" without feeling like a failure. You can acknowledge "this didn't go the way I planned" without interpreting it as evidence that you're doing something wrong.

Sometimes the detours are the path. Sometimes the delays are protection. Sometimes what looks like a closed door is actually God steering you away from something that would have destroyed you and toward something that will define you.

But you'll never know that if you're so busy trying to force your way through the door you wanted that you miss the one He's opening.

Surrender isn't weakness. Surrender is the most powerful thing you can do. Because it means you're finally admitting that you were never meant to carry everything alone. That you don't have to have all the answers. That you can release the burden of being both the author and the finisher of your story and trust the One who's been writing it all along.

This is where trusting and tracing come full circle. Tracing is safe but exhausting. It's following someone else's path and hoping it leads somewhere good. It's controlling every variable and still ending up anxious because there are variables you can't control.

Trusting is different. Trusting is stepping into the unknown with the confidence that you're not stepping alone. It's making the move even when you're scared. It's choosing faith over fear, possibility over safety, purpose over comfort.

And here's the magical thing that happens when you finally let go: you discover that the arms you've been afraid to fall into have been holding you the entire time. You realize that the God you've been trying to help has never needed your help. You understand that surrender doesn't lead to loss—it leads to freedom you couldn't manufacture on your own.

So take the step. Make the move. Release the grip. Step into the future you've been afraid to embrace.

Not because you have it all figured out. Not because you can see the whole path. Not because you're guaranteed it will be easy.

But because you're finally free. And free people don't live in cages of their own making. They don't stay stuck because they're afraid of the unknown. They don't let fear of what might go wrong keep them from discovering what could go right.

You've chased the demons long enough. You've named them. You've broken their chains. You've rewritten their narratives. You've become the author of your own story.

Now it's time to write the chapters they said you'd never get to write. The ones about joy. About peace. About purpose. About becoming exactly who you were created to be.

The future is waiting. And so is the version of yourself who's been waiting to meet you there—the one who's free, whole, and finally alive.

Are you ready to embrace it?

CHAPTER THIRTEEN
CHASE DESTINY

The Misdirection Of Demon-Chasing

There's something I need to tell you, and it might sting a little.

You can get so good at fighting demons that you forget why you're fighting them in the first place.

I've seen it happen. I've lived it myself. You spend so much time naming your demons, breaking your chains, rewriting your narratives, and creating systems for lasting change that the battle itself becomes your identity. You become the person who's always fighting. Always processing. Always healing. Always working on yourself.

And don't get me wrong—all of that work is necessary. You can't skip the chapters we've walked through together. You can't chase destiny while you're still chained to your past. You can't step into your calling while demons are stealing your present. You can't become who you're meant to be without confronting the forces that have kept you from it.

But here's the trap: at some point, you have to transition from fighting demons to chasing destiny. From breaking free to running toward. From defense to offense. From survival to purpose.

Because if you stay in battle mode forever, the demons win anyway. Not by defeating you, but by keeping you so focused on them that you never look up long enough to see where you're actually supposed to be going.

Let me tell you when I realized this.

I was in therapy—again—working through another layer of trauma, another pattern I'd discovered, another demon that needed naming. And my therapist, who'd been walking with me through this process for months, looked at me and said something that stopped me cold: "You're very good at identifying what's wrong. When are you going to start identifying what's right?"

In that moment it was like I was frozen in mid-thought. I didn't have an answer. Because somewhere along the way, self-awareness had become self-obsession. Healing had become my full-time job. Fighting demons had become my purpose instead of the thing clearing the way for my purpose.

I'd become so comfortable in the battle that I didn't know who I was without it.

The reality is this: demons love it when you stay focused on them. Even when you're fighting them. Even when you're winning. Because as long as your attention is on what you're running from, it's not on what you're running toward.

That's the misdirection. That's the trap. That's how they keep you from your destiny even after you've broken the chains—by convincing you that the fight is the point.

But the fight was never the point. Freedom is the point. And freedom isn't just about what you're free from. It's about what you're free for.

You weren't set free just to not be in bondage anymore. You were set free to step into something. To become someone. To do something that only you can do. To chase something that's been waiting for you to finally be ready.

You were set free for destiny.

And destiny doesn't wait for you to finish healing perfectly. Destiny doesn't require you to have all your patterns completely rewired and every trigger fully processed. Destiny doesn't demand that you never struggle again or that you become some polished, perfected version of yourself before you're qualified.

Destiny just requires that you're free enough to start running.

So let me ask you something: How much of your life is still about the demons? How much of your energy is still spent analyzing what's wrong, processing what happened, fighting what's attacking you? How much of your identity is wrapped up in being the person who survived trauma, who overcame obstacles, who broke chains?

And here's the harder question: What would you do if the demons weren't the center of your story anymore?

Because that's where we're going. That's what this chapter is about. We're transitioning from chasing demons to chasing destiny. From running away to running toward. From fighting for freedom to living in it.

The demons have been named. The chains have been broken. The narratives have been rewritten. The systems are in place. You've done the work. You've survived the battle. You've become the author of your own story.

Now it's time to write the chapters they said you'd never get to write. The ones about purpose. About calling. About becoming exactly who you were created to be.

The demons tried their hardest to keep you from this moment. They tried to convince you that you'd never be free. That you'd always be fighting. That survival was the best you could hope for. That your past disqualified you from your future.

But they were wrong. And you're still here. Right now. And you're ready.

So stop chasing demons and start chasing destiny.

Because your calling has been waiting, and it's tired of being ignored.

What Is Destiny?

Before we go any further, I want to ensure we are clear on something. Because the word "destiny" gets thrown around so much that it's lost its meaning. It's become this vague, inspirational concept that people put on motivational posters and Instagram quotes without actually understanding what it means.

So let me tell you what destiny is not.

Destiny is not a job title. It's not a salary bracket. It's not a corner office or a book deal or a certain number of followers or any external marker of success that the world uses to measure whether you've "made it."

Destiny is not about arriving at a destination where you finally get to rest because you've achieved everything you set out to achieve. It's not a finish line. It's not a trophy you earn and then put on a shelf.

Destiny is not even about accomplishing specific goals, though goals will be part of the journey. Goals are markers along the way. Destiny is the path itself.

So what is destiny?

Destiny is who you're called to become and what you're called to do because of who you are. It's the intersection between your gifts and the world's needs. It's what happens when you stop performing who you think you should be and start living as who you actually are. It's the thing that brings you alive—not applause, but life.

Let me say that again because it's important: destiny is about who you're becoming, not just what you're achieving.

The demons want you to confuse the two. They want you to think destiny is about external validation, about reaching certain milestones, about proving something to someone. Because if they can get you chasing the wrong thing, they can keep you running forever without ever actually arriving.

Greed whispers that destiny is about accumulation. That you'll finally be living your purpose when you have enough money, enough success, enough recognition. That there's always one more thing you need before you're ready. That your calling is something you earn through achievement rather than something you step into through obedience.

Envy tells you that destiny is what someone else has. That you're supposed to have their life, their opportunities, their platform. That your calling looks like theirs and if it doesn't, you must be doing something wrong. Envy keeps you so focused on everyone else's lane that you never run your own race.

Rejection convinces you that destiny is conditional. That if you've been rejected, overlooked, or passed over, it means you don't have one. That your calling is something people give you permission to pursue rather than something God placed inside you before you were even born.

Guilt says you're disqualified. That your past mistakes have forfeited your future purpose. That destiny is for people who got it right, not for people who got it wrong and are still figuring it out.

Selfishness makes destiny all about you. About your comfort, your convenience, your preferences. It turns calling into personal ambition and purpose into self-service. It makes you believe that destiny should revolve around what you want rather than who you're meant to serve.

All of it is a lie.

Your destiny is not about what you accumulate. It's not about matching someone else's path. It's not conditional on other people's approval. It's not forfeited by your past. And it's not just about you.

Your destiny is about alignment. It's about becoming so fully yourself that what you do naturally serves others powerfully. It's about discovering the thing that makes you come alive and realizing that the world needs that exact aliveness. It's about stepping into the space that was carved out specifically for you—not because you're perfect, but because you're you.

Frederick Buechner said it this way: "The place God calls you to is the place where your deep gladness and the world's deep hunger meet."

That's destiny. Not the thing that looks impressive. Not the thing that makes sense on paper. Not the thing everyone expects from you. The thing that brings you deep gladness while meeting the world's deep hunger.

For me, that looks like teaching. Like writing. Like creating space for people to see themselves clearly and believe they can change. That's what brings me alive. That's where my gifts meet the world's needs. That's my destiny— not because it's glamorous or because it's what I thought I'd be doing, but because it's what I'm called to do.

Your destiny will look different. It should look different. Because you're not me and no two destinies are exactly the same. You're not supposed to run my race or fulfill my calling. You're supposed to discover your own.

Through it all, here's what I've learned: your destiny has been leaving clues your entire life. There's a throughline in your story that keeps showing up. Things you're drawn to that you can't quite explain. Moments when you feel most alive. Situations where you show up as your best self without even trying. Problems you're uniquely positioned to solve because of what you've been through.

That's not random. That's your destiny trying to get your attention.

But you'll miss it if you're too busy chasing what the demons say destiny should look like. You'll miss it if you're comparing your calling to someone else's. You'll miss it if you're waiting for permission or validation or the perfect circumstances.

You'll miss it if you're still convinced that the battle is the point instead of recognizing that the battle was clearing the way for this.

So let me ask you: What brings you deep gladness? Not what impresses people. Not what makes money. Not what looks good on paper. What makes you come alive?

And where does that gladness meet the world's hunger? What problem can you solve? What gap can you fill? Who can you serve? What can you create?

That intersection? That's your destiny. And it's been waiting for you to be free enough to finally see it.

Identifying Your Destiny Markers

Here's the thing nobody tells you about destiny: it's not something you discover in a moment of divine revelation where the heavens open and a voice tells you exactly what you're supposed to do with your life.

I mean, maybe that happens for some people. But for most of us, destiny reveals itself slowly. Through patterns. Through preferences. Through the things we keep coming back to even when we try to ignore them. Through the problems that make us angry enough to do something about them.

Your destiny has been whispering to you your entire life. You've just been too busy surviving, or performing, or chasing what you thought you were supposed to chase, to hear it.

So how do you identify it? How do you separate what's actually your calling from what's just noise? How do you know the difference between your destiny and the version of success the world has been selling you?

Let me give you some markers. Some clues. Some questions that might help you recognize what's been there all along.

What Brings You Alive vs. What Brings You Applause

This is the first and most important distinction you need to make.

There are things you do that get you praise. That make people notice you. That earn you validation and recognition and all the external markers that say you're doing well.

And then there are things you do that make you feel alive. That you'd do even if nobody was watching. That energize you instead of draining you. That feel less like work and more like finally being yourself.

Those aren't always the same things.

For years, I chased applause. I pursued positions that looked impressive. I made career moves that would sound good when people asked what I did. I built a resume that checked all the right boxes. And I was good at it. People noticed. People validated. People told me I was successful.

But I wasn't alive. I was performing.

The moment I started teaching—actually teaching, not just lecturing but creating space for people to discover something about themselves—that's when I felt alive. Not because people applauded, though sometimes they did. But because something in me finally woke up. Something that had been dormant while I was busy chasing what looked like success.

That's the marker. That's the clue. The thing that makes you feel more like yourself, not less. The thing that energizes you even when it exhausts you. The thing you'd do for free if you had to because not doing it feels like suffocating.

So tell me, what is that for you? And be honest. Not what should bring you alive based on what you studied or what your parents wanted or what looks good on LinkedIn. What actually brings you alive?

The Throughline in Your Story

Here's another marker: look for the pattern.

When I look back at my life, there's a throughline I can trace all the way through. Even when I didn't recognize it. Even when I was trying to do something completely different. It kept showing up.

I've always been drawn to helping people see themselves more clearly. To creating space for honesty. To asking the questions that nobody else wants to ask. To writing things down in a way that makes people feel less alone. I think I got that from my mother. She had this passion for people and uplifting them that I didn't fully appreciate until later in life.

It first showed up when I was a kid writing in journals nobody would ever read. It showed up in college when I'd end up in deep conversations with people at 1 AM about things that actually mattered. It showed up in my career when the parts of my job I loved most were the moments of genuine connection, not the meetings or the politics or the performance.

Even when I tried to ignore it and chase what looked more impressive or more financially stable or more acceptable, that throughline kept appearing. Like it was saying, "This is who you are. This is what you're for. Pay attention."

So what's your throughline? What keeps showing up in your life even when you're trying to do something else? What themes, what interests, what passions have followed you through different seasons and different roles and different versions of yourself?

Can I tell you a little secret: that's not coincidence. That's destiny leaving breadcrumbs.

Where Your Pain Meets Your Purpose

This one is harder to accept, but it's often the most powerful marker.

The very things that broke you can become the things that equip you to help others. The pain you survived becomes the testimony that gives someone else permission to believe they can survive too. The demons you've fought give you the authority to teach others how to fight theirs.

I didn't want that to be true. For a long time, I resented it. I wanted my pain to just be pain. I wanted my trauma to just be trauma. I didn't want it to have a purpose because giving it purpose felt like saying it was okay that it happened.

But that's not what this means. Your pain isn't justified just because something good came from it. What happened to you was still wrong. The loss was still real. The damage was still damage.

But you get to decide what you do with it. You get to decide whether the demons that attacked you also get to define what you do with the rest of your life. You get to decide whether your survival means something beyond just making it through.

My mother's death nearly destroyed me. COVID nearly killed me. The discrimination I faced tried to silence me. The rejection I experienced tried to convince me I was fundamentally unlovable.

But now? Those experiences inform how I show up. They shape what I write. They give me the ability to speak to people in their pain without minimizing it or spiritualizing it or offering cheap comfort.

That's where my pain meets my purpose. Not because the pain was good. But because I'm not going to let the demons waste it.

Where does your pain meet your purpose? What have you survived that uniquely positions you to help someone else survive it? What have you learned in the dark that you can now use to help someone else find light?

That's a destiny marker.

What You Do Without Trying

Here's another clue: what comes naturally to you that others struggle with?

I don't mean the skills you learned or the degrees you earned. I mean the things that feel effortless. The things people compliment you on that you didn't even realize were noteworthy because they're just how you operate.

For some people, it's hospitality. They create space where people feel seen and welcomed without even thinking about it. For others, it's problem-solving. They look at a mess and immediately see solutions. For some, it's encouragement. They know exactly what to say to make someone believe in themselves again.

What's yours? What do people thank you for that you barely remember doing? What do you contribute to situations that feels so natural you don't think it counts as a gift?

That's a gift. And gifts aren't random. They're clues pointing you toward your calling.

The Problem That Makes You Angry

And finally, this one, one that I struggle with constantly: What injustice makes you angry enough to do something about it?

What breaks your heart? What keeps you up at night? What makes you want to flip tables and fight systems and refuse to accept "that's just how it is" as an answer?

That anger isn't a character flaw. It's a calling. Because the things that make you righteously angry are often connected to what you're here to change.

If you're angry about injustice in the workplace, maybe you're called to create better systems. If you're angry about people being silenced, maybe you're called to amplify voices. If you're angry about people being trapped in cycles they can't break, maybe you're called to show them the way out.

I've learned that anger is information. Pay attention to it.

So here's what I want you to do: Stop reading for a second and actually think about these questions. Not in a vague, "I'll think about it later" way. Right now.

What brings you alive? What's the throughline in your story? Where does your pain meet your purpose? What do you do without trying? What problem makes you angry?

Write it down if you need to. Journal it. Talk it out with someone who knows you well. But don't skip this. Because these aren't abstract exercises. These are the markers that point you toward your destiny.

And once you see them, once you recognize the pattern, you can't unsee it. You can't go back to pretending you don't know what you're called to do.

Your destiny has been leaving clues. It's time to start following them.

The Demons Vs. Destiny Test

Now that you're starting to see the markers, now that the pattern is becoming clearer, you're going to face a million decisions about what to pursue and what to let go. A million voices telling you what you should do, what makes sense, what's practical, what's safe.

And you need a way to filter through all that noise. You need a framework for discerning whether a choice is moving you toward your destiny or back toward captivity. Whether an opportunity is actually aligned with your calling or just another demon in disguise.

So let me give you a test. A series of questions you can run every decision through to help you separate what's from God and what's from the demons trying to distract you from your purpose.

I call it the Demons vs. Destiny Test. And I use it constantly. Every opportunity, every relationship, every choice that feels significant—I run it through these questions before I commit.

Does This Move Me Toward Freedom or Captivity?

Remember what we established all the way back in Chapter 2: where the Spirit of the Lord is, there is liberty. If something feels like captivity, it's not from God.

So when you're evaluating a decision, ask yourself: Does this expand my freedom or contract it? Does this make me feel more alive or more trapped? Does this give me room to breathe or does it feel like the walls are closing in?

I'm not talking about whether it's hard or whether it requires sacrifice. Destiny will absolutely cost you something. I'm talking about the quality of the challenge. Does it feel like growth or does it feel like bondage?

When I was climbing the education ladder, every promotion felt like captivity even though it looked like success. More responsibility, more visibility, more validation —but less freedom to be myself. Less room to breathe. More performance, less authenticity.

When I started teaching and writing, it was harder work. More vulnerable. More uncertain. But it felt like freedom. Like finally being able to exhale after holding my breath for years.

That's the difference. Destiny might be difficult, but it won't feel like a cage. Demons might offer you success, but it'll come with chains.

So, what are you considering right now? Does it feel like freedom or captivity?

Does This Align With Favor or Performance?

Here's another filter: Is this rooted in who you are or who you think you need to be?

Favor is God's positioning. It's about being placed where you belong because of who you are, not what you've proven. Performance is about earning your spot through achievement, validation, and exhaustion.

When you're living in favor, you show up as yourself and trust that's enough. When you're living in performance, you're constantly calculating, managing perceptions, trying to earn approval that was never yours to earn in the first place.

So ask yourself: Does this opportunity require me to be authentically myself, or does it require me to perform a version of myself that I think will be acceptable?

If it's the latter, that's not destiny. That's a demon wearing opportunity's garment.

I've turned down positions that looked impressive because they required me to hide parts of myself. I've walked away from opportunities that would've advanced my career but would've cost me my authenticity. And every single time, it hurt in the moment but freed me in the long run.

Because here's what I've learned: if you have to hide who you are to get it, you'll have to hide who you are to keep it. And that's not destiny. That's captivity with a better title.

So, what about you? Does this opportunity celebrate who you actually are, or does it require you to perform someone you're not?

Does This Honor Who God Made Me or Who Others Expect Me to Be?

Now, this one is related but different. It's about discerning between your calling and other people's expectations.

Your parents might have expectations. Your community might have expectations. Your culture, your church, your industry—they all have scripts for who you're supposed to be and what you're supposed to do.

And some of those expectations might align with your destiny. But some won't. And you have to be willing to disappoint people to pursue what you're actually called to do.

So when you're evaluating a path, ask: Is this honoring the person God created me to be, or am I trying to fulfill someone else's vision for my life?

I was supposed to be a lot of things according to other people's expectations. More corporate. More closeted. More acceptable. More manageable. More this. More that. You know the story.

But none of those expectations were my destiny. They were other people's comfort zones. And I had to choose between honoring who God made me to be and honoring who others expected me to be.

I finally chose myself. And it cost me relationships. It cost me opportunities. It cost me approval.

But it bought me freedom. And freedom is worth more than approval.

So tell me, what expectations are you carrying that aren't actually yours? What would you pursue if you stopped trying to fulfill other people's visions for your life?

Does This Produce Liberty or Exhaustion?

This one is critical: How does this feel in your body?

I know that sounds overly simplistic, but your body knows things your mind is still trying to rationalize. Your body knows the difference between good challenge and toxic stress. Your body knows when something is life-giving and when something is draining you.

Destiny will be challenging. It will stretch you. It will require more of you than you thought you had. But it won't chronically exhaust you. It won't make you feel like you're dying a slow death from the inside out.

That's the demons. That's captivity disguised as opportunity.

So pay attention to your body. When you think about this decision, do you feel energized or depleted? Do you feel a deep sense of "yes, this is right" even if it's scary, or do you feel dread?

I learned this the hard way. I spent years ignoring what my body was telling me because my mind was so committed to the path I thought I was supposed to be on. My body was screaming exhaustion, anxiety, depression—but I kept pushing because I thought that's what discipline looked like.

Turns out, it wasn't discipline. It was self-destruction. And my body was trying to tell me I was off course.

So now I listen. When an opportunity makes me feel alive, even if it's terrifying, I pay attention to that. When an opportunity makes me feel dread, even if it looks good on paper, I pay attention to that too.

What is your body telling you? And are you listening? Because if the body is exhausted, then nothing else matters.

The Final Question: Does This Help Me Chase My Destiny or Just Keep Me Busy?

And here's the last filter, the most important one: Is this actually moving me toward my calling, or is it just activity?

Because the demons are really good at keeping you busy. They'll fill your calendar with good things, productive things, important things—none of which are actually your things.

You can be incredibly busy and completely off course. You can be achieving a lot and still missing your destiny.

So before you say yes to something, ask yourself: Does this move me closer to where I'm supposed to be going, or is it just filling time? Does this align with the throughline I've identified in my story, or is it a detour? Does this serve the intersection of my gifts and the world's needs, or am I just saying yes because it's easier than saying no?

I've learned to be ruthless about this. I say no to a lot of good opportunities because they're not my opportunities. I turn down invitations, decline projects, and set boundaries that might seem harsh to people who don't understand that I'm protecting something more important than being liked.

I'm protecting my calling. I'm protecting the space and energy required to chase my actual destiny instead of just staying busy.

So, ask yourself, what are you saying yes to that's keeping you from what you're actually called to do? What needs to be cleared out to make room for your real purpose?

Run your decisions through this test. All of them. The big ones and the small ones. Because every choice either moves you toward your destiny or distracts you from it.

And despite what we all think, we don't have unlimited time or unlimited energy. You have to be intentional about what gets your yes and what gets your no.

Your destiny is waiting. But you won't get there if you're too busy chasing everything else.

The Cost Of Destiny

I need to be honest with you about something before we go any further.

Chasing your destiny will cost you something. It will require something from you. And I'd be doing you a disservice if I let you believe that once you identify your calling, everything just falls into place and life becomes easy.

That's simply not how this works.

Destiny demands sacrifice. It demands courage. It demands that you let go of things that feel safe so you can reach for things that feel uncertain. It demands that you disappoint some people so you can become who you're supposed to be. It demands that you trust favor when circumstances are screaming otherwise.

So let me tell you what it's going to cost you. Not to discourage you, but to prepare you. Because if you're going to chase your destiny, you need to know what you're signing up for.

It Will Cost You Safety

The first thing destiny will require is that you let go of what feels safe.

Safe jobs. Safe relationships. Safe versions of yourself that you've been performing for years. Safe paths that other people understand and approve of. Safe choices that guarantee predictable outcomes.

Destiny doesn't live in safety. It lives in risk. In uncertainty. In the space between where you are and where you're supposed to be, with no roadmap showing you exactly how to get there.

When I decided to embrace the fullness of my calling—administration, teaching, and writing together—I had to let go of the career trajectory that only valued the administrative titles and ignored the rest. I had to release the security of knowing exactly where I'd be in ten years. I had to give up the safety of positions that looked impressive on paper but felt like cages.

And that was terrifying. Because safety is comfortable. Safety is predictable. Safety is what we've been taught to value above almost everything else.

But you know what safety actually is? It's a trap. It's the thing that keeps you stuck in a life that's too small for who you actually are. It's the thing that convinces you to stay where you don't belong because at least you know what to expect.

And if you're going to chase your destiny, you're going to have to choose risk over safety. You're going to have to make moves that don't make sense to people who are still choosing comfort. You're going to have to step into the unknown and trust that the God who called you there will meet you.

That costs something. And you need to decide if you're willing to pay it.

It Will Cost You Relationships

Here's the part nobody wants to hear: some people won't make it into your destiny with you.

Not because they're bad people. Not because you don't love them. But because they're attached to the version of you that was safe, manageable, and predictable. They liked you better when you were small. When you were struggling. When you needed them in a way that made them feel important.

And when you start growing, when you start healing, when you start stepping into who you're actually meant to be, some people will feel threatened by that. They'll resist your transformation. They'll try to pull you back. They'll remind you of who you used to be as if that's who you're supposed to stay.

I've lost friendships over my healing. I've lost relationships over my authenticity. I've disappointed people who preferred the version of me that was performing, the version that was easier to control, the version that didn't ask too many questions or challenge too many systems.

And it hurt. God knows every single time, it hurt.

But you know what hurt more? Staying small to keep people comfortable. Hiding who I was to maintain relationships that required me to be someone I wasn't. Sacrificing my destiny to preserve connections with people who only loved the mask I was wearing.

So let me tell you what I learned: if someone can't celebrate your freedom, they don't belong in your future. If someone resents your growth, they're not your person. If someone requires you to stay broken to stay in their life, that's not love—that's bondage.

Destiny will cost you some relationships. And you have to be okay with that. You have to be willing to walk alone for a season if that's what it takes to walk in purpose.

Because the people who are supposed to be with you will celebrate who you're becoming. They'll champion your growth. They'll call you forward instead of calling you back. And those people? Those people are worth waiting for.

It Will Cost You Approval

Chasing your destiny means you're going to disappoint people. You're going to make choices that don't make sense to them. You're going to pursue things they don't understand. You're going to live in ways that challenge their comfort.

And they're going to let you know about it. Through criticism. Through concern. Through passive-aggressive comments disguised as care. Through withdrawal and silence and disappointment.

You're going to have to choose between their approval and your calling. And trust me that choice is harder than it sounds.

Because we're wired for approval. We want people to be proud of us. We want to make our parents happy. We want our community to validate our choices. We want to be understood and celebrated and affirmed.

But destiny doesn't wait for permission. Destiny doesn't require consensus. Destiny doesn't need everyone to agree before you're allowed to pursue it.

I had to make peace with disappointing people. Not everyone in my family understood some of my choices. My community questioned my path. People I respected thought I was making mistakes.

And maybe I was. Maybe I am. But they're my mistakes to make. This is my life to live. This is my calling to chase.

You're going to have to get comfortable with that too. You're going to have to release the need for everyone to understand your journey. You're going to have to be okay with people thinking you're crazy, or reckless, or wasting your potential.

Because their approval isn't the point. But your obedience to the process is.

It Will Cost You Control

And here's the hardest cost: destiny requires that you surrender control.

Remember what we talked about in Chapter 12? The difference between tracing and trusting? Tracing is safe because you can see the whole path. Trusting is terrifying because you can't.

Destiny is a trust exercise. It's stepping forward when you can't see the next step. It's making moves that don't guarantee outcomes. It's releasing your grip on how everything is supposed to happen and trusting that God is working even when you can't see it.

That goes against everything in you that wants to manage, plan, and control. That wants guarantees before you commit. That wants to see the whole staircase before you take the first step.

But control is an illusion. You were never actually in control. And the exhaustion you're feeling from trying to control everything? That's what happens when you try to carry something you were never meant to carry.

Destiny requires that you let go. That you surrender. That you trust the process you can't see and make peace with the uncertainty.

And that costs you the false comfort of believing you're in charge.

So Why Pay the Cost?

With all of that on the table, why would anyone choose to pay these costs? Why would you willingly give up safety, relationships, approval, and control?

Because what you gain is worth infinitely more than what you lose.

You gain freedom. I mean real freedom. Not the kind that's contingent on other people's approval or external circumstances, but the kind that lives in your bones. The kind that lets you breathe deeply for the first time in years. The kind that makes you feel alive instead of just surviving.

You gain purpose. A reason to get up in the morning that's bigger than just getting through the day. A calling that energizes you instead of draining you. Work that feels like worship instead of punishment.

You gain authenticity. The ability to show up as yourself without apology. To be fully known and still loved. To stop performing and start living.

You gain peace. Not the absence of struggle, but the deep knowing that you're exactly where you're supposed to be, doing exactly what you're supposed to do, becoming exactly who you're supposed to become.

And you gain the chance to become who you were created to be. Not who your parents wanted. Not who society expected. Not who your trauma convinced you that you were. But who God made you to be before the world got its hands on you.

That's worth the cost. Every single time, I promise you it's worth the cost.

So here's my question for you: Are you willing to pay it?

Are you willing to risk safety for purpose? Are you willing to release relationships that require you to stay small? Are you willing to disappoint people to obey God? Are you willing to surrender control to gain freedom?

Because your destiny is waiting. But it won't come to you. You have to chase it. And chasing it will cost you everything you've been holding onto that was never meant to be yours in the first place.

Running Your Race

So, now that you know the cost—and you're starting to see your destiny more clearly—there's one more trap I need to warn you about. One more way the demons will try to derail you, even after you've started running.

They'll get you to look at someone else's lane.

Because here's the thing: once you start chasing your destiny, you're going to notice other people chasing theirs. And some of them will look like they're further ahead. Like they're moving faster. Like their path is clearer, their progress more visible, their success more obvious.

And if you're not careful, you'll start comparing. You'll start measuring your beginning against their middle. You'll start wondering why your lane looks different from theirs. You'll start questioning whether you're even in the right race.

That's Envy. And Envy doesn't want you to quit the race entirely—that would be too obvious. Envy just wants you to run someone else's race instead of your own. Because if you're chasing their destiny, you're not chasing yours.

So let me tell you something you need to hear: your race has different terrain. Different obstacles. Different mile markers. And a different finish line.

Your Lane Is Not Their Lane

When I look at other writers, other administrators, other people doing work that looks similar to mine, it's easy to fall into comparison. They have bigger platforms. More followers. More opportunities. More visibility. More impact— or at least, what looks like more impact from the outside.

And for a long time, that messed with me. I'd look at their trajectory and wonder what I was doing wrong. Why wasn't I there yet? Why wasn't my path looking like theirs? Why wasn't I getting the same opportunities?

But here's what I had to learn: their lane is not my lane. Their race is not my race. Their calling is not my calling.

They're running the race God gave them. I'm running the race God gave me. And those races don't look the same because they're not supposed to.

Your lane has obstacles that are specific to you. Challenges that are meant to shape you into who you need to become to handle what's waiting at your finish line. Training that's preparing you for a calling that's uniquely yours.

So when you look at someone else's progress and start feeling like you're behind, remember this: you're not behind. You're exactly where you're supposed to be in your race. And their mile three is not your mile three. Their obstacles are not your obstacles. Their preparation is not your preparation.

Stop comparing your lane to theirs. Run your race.

Faithfulness Over Flash

Here's another thing I've learned: destiny is not about the big, flashy moments. It's about the small, faithful obediences that nobody sees.

It's showing up when you don't feel like it. It's doing the work when nobody's watching. It's staying consistent when there's no immediate reward. It's choosing your calling over comfort on a random Tuesday when it would be so much easier to just quit.

The world celebrates the highlight reel. The viral moment. The big break. The overnight success that actually took ten years of work nobody saw.

But destiny is built in the unsexy moments. In the daily grind. In the repetition of small choices that compound over time. In the faithfulness to your calling when it feels like nothing is happening.

I write when nobody's reading. I teach when the room is small. I lead as an executive even when the work goes unnoticed. I show up to my calling even when there's no applause, no recognition, no visible progress.

Because that's what faithfulness looks like. And faithfulness is what destiny requires.

You're not going to be famous tomorrow. You're probably not going to go viral. You're not going to wake up one day and suddenly have arrived at the destination.

But if you show up faithfully, consistently, obediently—if you keep running your race even when it feels like you're getting nowhere—you'll look back one day and realize you've traveled further than you thought possible.

Destiny is a marathon, not a sprint. And marathons are won by the people who keep running when everyone else quits.

The Danger of Distraction

The demons know they probably can't get you to quit entirely. You've come too far. You've done too much work. You've seen too much freedom to go back to captivity willingly.

So they'll try a different strategy: distraction.

They'll show you opportunities that aren't bad, just not yours. They'll present doors that look impressive but lead away from your actual calling. They'll dangle shiny objects that pull your attention away from the race you're supposed to be running.

And before you know it, you're busy but not purposeful. Active but not obedient. Running but in the wrong direction.

I've had to turn down opportunities that looked good on paper because they weren't aligned with my actual calling. Speaking engagements that would've expanded my platform but pulled me away from writing. Projects that would've paid well but drained the energy I needed for teaching and enhancing student success. Positions that would've looked impressive but required me to be someone I'm not.

Every single one of those was a distraction. And saying no to them protected my yes for what actually matters.

You're going to face the same thing. Opportunities that aren't bad, just not yours. Doors that open but lead somewhere you're not supposed to go. Invitations that look like advancement but are actually detours.

And you're going to have to be ruthless about protecting your lane. About saying no to good things so you can say yes to your things. About staying focused on your race instead of getting distracted by everyone else's.

Because distraction doesn't always look like procrastination or laziness. Sometimes distraction looks like productivity. Like busyness. Like success.

But if it's not moving you toward your actual destiny, it's a distraction. And you need to let it go.

Trusting God's Timing

And here's the last part about running your race: you have to trust God's timing even when it doesn't make sense.

Some people's destinies unfold quickly. Doors open. Opportunities appear. Progress is visible and rapid.

Yours might not work that way. It certainly didn't for me. And that doesn't mean you're doing something wrong.

Abraham didn't get to the promised land overnight. Moses wandered in the wilderness for forty years. Joseph spent years in prison before he stepped into his purpose. David was anointed as king long before he wore the crown.

Delay doesn't mean denial. Waiting doesn't mean you're off course. The wilderness isn't punishment—it's preparation.

Maybe you're in a season where nothing seems to be moving. Where you're doing all the right things but seeing no visible progress. Where you're showing up faithfully but the doors aren't opening. Where you're running your race but it feels like you're running in place.

That's not wasted time. That's not evidence that you've missed your calling. That's not proof that the demons were right.

That's the season where God is building your character to match your calling. Where He's preparing you for what

He's preparing for you. Where He's teaching you to trust Him in the waiting so you can handle what happens in the acceleration.

So don't compare your timeline to anyone else's. Don't assume that because their door opened quickly, yours should too. Don't interpret delay as rejection.

Just keep running your race. Keep showing up. Keep being faithful. And trust that the God who called you to this lane knows exactly when to bring you across the finish line.

Your Race, Your Pace, Your Purpose

So here's what I want you to remember when comparison starts creeping in, when distraction starts calling, when you're tempted to look at someone else's lane and wonder why yours looks different:

You're not running their race. You're running yours. And your race is exactly what it needs to be to turn you into who you need to become.

Stop measuring your progress by their milestones. Stop questioning your calling because it doesn't look like theirs. Stop trying to run at their pace when God has given you a different rhythm.

Just run your race. Stay in your lane. Be faithful to your calling. And trust that the finish line you're running toward is exactly where you're supposed to end up.

Because your destiny isn't about being like anyone else. It's about being exactly who God created you to be, doing exactly what He called you to do, in exactly the way only you can do it.

The Final Stand

So here we are. At the end of this book. At the beginning of what comes next.

You've done the work. You've named the demons. You've broken the chains. You've rewritten the narratives. You've built systems for lasting change. You've embraced a new future. And now you're standing at the edge of something you've been running toward this entire time.

Your destiny.

And I need you to understand something before you close this book and step into what's waiting: you're ready.

Not because you're perfect. Not because you've figured everything out. Not because the demons are gone forever or the struggles are over or the journey is complete.

You're ready because you're free. And free people don't need permission to chase what they were created for.

Coming Full Circle

Remember where we started? All the way back in Chapter 1, standing in front of that bathroom mirror at 3 AM, confronting the person in the reflection and asking the question that changed everything: What demons are you carrying?

That moment wasn't just about identifying what was chasing you. It was about deciding whether you were going to keep running from them or turn around and face them. Whether you were going to stay prey or become the hunter.

And look at you now. You're not the same person who started this journey. You're not carrying the same weight. You're not bound by the same lies. You're not living in the same captivity.

You've learned the difference between tracing and trusting. Between favor and performance. Between captivity and liberty. Between being a victim, a survivor, and an author.

You've learned that where the Spirit of the Lord is, there is liberty. And if something feels like bondage—even if it looks like success—it's not from God.

You've learned that Guilt doesn't get to define you. That Envy's comparison is poison. That Greed's appetite is never satisfied. That Selfishness isolates. That Rejection doesn't have the authority to write your story.

You've learned that your past doesn't disqualify you. Your pain has purpose. Your test is becoming your testimony. And your survival means something beyond just making it through.

You've learned that transformation requires systems, not just willpower. That change sticks when you build it into your daily rhythm. That you can't do this alone—you need people who call you forward instead of calling you back.

And you've learned that freedom isn't just about what you're free from. It's about what you're free for.

Come What May

You remember Mama's phrase? The one that's carried me through every storm, every loss, every moment when I didn't think I could keep going?

Come what may.

Not as resignation. Not as passive acceptance of whatever life throws at you. But as defiant confidence that no matter what comes, you're standing on something solid. That no matter what the demons throw at you, they don't get the final word. That no matter what circumstances look like, you're held by favor that can't be shaken.

Come what may, you're ready.

The demons will still show up. They're not gone forever. Guilt will try to remind you of your past. Envy will whisper that someone else has what should be yours. Greed will convince you that you need more before you can start.

Selfishness will try to isolate you. Rejection will attempt to make you believe you're unworthy.

But here's what's different now: you know their names. You know their strategies. You know their lies. And you know that their presence doesn't mean you've failed. It means you're still in the fight. It means you're still moving toward something they don't want you to have.

And come what may, you're not backing down.

Favor Has Positioned You, Liberty Has Freed You

Throughout this journey, we've talked about favor and liberty as the foundation of everything. And now, standing at the threshold of your destiny, I need you to remember what those words actually mean.

Favor isn't something you earn. It's something you're given. It's God's positioning—placing you where you belong not because of what you've proven but because of who you are. Favor is why you survived what should have destroyed you. Why doors opened that you didn't even knock on. Why you're still here when the demons tried their hardest to take you out.

You didn't earn your survival. You didn't work your way into worthiness. You didn't perform your way into purpose.

You were favored. And that favor has been positioning you for this moment your entire life.

Liberty is what happens when favor does its work. Where the Spirit of the Lord is, there is liberty. Not someday. Not when you've earned it. Not after you've proven yourself. Right now. In this moment. You are free.

Free to be yourself. Free to pursue your calling. Free to disappoint people who need you to stay small. Free to make mistakes. Free to take risks. Free to trust the process you can't see. Free to run your race at your pace in your lane.

The demons tried to convince you that freedom was something you had to fight for forever. That you'd always be in battle mode. That captivity was your permanent address.

But they lied. You're free. And nothing they say or do can change that.

Your Destiny Is Calling

So now what?

Now you chase it. The thing you were created for. The calling that's been waiting for you to be free enough to answer. The destiny that has your name on it.

Not someone else's destiny. Not the version of success the world has been selling. Not what your parents wanted or your community expected or your trauma convinced you was the best you could hope for.

Your destiny. The one where your deep gladness meets the world's deep hunger. The one where your gifts serve others powerfully. The one where you become exactly who God created you to be.

And yes, it will cost you something. It will require sacrifice. It will demand that you let go of safety, relationships that require you to stay small, approval from people who don't understand, and control over how everything unfolds.

But what you gain is worth infinitely more than what you lose.

You gain freedom. Purpose. Authenticity. Peace. The chance to live fully alive instead of just surviving.

And you gain the opportunity to become the person who helps someone else break free. To let your test become your testimony. To show others that the demons don't get the last word. To be living proof that transformation is possible and freedom is real.

The Challenge

So here's my final challenge to you: Don't waste what you've learned. Don't go back to sleep. Don't let the comfort of the familiar pull you back into patterns you've already broken. Don't let the demons convince you that the battle is the point instead of recognizing that the battle was clearing the way for this.

Chase your destiny with the same intensity you used to chase the demons.

Run your race with faithfulness, not flash. Stay in your lane. Trust God's timing even when it doesn't make sense. Show up when nobody's watching. Make the small, daily choices that compound into transformation.

Protect your calling ruthlessly. Say no to opportunities that aren't yours so you can say yes to what actually matters. Don't get distracted by the shiny objects the demons dangle in front of you.

And when the demons show up—because they will—don't panic. Don't assume you've failed. Don't go back to believing their lies.

Just remind them: you know their names. You've broken their chains. You've rewritten their narratives. And they don't get to keep you from your destiny.

Then keep running.

You Were Made For This

Listen to me: You were made for this. Not the struggle. Not the battle. Not the surviving.

You were made for the destiny that's waiting on the other side of your freedom.

You were made to be fully yourself—authentic, whole, and alive. You were made to use your gifts in service of something bigger than yourself. You were made to step into the calling that only you can fulfill. You were made to chase what brings you deep gladness while meeting the world's deep hunger.

The demons tried to steal that from you. They tried to convince you that you were made for captivity, for shame, for smallness, for survival at best.

But they were wrong.

You were made for freedom. For purpose. For destiny.

And you're finally free enough to chase it.

The Invitation

So here's what I want you to do when you close this book:

Take a moment. Take a breath. Look at where you've been and where you're going.

Then make a choice.

Are you going to stay in the safety of survival, or are you going to chase the destiny that's calling your name?

Are you going to keep focusing on the demons, or are you going to focus on what you're running toward?

Are you going to live small to keep people comfortable, or are you going to live fully alive?

The choice is yours. It always has been. But now you're free enough to actually make it.

The Final Word

The demons have been named. The chains have been broken. The narratives have been rewritten. The future is waiting.

And you? You're no longer prey. You're the hunter. You're no longer a victim of your circumstances. You're the author of what comes next. You're no longer running from what's chasing you. You're running toward what you were created for.

Come what may, you're ready.

The demons tried to keep you from this moment. They failed.

Your calling has been waiting. It's tired of being ignored.

So stop chasing demons.

Start chasing destiny.

Your life—your real life, the one you were always meant to live—is waiting.

Go get it.

AFTERWORD

Let me be honest with you one last time.

This book didn't fix me. Writing it didn't exorcise my demons. Publishing it didn't mean I've "arrived" at some peaceful place where Guilt doesn't whisper, Envy doesn't sting, or Rejection doesn't hurt.

What it did was give me language. It gave me permission to stop pretending I had it all together. It forced me to look at the patterns I'd been running from and finally turn around to face them. It reminded me that I'm not crazy, I'm not alone, and I'm not beyond redemption.

And neither are you.

In the Book of Revelation, John writes about a war in heaven—Michael and his angels fighting against the dragon and his angels. The dragon was hurled down to earth, and with him went his demons. That ancient battle continues today, not just in cosmic spaces but in the intimate spaces of our hearts, minds, and lives.

This book has been about earthly demons—the ones that wear familiar faces and speak in our own voices. Guilt. Envy. Greed. Selfishness. Rejection. But make no mistake: the war is still spiritual. It's still real. And it still requires us to fight with weapons both practical and divine.

The reality is, I'm still chasing my demons. Some days I'm winning. Other days I'm just surviving. But I'm still here, still fighting, still believing that the life they stole can be reclaimed. Not because I have it all figured out, but because I've learned how to confront them. I'm wiser now. I know their tactics. I recognize their voices. And I know I can't do this alone.

Neither can you.

Prayer without action is hope without legs. Action without prayer is effort without covering. You need both. You need the wisdom to identify your demons AND the strength to chase them down. You need the vulnerability to admit you're struggling AND the faith to believe God hasn't abandoned you in the struggle.

Here's what I need you to know: this is a daily fight. Every single day you'll have to choose—will you let your demons chase you, or will you turn around and chase them down? Some mornings you'll wake up ready for battle. Other mornings you'll barely have the strength to get out of bed. Both are valid. Both are part of the journey.

But God gives us brand new mercies day after day. His compassion never fails. It's new every morning. The Psalmist said, "Weeping may endure for the night, but joy comes in the morning." Notice he didn't say weeping wouldn't come. He said it wouldn't stay. The night doesn't get the final word. Your demons don't get to write the ending.

God allowed me to survive COVID, to lose my mother, to face discrimination, to wrestle with identity—not because He was punishing me, but because He was preparing me. Every test became a testimony. Every wound became wisdom. Every demon I chased became a chapter in a story bigger than my pain.

Your story is still being written too. And the Author of life is still working, still writing, still making a way where there seems to be no way. You don't have to have it all together to start chasing. You just have to be willing to take the first step, then the next one, then the one after that.

You're not alone in this fight. I'm still in it with you. And more importantly, God is with you—not watching from a distance, but right there in the trenches, giving you new mercies for each new battle.

Weeping may endure for the night, but it has to give way to the morning light.

Trust the process. Chase the demons. Claim your life.

So again, I say to you as my grandmother said to me, "come what may."

ABOUT THE AUTHOR

J. Michael Williams, DBA is an author, award-winning higher education administrator, educator, and inspirational voice for those who have wrestled with their own demons. Born in Gainesville, Florida, as the middle child of James C. Williams, Jr., and Wenda G. Williams, he was raised in a home where love, faith, and the wisdom of generations shaped everything he would become.

His gift for writing emerged early. As a child, he found expression through poetry and crafting sermons, discovering that words had the power to reach places nothing else could. That gift was recognized during his high school years when one of his poems was featured in *Torchlights*, and it deepened during his undergraduate years at Bethune-Cookman University, where he delivered his first public sermon, "Delayed Not Denied"—a title that would prove prophetic for his own journey.

Dr. Williams' path wasn't a straight line. He started as a pre-med student at Xavier University of Louisiana, pursuing his dream of becoming a cardiothoracic surgeon. But when he discovered his mother had sacrificed her truck to cover his unmet tuition, he transferred to Bethune-Cookman to ease her burden—a decision that would redirect his calling in ways he couldn't have imagined. He eventually became a different kind of doctor, earning a Doctor of Business Administration and building a career as a higher education executive. His work is rooted in a commitment to equity, enablement, and excellence—dedicated to student success, innovation that elevates learning and growth, and institutional advancement.

In 2023, he released his first book, *The What If Factor: Living Beyond The Question Mark*, a transformational work years in the making that challenged readers to move past the paralysis of uncertainty. In 2024, he released *7 Days of Grace: A Devotional On Grace*, which became an Amazon bestseller and established his voice in the devotional space.

But the work you hold in your hands required more than expertise. It required lived experience.

In 2020, Dr. Williams faced battles that nearly broke him. He survived COVID-19 when doctors didn't expect him to, lying in a hospital bed surrounded by death, unable to move his arms or speak, convinced he wouldn't make it. Months later, he lost his mother—the only person who had read the manuscript he'd been working on for years. By October of that year, his grandmother Mama died of a heart attack, adding another layer of loss to a grief he couldn't process.

The demons he writes about in these pages aren't theoretical. They're the voices that whispered he was done, that his story ended when hers did, that survival wasn't the same as living. And they would have been right—if he hadn't learned to chase them instead of letting them chase him.

Dr. Williams currently serves as a higher education administrator while also teaching and writing—embracing the fullness of a calling his mother always saw in him. He creates inspirational content for social media, speaks to audiences navigating their own internal battles, and continues the work of helping people recognize the demons that hold them captive and find the courage to reclaim what was stolen.

This book is his testimony. Witness work from the trenches. The message he couldn't write until he lived it first.

He resides in Florida, still standing on the foundation built by those who saw something in him before he saw it in himself—and invested in his becoming anyway.

Come what may.

OTHER BOOKS

The What If Factor: Living Beyond The Question Mark

What if the questions holding you back are actually invitations forward? This transformational work challenges readers to move past the paralysis of uncertainty and into the life they were meant to live. Stop letting "what if" be the period at the end of your story—and start letting it be the beginning of your next chapter.

7 Days of Grace: A Devotional On Grace *(Amazon Bestseller)*

A week-long journey into the depths of grace that has touched thousands of readers. Each day offers reflection, scripture, and practical application designed to help you experience grace not as a concept, but as a daily reality. Because grace isn't just something you receive—it's something you learn to live in.

For more information, visit https://www.jmwdba.us or connect on social media.

www.ingramcontent.com/pod-product-compliance
Lightning Source LLC
Chambersburg PA
CBHW070908130626
46555CB00001B/50